SPECIAL EDITION

EDITED by
CHAS. BALUN

Our Deepest, Reddest Thanks to: Dario Argento, Luigi Cozzi, Profondo Rosso Bookstore, KNB EFX Group, Shaun Hutson, Bill Lustig, John McNaughton, Jorg Buttgereit, Sergio Stivaletti, Southgate Entertainment, Troma, Inc., Trio Entertainment, Inc., Eric Caidin, Samhain Magazine, and Blue Cheer.

EDITOR / DESIGN / LAYOUT
Chas. Balun
WRITERS
Chas. Balun
Stephen R. Bissette
Shane M. Dallman
Dennis Daniel
Walter Gay
Kris Gilpin
Greg Goodsell
Steven R. Johnson
John Martin
Thomas Nilsson
Paul Sammon
GRAPHIC ARTISTS
Chas. Balun
Gurchain Singh
Bruce Spaulding Fuller
TYPOGRAPHY / DESIGN
Eric Hausmann
Hank Jansen
PUBLISHER
FantaCo Enterprises, Inc.
21 Central Avenue
Albany, New York 12210

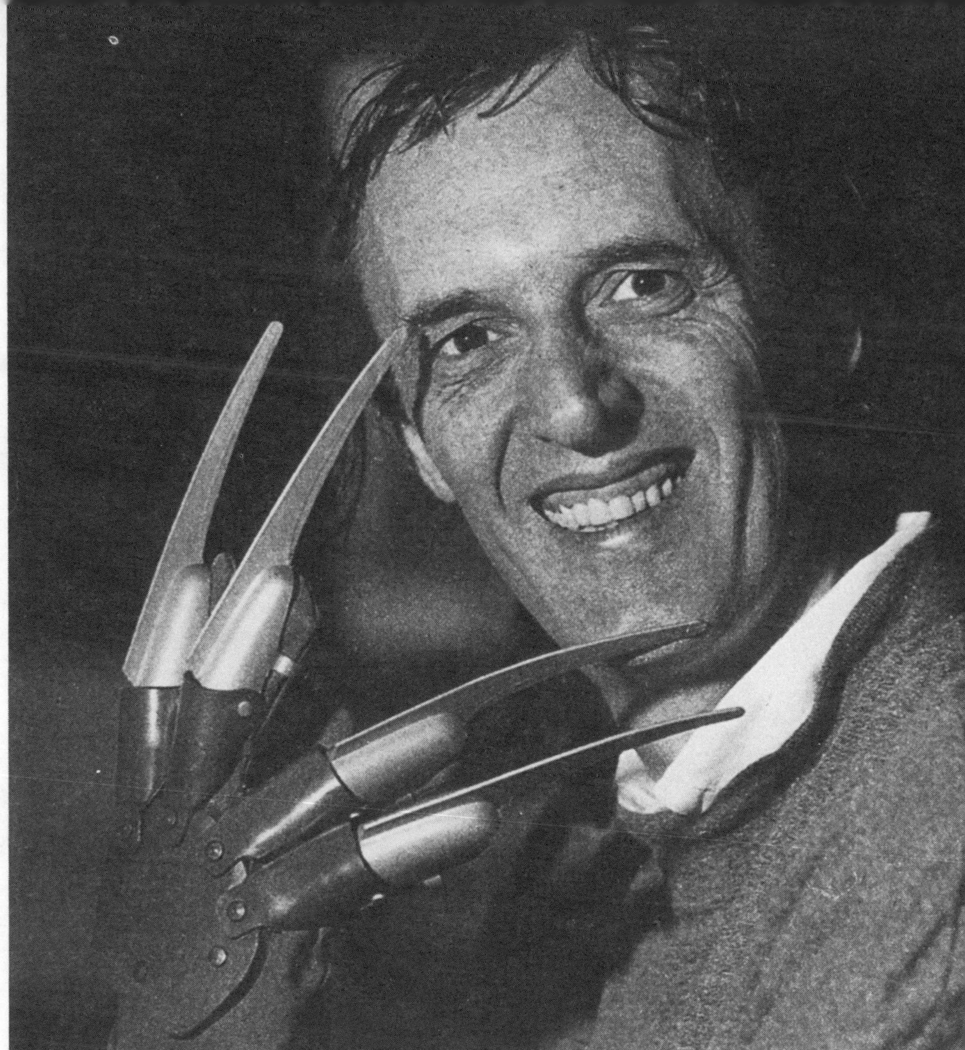

ISBN 0-938782-16-9 Printed and stitched in the United States. A limited hardcover edition of 100 copies was simultaneously released, ISBN 0-938782-17-7

INTRODUCTION

Much like the genre itself, *Deep Red* magazine has undergone a fairly radical metamorphosis since our first issue appeared in the summer of 1986. Then, there was much to be happy, enthusiastic and hopeful about. For awhile, it seemed as though the immediate future of horror was assured. There was plenty of the New Blood to go around and many veteran genre directors seemed to be just hitting their stride. Newcomers like Stuart Gordon, Clive Barker, Peter Jackson, John McNaughton and Michele Soavi were twisting the parameters of horror alongside established directors like David Cronenberg, George Romero and Dario Argento, who appeared at the peak of their powers.

"Splatterpunk" was born and young, talented writers like David J. Schow, John Skipp, Craig Spector and Ray Garton injected contemporary horror fiction with a rabidly eclectic mix of rock 'n' roll, splatter, sex and shocks that established a new beachhead for explicit genre literature.

Horror was trés hot and soon the genre would be supporting a half dozen glossy, mass-market magazines chock full of eyepopping makeups, special effects and behind-the-scenes peeks at dozens of films that just seemed *too* good to be true.

However, the accumulated effect of all this activity within the community proved to have quite an unexpected result. Instead of a renaissance in genre filmmaking, the bottom fell out. Horror films were being hamstrung by not only the MPAA's ever-tightening reins, but by distributors who were unable to move the product. " 'B' movies were dead," they said and according to many, "you couldn't give away a gore film." Many noteworthy genre efforts including John McNaughton's *Henry: Portrait of a Serial Killer* and *The Borrower*, Jim Van Bebber's *Deadbeat at Dawn* and Peter Jackson's *Bad Taste* faced a long, uphill struggle against anal-retentive, chickenshit distributors who had no idea how to market films that defied simple classification.

The cost of moviemaking again began to skyrocket; and as the 90's approached, the Motion Picture Association of America estimated that the average Hollywood production was costing a cool $23.4 million.

Audiences expected a certain "production sheen" to be seen in films and soon the grittier, low-budget splatterfests so prevalent in the early 80's began to become an endangered species. Even video distributors, who became the defacto drive-in market of the decade, were stocking multiple copies of the mainstream blockbusters at the expense of their usually reliable assortment of "B" movies.

Filmmakers were taking fewer chances with their material in hopes of snaring an even wider audience and sequels to established hits were becoming the order of the day. Then, expensive remakes of 50's hits became the rage.

By decade's end, the prime movers and shakers of the early 80's—John Carpenter, Tobe Hooper, Wes Craven, Sean Cunningham, Joe Dante and George Romero—seemed to have already put their best work behind them. More filmmakers seemed eager to shed their horror reputations for a chance at a multi-picture deal and an opportunity to work with a more generous budget. Many simply denied they were genre directors at all and actually *resented* the association.

Horror escaped from the theaters and splashed across the nation's TV screens for a time, resulting in lackluster, ball-less fodder like *Freddy's Nightmares*, *Friday the 13th: The Series*, *Tales from the Darkside* and *Monsters*. Cable horror films like Tobe Hooper's *I'm Dangerous Tonight* proved just as lame as network TV's *Daughter of Darkness* (directed by Stuart Gordon) and any number of other prime-time cathode ray abortions helmed by Wes Craven.

For years, no single film galvanized the horror community like *Re-Animator* did in 1985 and *Evil Dead* in 1983. *Bad Taste* came closest, but American audiences were deprived of a theatrical experience and had to settle for splatter served up cold and on the little screen.

Even the slick New York magazines were beginning to fight over the scraps of such inconsequential films as *Halloween 4*, *Nightmare on Elm Street 5*, *Fright Night 2*, *Dream Demon* or *Friday the 13th VIII*. Same gory photos, same tired set visits. In less than a year, magazines like *Slaughterhouse*, *Horror Fan* and *Toxic Horror* went down for the count. Although the nonprofessional fanzine scene continued to flourish, thanks in part to their ever-vigilant search for mondo bizarro, sleaze rarities, the remaining "pro zines" continued to flounder and fight for direction. Everyone copped an attitude. Some turned their noses up at the mention of Argento, Bava or Deodato. Others refused films without flashy FX. Some became so fucking hip it hurt.

It was approximately at this point that *Deep Red* took a vacation. Not only was there less and less of merit to write about, but even hardcore, unreconstructed splatter hounds rapidly tire of editorials bemoaning the current state of affairs while waxing nostalgic about the good ol' days. *Deep Red*, the magazine, had made its mark. It was time for a change.

Sensing the disposable and topical nature of all magazines, both editor and publisher of *Deep Red* agreed that the future demanded something more versatile in the way of contemporary horror criticism. Besides, small press publishers are always at a decided disadvantage when competing with mainstream, newsstand publications and cannot hope to compete with periodicals that offer full-on, four-color art throughout and hope to maintain a manageable cover price.

Despite the cult appeal and relative success of a small-press product like *Deep Red*, we were unable to meet the financial demands incurred by the ever-changing forces at work in both the printing and distribution arenas and each issue became more costly to produce. While our ambitions and hopes for the future soared, budgetary limitations hit us in the face like a back alley sucker-punch. And frankly, your editor was rapidly approaching burnout after writing regularly for both *Fangoria* and *GoreZone* for several years, editing and laying out six issues of *Deep Red*, as well as being involved in numerous related book projects.

It got to the point that I had run out of things to say. Perhaps that should be rephrased to read something "positive" to say. I had always enjoyed a relatively free forum in which to shoot my mouth off, but soon the message became tired and redundant. There simply was little going on to get excited about. I also wanted to explore other opportunities where I felt I might make a positive contribution to the genre rather than just rely on acerbic, vindictive criticism of others' work to sustain my position in the field. Writing a horror novel, *Ninth and Hell Street*, as well as co-scripting the feature film *Chunkblower* for Canada's Plasma Films provided me the chance to put my money where my mouth was. *Deep Red* was never far from mind, though, and plans were always afoot to resurrect the Beast in one form or another.

The Deep Red Horror Handbook became our first real attempt at metamorphosis, shape-shifting if you will. True, *Deep Red* the *magazine* appeared dead and buried, but its spirit remained totally viable and highly operative. Other projects were soon discussed and both editor and publisher again agreed that *Deed Red* should and *would* continue, in one form or another.

As other magazines and publications continued to rely upon bullshit fluff pieces that shamelessly hyped a plethora of boneheaded genre entries and the attending legions of self-serving, publicity-hungry filmmakers, *Deep Red* again became relevant and necessary. Sure, we played favorites in the past, but much of our reputation was earned by the many critical, sometimes scurrilous, features we ran that openly attacked many of the genre's most sacred cows. We were biting the hand that was feeding us, but we *liked* it that way, and so did our readers.

Our staff writers were fans *first* and critics second. So, despite the blatant hostility and razor-sharp cynicism displayed in many of our features, our writers remained motivated primarily by their obsessive love for the horror film and were only venting their frustrations over their beloved genre gone astray. *Deep Red* gave free rein to its writers and encouraged them to tell the truth–be painfully honest if need be–but above all, get down to the meat of the matter regardless of whose toes got stomped on.

Well, our job is not yet finished. At the dawn of a new decade, the genre has been sending out a series of mixed signals. Though most fans believed the MPAA was at least partially responsible for the decline in graphic horror, the new NC-17 rating has not proven to be the panacea that many were hoping for. Some newspapers and several theatres have still refused to promote films with the controversial new rating and plenty of studios continue to insist on a contractually-established "R" rating on a completed film.

Other films like Brian Yuzna's *Society* and *Bride of Re-Animator*, Peter Jackson's *Meet the Feebles*, and Dario Argento's *Opera* and *Two Evil Eyes* are languishing in Distribution Hell. American audiences remain staunchly xenophobic and the rare foreign gore film that makes it to stateside theaters is usually heavily cut, carelessly dubbed and indifferently distributed. Besides Argento and Jackson, other high-profile overseas auteurs like Michael Soavi (*Stage Fright*, *The Church*), Lucio Fulci (*Zombie 3*, *The Red Monks*, *Aenigma*, *Murderock*, etc.) or Ruggero Deodato (*Dial Help*, *Phantom of Death*) have not exactly been afforded the red carpet treatment by either the theatrical outlets nor the video cassette marketplace.

Though sequels and remakes to established hits continue their stranglehold on the genre, there are promising signs that the trend may be withering on the vine. The unspectacular box office receipts to *Halloween 5*, *Nightmare on Elm Street 5*,

Friday the 13th VIII, *Predator 2*, and *Gremlins 2* have led greedy, opportunistic studios to the inevitable–the final chapter. New Line's last gasp in the Krueger Killathon now appears to be *Nightmare 6: Freddy's Dead*. Let's hope so. Expensive remakes like *The Blob*, *The Thing* and *Invaders From Mars* failed to generate much heat at the box office. Even the George Romero/Tom Savini can't-miss-sure-as-shit remake of *Night of the Living Dead* bit zombie dick in a big way.

The sequel and the remake may be at least partially extinct by decade's end, but it appears that the pesky horror comedy may be here to stay. The closest thing to a box office success within the genre in 1990 was the "thrill-omedy" *Arachnophobia*, a marginal horror film at best, but a $50.7 million winner in the column that counts. It's actually becoming quite difficult to remember the last genuinely scary moment spent inside a theater during the last five years or so. Now *that's* a truly horrifying thought.

Despite solid evidence to the contrary, the contemporary horror film is in no real danger. The genre has proven again and again throughout the *century* that it is one tough, resilient and tenacious motherfucker. It may appear dead at times, but revenge from beyond the grave is an established, revered tradition within the genre.

So, at the beginning of the last decade in the twentieth century, the horror film may be down, but it's hardly out of the picture. Westerns, detective thrillers, film noir, war pictures and musicals have suffered far more through the years than the venerable horror film. From cinema's inception, with Georges Melies' *Le Manoir du Diablo* (*The Manor of the Devil*) in 1896 and Thomas Edison's 16-minute *Frankenstein* shot in 1910, the horror film has proven itself capable of constantly reinventing, redefining and resurrecting itself no matter what the odds nor circumstances may be.

Despite the overt cynicism and crass commercial instincts prevalent in the film business, there still seems a nearly inexhaustible flow of New Blood into the genre–people whose fierce dedication and love for the horror film will not be compromised. Some of these people eat, breathe and sleep filmmaking and their faith and perseverance is the kind that moves mountains. They believe in miracles. There is simply too much talent and wildeyed, unflappable enthusiasm out there to be denied.

People become fans. Fans become super fans and many of those go on to become writers, artists, actors, directors and producers. The regular cyclical pattern of rebirth and regeneration within the genre remains the most promising and encouraging sign of the things to come.

Deep Red will be right there with you...in the front row.

CHAS. BALUN, WINTER 1991

DARIO ARGENTO

FACE TO FACE

by Chas. Balun

Additional material by Dennis Daniel and Thomas Nilsson

It needs to be said in print and without further delay. What has been merely hinted at and alluded to for years can now be safely stated for all to hear. Dario Argento is the genre's Greatest Living Director. And, I'll go to the mat on this one, too.

With a career spanning well over two decades, Argento has produced an unbroken body of work that is unparalleled in the genre. His consistency of vision, his unbridled, deeply-felt passions and masterful control of his medium have produced a series of films that showcase many of the finest moments ever seen in genre filmmaking. He alone remains a true Maestro in a kingdom of Mediocrity.

Argento is practically an anomaly in a field that has ever-so-consistently placed a premium on established formulas and commercial viability of its product. In a world filled with high-profile horror icons like Freddy Krueger, Jason Voorhees, Leatherface and Michael Myers, there seems to be no room at the inn for a man who is really and truly deadly *serious about his work. He unashamedly professes a genuine and heartrending love for his art and, contrary to most of his contemporaries, doesn't find working within the parameters of the horror film to be the least bit restrictive or unfulfilling. When his camera soars, pirouettes or glides serpentlike down the tunnels of his dreams, we see sights that none have seen before. The spectacular aerial acrobatics seen in such films as* Suspiria, Tenebrae, Phenomena *and* Opera *show us a master whose obsessions cannot be contained by the usual conventions of his craft. Argento has consistently and* relentlessly *pursued a pure, unadulterated personal vision of genre grandeur that exposes most other horror filmmakers for the studio hacks they are.*

It is, indeed, a rare bit of luck, a privilege *even, that contemporary audiences have been able to "grow up" along with Argento's oeuvre. The fact that Argento has never denigrated nor trivialized his work within the genre further endears him to an audience grown accustomed to opportunistic journeymen filmmakers who jump ship as soon as they're offered their first "real Hollywood film."*

Argento is obviously very proud of what he has accomplished. He makes no excuses. He is not trying to be popular; he's never, ever been the "Flavor of the Month." He places demands upon his audiences—many of his films are far from being

The Sect (La Setta)

"userfriendly." While others routinely offer up shovelsful of the latest fast-food designer frights with alarming regularity, Argento has continued to confound, styme and challenge his audience for well over two decades.

He has brought magic back to a constipated and weary world that has little time for flights of fancy of any kind. *Not only has he revived the ancient art, but as in* Suspiria, *he has proven that, indeed, "there is magic all around us."*

From his modest beginnings as a journalist for one of Italy's foremost newspapers, Paese Sera, *Argento has risen from the ranks of film criticism, screenwriting and musical composition to become one of the few genuine auteurs in the genre. After writing several westerns in the 60's, including Sergio Leone's classic* Once Upon A Time in the West *(1969), Argento made his directorial debut with* The Bird With the Crystal Plumage *in 1970 and was awarded trophies proclaiming him Italy's "Best New Director" and maker of the "Year's Best Film."*

For the next twenty years, Argento produced a prodigious body of work that climaxed at decade's end with a flurry of projects including Opera, Two Evil Eyes, *Michele Soavi's* The Church *and Lamberto Bava's two* Demons *films. Argento still shows no signs of disenfranchisement with the genre and remains a highly animated, enthusiastic "traveler" who feels as though he has completed only part of his voyage.*

In person, Argento is a warm, engaging, romantic *man. Despite the cruelty and violence in his work, his manner is that of a poet, delicate, even. It is soon made quite clear, though, that Argento is a man possessed. An artisté driven by passions and obsessions that even he may not understand fully. Regardless, those fleeting and elusive glimpses we have seen of Argento's private Heaven and Hell have provided the genre with enough raw material to fuel a thousand nightmares.*

Perhaps Stephen King had it all wrong *when he declared Clive Barker "the future of horror." Maybe, just maybe, it should have read, "I have seen the past, present,* and *the future of horror and it's name has been, will be, and ever shall be...Dario Argento."*

[This interview was conducted both before and during the 1990 FantaCon in Albany, New York.]

"I concentrate on cruelty," says Argento, "not blood. The psychological aspect of human cruelty is extremely fascinating. Violence is a means of communication, a way of expressing myself. I don't know why I love this; perhaps, in part, because life is too boring, people are too boring. In the movies, in the dark, the love, the emotions become my reality. *Real* reality I do not love."

Though not completely fluent nor at ease with speaking in English, Argento nonetheless painstakingly assembles then delivers his thoughts slowly and thoughtfully, constantly punctuating his statements with graceful, animated hand gestures. He explains that he "learned English from songs" that he'd heard on the radio. "I love Bob Dylan especially," Argento adds.

Before Argento would dazzle both critics and audiences alike with his first effort, *Bird With the Crystal Plumage*, he worked with a variety of collaborators writing westerns and action picture like *Five Man Army, Cemetery Without Crosses,* and *Today It's Me...Tomorrow You.* Both Argento and Bernardo (*1900, Last Tango in Paris*) Bertolucci worked with Sergio Leone on the epic western *Once Upon A Time in the West*, which starred Henry Fonda, Jason Robards, Charles Bronson and Keenan Wynn amongst an all-star, international cast. "I did an original treatment for the film, inspired mainly by two films—*Johnny Guitar* and *The Searchers*."

The Church

Dario Argento
PROFONDO ROSSO
MENSILE - N. 1 - L. 2.500
AAAAHH...
VAN NINI 90
LA PICCOLA
BOTTEGA
DEGLI ORRORI

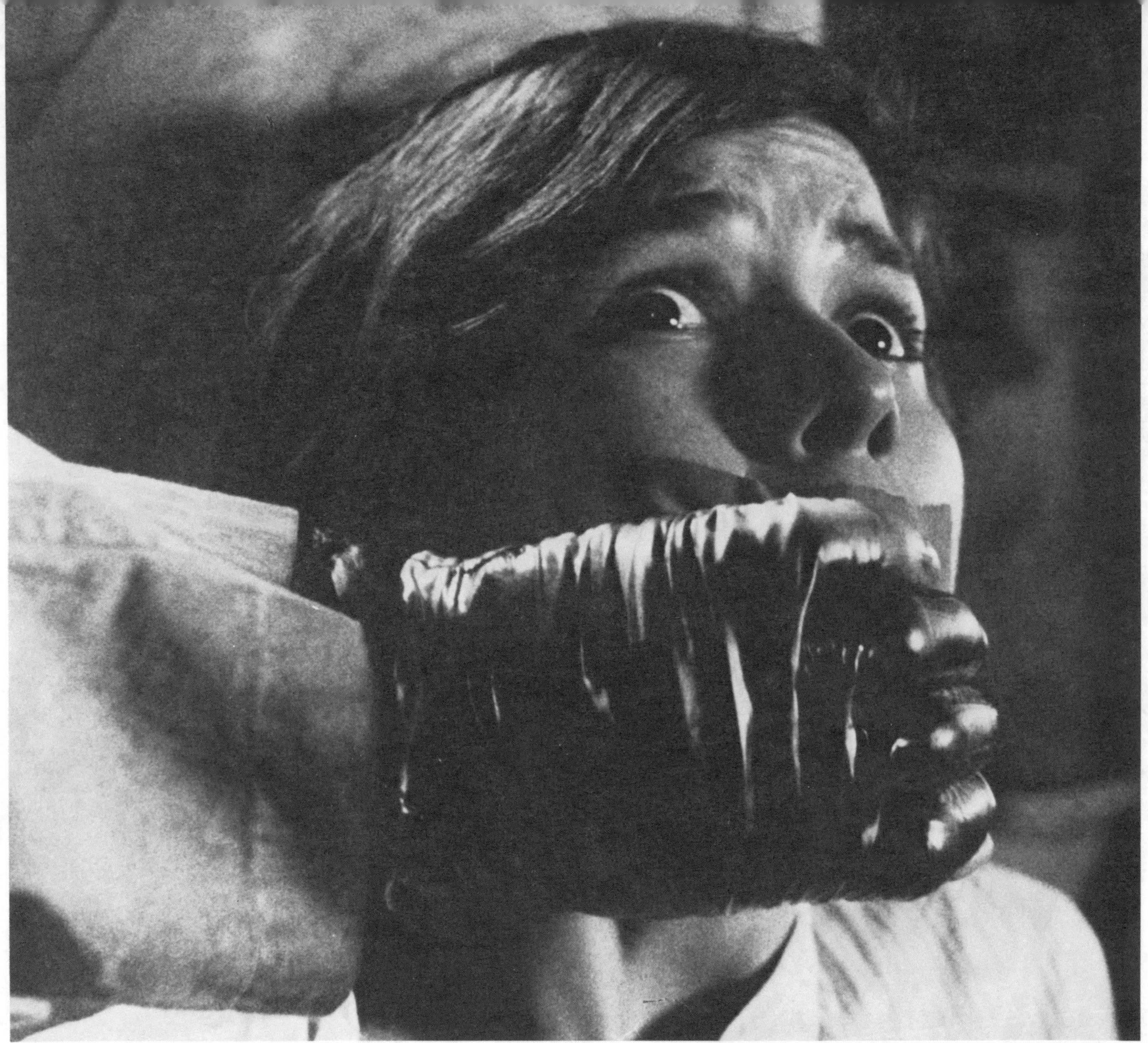

Opera: A Triumph of Will.

While *Bird With the Crystal Plumage* tantalized the curious public, both *Cat O'Nine Tails* (1971) and *Four Flies on Grey Velvet* (1971) cemented Argento's reputation as "the Italian Hitchcock." *Four Flies on Grey Velvet* climaxes with

"Violence is a means of communication; a way of expressing myself. I don't know why I love this; perhaps, in part because life is too boring, people are too boring."

one of the most spectacular slow-motion decapitations in screen history. (Richard Donner was later to reprise the trick six years later in *The Omen* when David Warner is rendered headless by flying sheet glass.)

Mimsy Farmer co-starred with Michael Brandon partly because "she reminded me of my wife at the time," Argento admits. "She was very good in it, too, by the way; but she did have a similar voice, hair and face."

Argento changed directions after *Grey Velvet*, pursuing a more operatic and gothic approach in such films as *Deep Red* (1975), *Suspiria* (1976) and *Inferno* (1979). He frequently changed cinematographers as well as composers from film to film in order to better accommodate his ever-evolving vision. "Ennio Morricone was a friend of the family," Argento remembers. "For many, many years he would come to the house. When I made my first picture, my father called Morricone and said 'take a look.' That began a collaboration that lasted for three pictures."

To compose the soundtracks for his next films, Argento "invented" the group Goblin. "I put this group together; they never existed before," he says. "I knew many young musicians then that came from the conservatory directly to our studios."

Argento would also compose much of the film's music in his head long before he would shoot his first reel of film. "Before Suspiria, I took a week's vacation in Greece and I saw a wonderful musician playing a bazuki," he recalls. "It was the first time I had ever heard one so I bought one and brought it back with me. I experimented with it before I shot anything. About a month before shooting, I composed the main title theme."

With *Inferno,* he also employed the talents of Keith Emerson to further embellish the lush, orchestral scores that were to become his trademark until 1984's *Phenomena* again broke the mold. "I was a rock-'n'-roll fan," Argento says, "but I especially enjoyed the music of Emerson, Lake and Palmer. When I met Keith, the group was already finished. He played no rock-'n'-roll on *Inferno,* though; it was more classically inspired."

"Every picture I change the music and with every picture I change the cinematographer. Though the vision is still mine, it is exciting to have a new experience with another person."

Deep Red also began Argento's flirtation with the dramatic candy-colored technicolor feasts that have steadfastly remained an earmark of most of his subsequent work. The inspiration for some of Argento's most audacious color schemes is revealed to come from a most unlikely source. "Color cartoons, especially the Disney ones, have *fantastic* colors," enthuses Argento. "The movie that most influenced me as far as color was *Snow White.* In fact, *Suspiria* was inspired by the coloring in that film.

"I concentrate on cruelty, not blood. The psychological aspect of human cruelty is extremely fascinating."

During the filming of *Inferno*, Argento remembers and describes in tender and wistful terms his working relationship with his aging mentor, Mario Bava. "I had known Mario for many, many years. His son, Lamberto, and I dated girls in the same class who were also friends. Mario was one of my best friends. Mario made the special effects for the last part of *Inferno*...the windows, the glass (and the stunning room underwater). This was all his wonderful work. Then right after the film, he died."

During the 80's, Argento's films were rarely seen on theatre screens in the United States; once they did surface on videocassette, they were indiscriminately cut and retitled. *Tenebrae* was shorn of most of its explicit scenes of violence

(including the justifiably famous "spurting stump") and released in truncated form as *Unsane*. *Phenomena* suffered an even harsher fate, as close to a half hour of footage was lost before it was released on stateside cassette as *Creepers.* Argento is clearly nonplussed by the reactions his films have received in the United States. "When someone cuts

(Previous page)
John (The Man of a Thousand Cuts) Morghen with heart-on from The Sect.

my films, takes out particular scenes, I ask why? It makes no sense," he shrugs.

"If one picture is made in Europe—my style, Argento style—it's difficult to make it appear like an American film. The American "machinery" of movie making is different. It is easy to make films here, everything is modern and very professionally handled. It was wonderful to work for six months in Pittsburg with George Romero on *Two Evil Eyes.* There are great technicians and engineers. And the cameras are...beautiful."

Argento, however, is definitely at odds with the other aspect of stateside moviemaking—the business and distribution end that has consistently failed to properly market an Argento film. "I do not love the American horror picture; they always include comedy and laughter. The killer, he's nice, or he's a joke. The U.S. distributors are very hypocritical. They do not love movies; they love only money. They are far too commercial and this is not the way. They don't care how the film is cut; they only think by editing my work they can get more of an audience."

> **"I do not love the American horror picture; they always include comedy and laughter. The killer, he's nice, or he's a joke."**

Argento clearly enjoys the fanaticism expressed in some corners for his work and always includes little telltale touches and tributes to those perceptive enough to catch them in each of his films. "I was always inspired by the German Expressionists and their strange corners, lights and movements. *The Cabinet of Dr. Caligari, Metropolis* and *M* are masterpieces. In *Four Flies on Grey Velvet*, I named the main thoroughfare 'Fritz Lang Street.' People who know my work understand there is always a piece of me in all my films. The fly in *Opera* is a tribute to *Phenomena.* In every picture I try to put something in it—a sequence, a shot that is my signature. The things of my obsessions—the lighting, the corridors, the stairs *and* the blood and love. In every picture I have at least one spectacular, acrobatic camera shot, like in *Tenebrae* and *Opera* that remains mine alone."

In both *Opera* and *Tenebrae* Argento also makes several comments about both fan obsessions and directorial passions. "In *Tenebrae* there are some answers to those who have been critical of my work. The same applies to *Opera* where a newspaper critic is telling the director to 'return to his old horror pictures.' I put things from my *real* life in both these pictures."

Snaky demon-sex in *The Church.*

He also reveals the source for many of his trademark sequences—his subconscious. "They really come from my nightmares. And sometimes in the night, before I fall asleep, I think these strange thoughts and then write them down. I remember one obsessive dream about remaining in a room alone and hearing an airplane overhead in the night sky. I fantasized about it crashing into the room and devouring it." That particular dream became the helicopter-through-the-roof sequence in *Demons*.

"Maybe we should be careful with the adults instead. Kids understand movies are a world of the nightmare, of dreams, inventions and music."

Both *Demons* films were produced by Argento and directed by Lamberto Bava. Argento is clearly ambivalent about Bava's most recent independent efforts. There have been numerous reports that Argento was none too pleased to see Bava attempt to release his film *The Ogre* as sort of an unofficial *Demons 3*. Michele Soavi's most recent film, *The Church* (also produced by Argento), was always intended as the official successor to Bava's series. "I did not see his picture *The Ogre*. For three years I have not collaborated with Bava. He's just recently finished another picture for television. He has made many, many short pictures for TV. That's what he wanted to do for a few years. We were a *group*," Argento sighs, "Michele Soavi, Bava and me. We were regularly making a couple of pictures every year."

The Church

After producing both of Bava's films in short succession, Argento returned to directing what was to become his most problematic film. *Opera,* budgeted at $7 million and requiring nearly 15 weeks of principal photography at Italy's famed De Paolis Studios, was, by far, Argento's most elaborate and costly production. The high costs were not merely financial; the film exacted a heavy personal toll from the filmmaker as well. Besides suffering one of the worst critical drubbings of his career, Argento's father, long-time producer Salvatore Argento, died during the filming of *Opera*; another actor was killed in an automobile accident; Vanessa Redgrave pulled out at the very last minute; and Argento's engagement was on the rocks by film's end. *Opera* was further plagued by censorship controversies, indifferent distribution and a lackluster box office.

The film is clearly very close to Argento's heart. "I think *Opera, Deep Red* and *Suspiria* are the three pictures that are very close to my original vision."

"The movie that most influenced me as far as color was *Snow White*. In fact, *Suspiria* was inspired by the coloring in that film."

"The ending of *Opera* was important to me. The distributors don't care. Orion cut it; maybe it bored them."

Orion Pictures cut hefty chunks from *Opera* (though retaining *all* acts of graphic violence) and eliminated Argento's original ending. "The ending was important to me. The distributors don't care. Orion cut it; maybe it bored them."

"The picture is very cruel, sadistic," he admits, "it is one of my most cruel pictures. You see so many films filled with blood and things, but they're like a joke. *Opera* is real, something deeper."

In keeping with his tradition of changing cinematographers and composers for each of his films, Argento presents a heady, eclectic music mix in *Opera*. "I think the different kinds of music worked well. We had so many composers, but I think the music worked comfortably together. It was difficult, though. We had Verdi, Puccini and Bellini, Bill Wyman of the Rolling Stones, Brian Eno, "new age" music and three heavy metal groups. I used metal especially because of the energy. It's perfect when you're very hungry in your soul and feeling the blood and the aggression."

After *Opera,* Argento once again turned producer and worked with long-time acolyte Michele Soavi on *The Church*, a supernatural thriller about a cathedral of the damned. Though *The Church* is only Soavi's second full-length feature film, his genre credentials are staggering for a man still in his very early 30's. Besides directing the critically-acclaimed *Stagefright* (*Aquarius, Deliria*) in 1987, Soavi served as Argento's assistant on *Tenebrae, Phenomena* and *Opera*; worked with Joe D'Amato, Lamberto Bava and Ruggero Deodato on such films as *Endgame, 2020 / Texas Gladiators, I Predatori de Atlantide, Blastfighter* and *House of the Dark Staircase*; and was Terry Gilliam's second unit director on *The Adventures of Baron Munchausen*. He has appeared in both *Demons* (as the punk giving out tickets) and Lucio Fulci's *The Gates of Hell* (he watches his chunkblowing girlfriend lose her entire intestinal tract out her mouth) as well as directing the essential documentary on his mentor, *The Horror World of Dario Argento*. Soavi is currently the second hottest horror director in Italy, and no wonder.

The Church also features Asia Argento, who, along with her sister Fiore, have made a family tradition out of appearing in their father's films (*Phenomena, Demons 2*).

The Sect (La Setta)

The Sect

In July, 1989, Argento began principal photography on *Two Evil Eyes*, a two-part Edgar Allen Poe tribute co-directed by George Romero, whom Argento had worked with ten years prior on *Dawn of the Dead*. Though their cinematic styles seem quite incompatible, Argento knows that it is something much deeper that draws them together. "It is strange, but it is something that comes from the soul. Our friendship is something mysterious, something nearly impossible to describe. Even we do not know exactly."

While Romero's segment, "The Facts in the Case of M. Valdemar," has been dismissed by most critics, many feel Argento's "The Black Cat" to be one of his most accessible, albeit gruesome, efforts. "At first, I decided to make *The Pit and the Pendulum* ('The Black Cat' contains an especially meaty tribute), but after some time in writing, I changed my mind. 'The Black Cat' is more of a complete story and I think it is one of Poe's best. He has always been my greatest source of inspiration. I love Poe because I can understand his

"I used heavy-metal especially because of the energy. It's perfect when you're hungry in your soul and feeling the blood and the aggression."

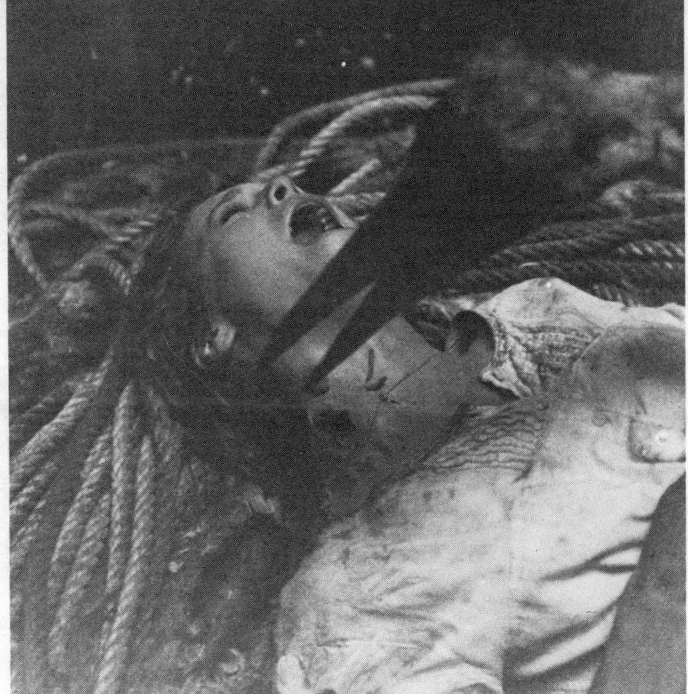

pain. He is the one who pushed me into the horror genre."

Argento also acknowledges Die and Lieb, his two cats at home, for additional inspiration while writing his segment of the film. (Contrary to filmic evidence, Argento does, indeed, seem to really like cats.)

Two Evil Eyes caps off two decades of filmmaking for Argento and, unlike most of his contemporaries, he relishes future excursions in the genre. He acknowledges the fact that many "genre" directors have merely used the field as a stepping stone and that several others have expressed fatigue from working within genre boundaries. But "burn-out" is most definitely not part of Argento's vocabulary. "Some have wanted to use the horror film to go on to the next thing. Like Brian DePalma, with *Casualties of War*; he has changed. He does not love the horror film like I do."

Argento also seems unruffled by the reputation most horror directors have in the eyes of the critical press. "This does not bother me. It is not important. I have come to realize that it's very hard to change people's ideas about horror films. It's okay. I am not desperate to be recognized as a so-called 'serious filmmaker'."

"The U.S. distributors are very hypocritical. The do not love movies; they love only money."

Argento is also acutely aware of the problems his films have always had with the censors because of his lingering portrayals of ghastly and explicit scenes of violence. He summarily dismisses the critics' claim that on-screen violence is tangentially related to similar

> **"*Opera, Deep Red* and *Suspiria* are the three pictures that are very close to my original vision."**

activity in the *real* world. Argento feels that even his youngest audiences are perceptive enough to distinguish the difference.

"Maybe we should be careful with the *adults* instead," he smiles. "The kids understand movies are a world of the nightmare, of dreams, inventions and music. They see a horror film and say 'I love this.' It is not real; it is a joke. When you make it too realistic in terms of story and setting, they don't like it because it is real. The young people, they know by their souls that this is the nightmare. The horror picture—it is not life."

For the future, Argento expresses a studied interest in pursuing a direction he began while shooting *Phenomena*. He remains very fascinated and curious about the world of entymology. "I want to make a picture seen through the eyes of a lizard with all these strange angles and perspectives. I knew when I made *Phenomena* that I wanted this. An entymologist made a study years ago and claimed he knew what the animals were saying and what they were seeing. Their vision, like that of a

La Setta

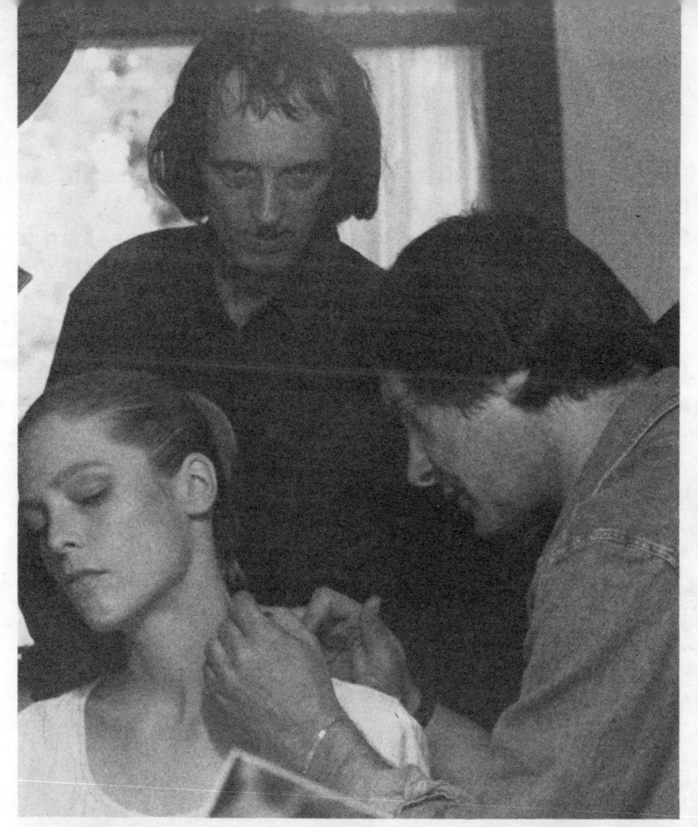

fly, is strange—so different from ours. Now, I want to explore the vision of a lizard."

"I am an explorer," concludes Argento, "and there are still many, many things to show, to represent on film. I have explored but a piece of this forest and it's a big, big forest."

In Johann Peter Eckermann's *Conversations with Goethe* (January 2, 1824), the German author asks, "Where do we now meet an original nature? And where is the man who has the strength to be true and show himself as he is?"

We *have* found him...and with him, the magic all around us.

FILMOGRAPHY

1967 ***Cemetery Without Crosses (Cementerio sin cruces)*** Story by Dario Argento. Directed by Robert Hossein. With Robert Hossein, Michele Mercier and Ann Marie Balin.

1968 ***Today Me...Tomorrow You...(Oggi A Me...Domani A Te...)*** Story and screenplay by Dario Argento. Directed by Tonino Cervini.

1968 ***One Night at Dinner (Metti, Una Sera a Cena)*** Screenplay by Dario Argento. Directed by Guiseppe Patroni Griffi.

1968 ***Sex Revolution (La Rivoluzione Sessuale)*** Story and screenplay by Dario Argento. Directed by Riccardo Ghione.

1968 ***Zero Probability (Probabilita' Zero)*** Story and screenplay by Dario Argento. Directed by Maurizio Lucidi.

1969 ***Five Man Army (Un Esercito di Cinque)*** Story and screenplay by Dario Argento. Directed by Don Taylor.

1969 ***Commandos*** Story by Dario Argento. Directed by Amando Crispino.

1969 ***Legion of the Damned (La Legione dei Dannati)*** Dialog supervision by Dario Argento. Directed by Umberto Lenzi.

1969 ***Season of Loves (La Stagione dei Sensi)*** Story supervision by Dario Argento. Directed by Massimo Franciosa.

1969 ***Once Upon a Time in the West*** Story by Dario Argento, Sergio Leone and Bernardo Bertolucci. Directed by Sergio Leone. With Henry Fonda, Jason Robards and Charles Bronson.

1970 ***Five Man Army (Ejercito de Cinco)*** Story by Dario Argento and Marc Richards. Directed by Don Taylor. With Peter Graves, James Daly, and Bud Spencer.

1970 ***Bird With the Crystal Plumage (L'Uccello dalle Piume di Cristallo)*** With Tony Musante, Suzy Kendall and Eva Renzi.

1971 ***The Cat O'Nine Tails (Il Gatto a Nove Code)*** With Karl Malden and James Franciscus.

1971 ***Four Flies on Grey Velvet (Quattro Mosche di Velutto Grigio)*** With Michael Brandon, Mimsy Farmer and Jean-Pierre Marielle.

1972 ***Door Into Darkness (La Porta Sul Buio)*** TV series included: ***The Bus (Il Tram)*** Written and directed by Dario Argento. ***Home Neighbor (Il Vicino di Casa)*** Written and directed by Luigi Cozzi. ***The Doll (La Bambola)*** Written and directed by Mario Foglietti. ***Eyewitness (Testimone Oculare)*** Written by Luigi Cozzi and Dario Argento. Directed by Dario Argento.

1973 ***Five Days of Milan (Le Cinque Giornate)*** Screenplay and direction with Adriano Callentano, Ennio Cerusico, Marilu Tollo.

1975 ***Deep Red (Profondo Rosso)*** With David Hemmings, Daria Nicolodi and Gabriele Lavia.

1976 ***Suspiria*** With Jessica Harper, Stefania Casini and Udo Keir.

1979 ***Dawn of the Dead (Zombi)*** Dario Argento as co-producer and composer. Directed by George A. Romero. With David Enge, Ken Foree, Scott Reiniger and Gaylen Ross.

The Sect-- Argento and Soavi,together again.

1980 ***Inferno*** With Irene Miracle, Leigh McCloskey and Daria Nicolodi.

1982 ***Tenebrae (aka Unsane) (Sotto gli Occhi dell'Assassino)*** With Anthony Franciosa, John Saxon and Daria Nicolodi.

1985 ***Phenomena (aka Creepers)*** With Jennifer Connelly, Daria Nicolodi and Donald Pleasence.

1986 ***Demons (Demoni)*** Produced by Dario Argento. Directed by Lamberto Bava. With Urbano Barberini and Natasha Hovey.

1987 ***Demons 2 (Demoni 2)*** Produced by Dario Argento. Directed by Lamberto Bava.

1987 ***The Horror World of Dario Argento*** Directed by Michele Soavi.

1987 ***Mystery (Giallo)*** Weekly TV program produced by Dario Argento. Included ***Night Shift (Turno di Notte)***. Episodes directed by Lamberto Bava and Luigi Cozzi.

1988 ***Opera (aka Terror at the Opera)*** With Cristina Marsillach, Ian Charleson, Urbano Barberini and Daria Nicolodi.

1989 ***The Church (La Chiesa)*** Produced by Dario Argento. Directed by Michele Soavi. With Hugh Quayshie, Tomas Arana, Fedor Chaliapin.

1989 ***Two Evil Eyes (Due Occhi Diabolici)*** Co-directed by George A. Romero. With Adrienne Barbeau, Harvey Keitel and Madeleine Potter.

1990 ***The Sect (La Setta)*** Written and produced by Dario Argento. Directed by Michele Soavi.

1991 Untitled film written and directed by Dario Argento. Scheduled to be shot in the United States.

ON YOUR KNEES IN *THE CHURCH*

by

Chas. Balun

THE CHURCH (1990) DIRECTED BY MICHELE SOAVI 110 Minutes (Uncut version)

After Michele Soavi's superlative, affectionate documentary, *The Horror World of Dario Argento*, and his self-assured, stunning debut feature, *Stagefright* (*Aquarius*, *Deliria*), many critics began to regard him as heir-apparent to the unchallenged throne of Argento. With his second feature film, *The Church* (*La Chiesa*), Soavi has triumphantly fulfilled those expectations. Co-written and co-produced by Dario Argento, *The Church* is a stately, classy supernatural thriller that boasts bravura cinematography, entrancing set pieces, generous doses of splatter and creature FX, a stirring score (by Keith Emerson, Simon Boswell, Phillip Glass and Goblins) and haunting imagery that stays with you long after the closing credits.

The Church originally began as *Demons 3*, with Lamberto Bava again slated to direct, but the dismal box-office of *Demons 2* forced wary producer-investors to replace both Bava and the original script. When Bava went on to direct an insipid Italian TV movie called *The Ogre*, he subtitled it *Demons 3*, so Soavi and Argento had to settle for an alternate title for their joint project.

The Church begins in the Middle Ages, when hundreds of suspected devil worshippers are brutally massacred and buried in a mass grave that later becomes the site of a massive Gothic cathedral. Soavi then propels the action forward by hundreds of years with a dizzying, show-stopping camera tour de force that recalls the spectacular acrobatic cinematography seen in such Argento films as *Suspiria*, *Tenebrae* and *Opera*.

When a new research librarian is cut and infected during an archeological dig, evil forces trapped within the cathedral begin to manifest themselves: a priest is impaled on a fence post, a worker is gutted by a possessed jackhammer,a teacher is skewered by a rampaging madman while another claws her face to ribbons. The chaos continues to escalate and before Sergio Stivaletti's horned and winged demon makes the beast-with-two -backs with the heroine (Barbara Cupisti) in an eery, candlelit sepulchre, we are treated to a weeping woman banging a decapitated head against a church bell while yet another struggling damsel gets her face smashed to pumpkin pulp by a speeding train.

The uncut print spares little, and other graphic shots including a man pulling out his beating heart and the gory, jackhammer evisceration are both sure to be missing in the "R" rated version. (Southgate Entertainment plans to release an uncut, unrated version as well, so relax.)

Argento's daughter, Asia, is also featured in a co-starring role as is Italian Sleaze Legend, John Morghen, who is once again inexplicably cast as a priest. (Check out Ruggero Deodato's *Phantom of Death* for yet another side of Monsignor Morghen.)

Though the film suffers somewhat from the clumsy, distracting dubbing and the protracted running time, (just under two hours) *The Church* remains a satisfying, occasionally transcendent viewing experience that further reinforces both Argento and Soavi's mastery of the medium.

Fans of the newly annoited Royal Italian Court of Connoisseur Horror will no doubt have still another reason for rejoicing: Argento has just finished writing and producing Soavi's latest film, *La Setta (The Sect)*, starring Herbert Lom and Kelly Leigh Curtis (Jamie Lee's sister).

The Church

I DREAM OF DEMONS

Profile of Italian F/X Maestro Sergio Stivaletti

by Thomas Nilsson

Horny devil makes the beast with two backs in *The Church*.

Sergio Stivaletti is one of a handful of the few really great FX wizards in Europe. When, for instance, Dario Argento — the Master of the Macabre himself — needs someone to visualize his famous tales of terror, he calls Stivaletti. Still, the modest, softspoken Rome-based FX Supremo — who has supplied the red stuff for some of Pastaland's most notorious splatter-feasts — is still delivering his meaty shocks in the shadows of his more renowned American colleagues.

In 1986 Stivaletti and his FX disciples shocked audiences everywhere with eye-popping, jaw-dropping scenes of ultraviolent, explicit guts n' gore-orgies in Lamberto Bava's Demons *— a bloodred story of a haunted movie theatre where moviegoers turn into flesheating zombies. Today — as much in demand as ever in his native Italy — Sergio Stivaletti is hard at work, creating more of that which our darkest nightmares are made of. Thomas Nilsson has tracked down signore Grand Guignol who talks openly about his work, hopes and dreams in this rare interview.*

In Italy — as in most other parts of Europe — you rarely, if ever, hear about the talented make-up artists that reside and work on *this* side of the Atlantic. The word simply doesn't seem to get around as much as in the States where creators of this bloody, often illfated craft more often receive the attention they crave. The likes of Tom Savini, Rick Baker, Rob Bottin and Dick Smith are — deservedly — treated like superstars while (most of) their European colleagues have yet to step out in the limelight. Maybe it is, in some ways, due to the various censorship Boards that are pestering the horror movie makers on both continents. True, the MPAA do seem to become more powerful each year now, but those scissor-happy celluloid-saboteurs have plenty of like-minded bureaucrats spread across the globe, situated particularly in places like Sweden, Norway, Germany and Britain. So, bearing this in mind, one really shouldn't be too surprised to learn that only a handful of dedicated Splatter-afficionados have heard of people like Segio Stivaletti, Rosario Prestopino, Gianetto De Rossi and others. OK, maybe you've heard of their grisly handywork, but thanks to the corrupt censors, you've never got a fair chance of watching their stuff in action, so to speak.

> **"In Italy, if you wanted to become an FX artist, the guts n' gore business was where you put your money."**

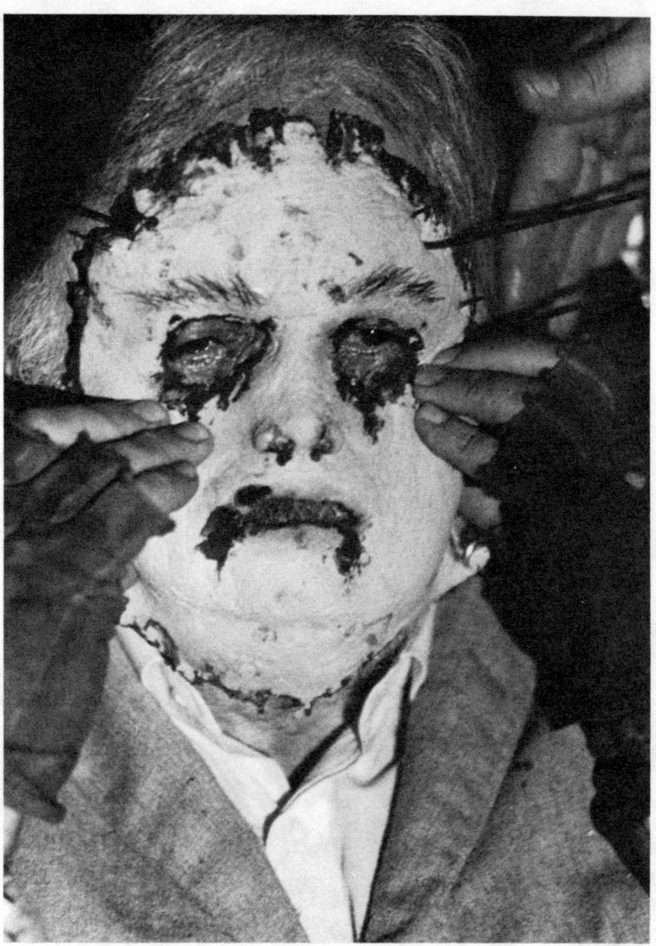

The Sect specializes in easily affordable face-jobs.

When in the early 80's, a tidal wave of megaviolent, gutsy Italian gorefeasts, crammed with never before seen explicit shockscenes of the macabre, suddenly swept over us, European gore-meisters like Lucio Fúlci, Dario Argento, Lamberto Bava, Ruggero Deodato, Umberto Lenzi and Andrea Bianchi had us all cheering, laughing and vomiting in our seats.

The term "Spaghetti-horror" would soon become a household expression of those unnerving, brutal excursions into the dark and the "zombie" and "cannibal" movies spread like wildfire. Gorehounds everywhere were applauding while the censors called for overtime in the cutting-rooms. But Fulci, Argento and friends were HOT items at the time. Sure enough, those guys were seated in the director's chairs, but the ones who really delivered the meaty shocks, were, of course, the crews working in the shadows.

"I landed my first professional make-up assignment back in 1983," remembers Sergio Stivaletti from his Rome studio, situated just around the corner from Italy's first, already famous, Horror/Fantasy shop "Profondo Rosso".

"I was offered a chance to deliver the special effects for Dario Argento's *Phenomena* (a.k.a.

Creepers — the butchered U.S. version of the film) and I was very flattered. Argento was, of course, very big and famous in Italy already at the time.

"Before that," Sergio continues in surprisingly good English, "I had been experimenting on my own as far as special effects were concerned. I am totally self-taught. For a while I was very much into space movies, *Star Wars* and movies like that, you know, and I also built litle miniatures of spaceships. But in Italy, at least in the past, horror films were THE main issue in moviemaking, and if you wanted to become an FX artist — and to get to work in that field — the guts n' gore business was where you had to put your money. That's why I too got going doing those gore effects. It was just a natural turn for me. And really, I didn't mind at all. I have always been very interested in horror movies — well, I do love them — so when I got to be involved in making them too, I simply couldn't be happier. And again, working for Dario already that early in my career, was fantastic.

After working for Argento on *Phenomena*, Sergio Stivaletti took his bloody toolbox to the set of *Demons* and turned this violent tale of terror, directed by Lamberto Bava and produced by Argento, into a gruesomly explicit, jaw-dropping splatter-feast that amazed horror buffs everywhere. Thanks to the film's heavy FX, *Demons* turned out to become a major success at the box offices, especially in the south of Europe.

"The transformation scene is arguably the best effect I have created as of yet," says Stivaletti. "It wasn't all that complicated to perform, but the effect turns out very well, very realistic on the big screen. when I look back on all of my previous work, I'm still very pleased — and proud — of what we accomplished in *Demons*.

Stivaletti also handled the FX – together with Rosario Prestopino – in Bava's *Demons 2*, released in 1987, but for various reasons neither Bava nor Stivaletti managed to repeat the tremendous success of the original movie.

"Personally, I wasn't happy with the film at all," Stivaletti admits. I felt that they screwed it up in the cutting-room while editing the film. It just lacks continuity."

In the States, *Demons 2* bombed for another reason too, thanks to the MPAA who forced the distributors to cut out most of the explicit scenes in order to secure an "R" rating. Sitivletti also reveals that he is very happy with his work in Argento protége Michele Soavi's horror film, *The Church*.

"The enormous mechanical demon that we provided for the film is another highlight of my career as a make-up artist and I regard this work right up there with the *Demons* FX. This giant demon is also the most technically advanced prop I have created as of yet," Stivaletti says.

"I wasn't happy with *Demons 2* at all. They screwed it up in the cutting room. It lacks continuity."

"But when I see what my American colleagues have accomplished in the FX field, I can't say that I'm too impressed with my own work," Sergio says modestly.

The Americans are so advanced and so clever, way ahead of the rest of us," Stivaletti goes on. "I love to watch their magic. Rick Baker's "ape suits" in *Greystoke*, for instance, are probably the best FX I have ever seen.

Apart from minor contributions for a film shooting in Cuba, Sergio Stivaletti has yet to work outside Italy, but he has his hopes and dreams.

"Naturally I would just love to work in the USA," he says. "I think that is what all Italian (European) make-up artists dream of. But the competition is so tough over there."

"Then again, you never know, do you? Maybe someone will see my work in a film and like it enough to offer me a job in an American production," Stivaletti laughs.

He speaks openly about his past, present and future, and talks enthusiastically about a trip he made to the States not long ago.

"It was fantastic," he remembers. "Stepping into a place like Rick Baker's studio was like entering another dimension. Rick is marvelous and probably THE best all-around FX artist in the business today.

"Besides a most interesting visit to the ILM studio, I also got to meet with people like Tom Savini and Dick Smith."

Stivaletti admits that he hopes that his visit to the USA eventually will open up some doors for him there. And why not? The man has proven his skills more than once, at least over here in Europe. In the States, the censors made sure that nobody caught his talents in the hacked-up version of Argento's *Phenomena / Creepers,* but if that uncut version of *Opera* – as rumoured – actually turns up unrated in the USA, people will sure as Hell notice this Italian FX maestro!

And speaking of *Opera*, this controversial journey into the dark corners of a bloodsoaked Italian opera house, the film also turned out to become a nightmare for everyone involved, even behind the cameras. Director Dario Argento had his fair share of accidents and mishaps. Sergio Stivaletti – who provided the FX for the film – also recalls that working on the set was a gruelling experience. Rumour has it that Argento wasn't all that happy with Stivaletti's work, but no one seems too eager to dwell on the subject anymore.

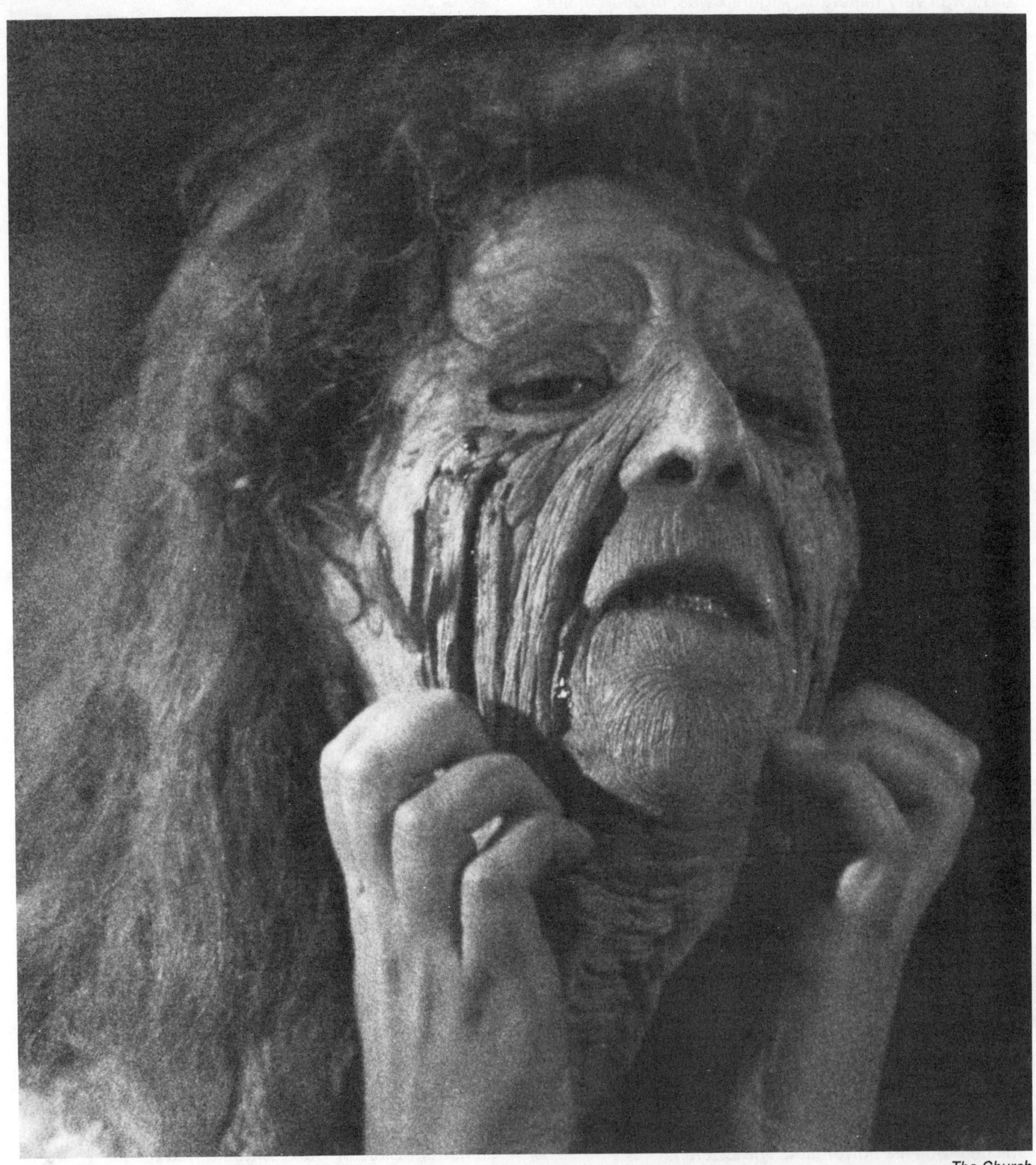

The Church

Whatever happened during the making of *Opera* has been buried in the past and both Argento and Stivaletti still work together, in one way or another. Stivaletti has recently completed the FX for another horror film, called *La Setta*, directed by Michele Soavi and produced by Argento. One also feels that despite whatever dissension occured

> "Rick Baker's ape-suits in *Greystoke* are probably the best FX I have ever seen."

"When I see what my American colleagues have accomplished, I can't say that I'm too impressed with my own work. They are so advanced and so clever, way ahead of the rest of us."

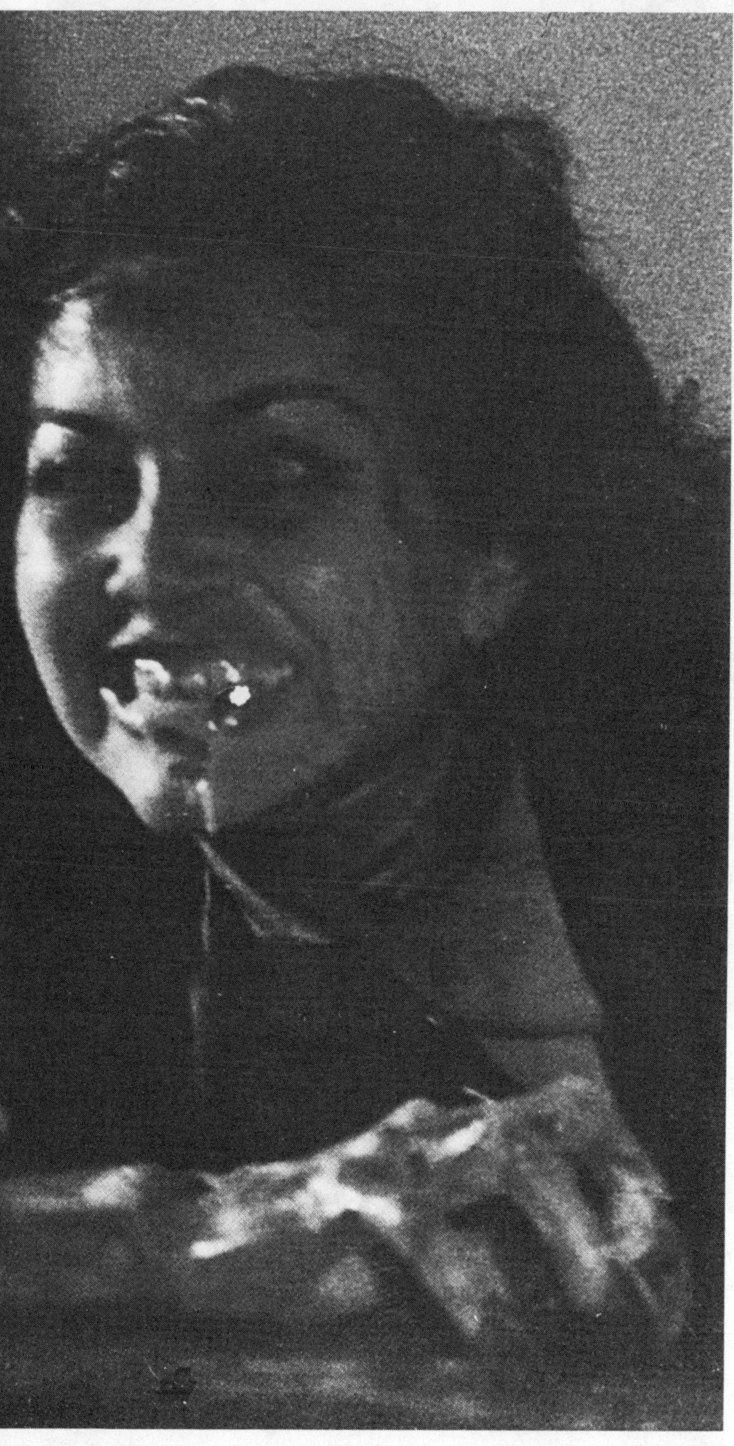

Argento and Stivaletti still have the highest regard and respect for each other. In the now already legendary basement of Argento's Profondo Rosso shop in Rome, Sergio Stivaletti has displayed an impressive collection of props used in some of Argento's most famous movies.

In this gruesome Chamber of Horrors, Stivaletti has reconstructed scenes from such classics as *Demons*, *Opera*, *Phenomena* and *The Church* – stuff guaranteed to make your eyes pop !

Talking to Stivaletti about horror movies and explicit FX, it is of course (absolutely) unavoidable not to bring up a certain subject – film censorship. Like Argento, Stivaletti objects very strongly to all forms of censorship, and he can hardly believe my stories of the infamous Swedish censors.

"I cannot understand why you have to cut horror films," he says. "Horror films are just a joke, they are visions of fantasy! There are so many people who go watch horror movies only for the sake of exciting, mind-bending special effects. The people are curious and they want to be amazed, but when you cut out the stuff, there's nothing."

At the moment, Sergio Stivaletti is hard at work, providing the effects for TV movie, produced for Italian television and directed by Lamberto Bava, due to be aired around Christmas 1990.

"It's not a big production," Stivaletti reveals, "But I enjoy this kind of work too. It's a fantasy tale and I have been making some funny little props; talking fish, trees and various animals."

"I don't mind working with splatter FX," he continues, "but sometimes this line of blood, guts n' gore becomes a little monotonous. I, for one, can well understand why Tom Savini, for instance, admits that he is tired of producing splatter FX. I too wouldn't mind doing other stuff, for instance making effects for sci-fi movies. I love science-fiction films too.

"Once I was offered to supply the FX for a porno movie," Stivaletti laughs. "But I decided to decline the offer. I simply couldn't see where the challenge was."

Right, it's not that kind of flesh we want one of the most skilled and original FX artists in Europe to be messing with. His supreme talents shouldn't be wasted with latex cocks and fake cum. Sergio Stivaletti is a man for zombies, demons and other gruelling creatures of the dark. And he *is* available, so listen up, Stateside-based producers. Here's a man capable of scaring the socks off of anyone, and he's ready to bring the deep red stuff to your shores, too.

Drooling *Demons* of Doom.

HAND IT TO REMO

by Shane Dallman

No, not Remo Williams...Remo D., comedian at large, at your service. The twelve of you who've managed to catch my act know me for one thing in particular. For the rest of you, I'll explain. My stage persona (not my offstage one, I admit) is equipped with an iron hook instead of a right hand and delights in offering many florid explanations of how this came to be. It wasn't long before I started using clips from my favorite movies to illustrate these explanations.

Well, you know how these things work out. My casual quest for the best hand-loss clips became an obsessive undertaking. As Tim Lucas searches for Jess Franco, as Shane Dallmann hunts for Paul Naschy, I look for anyone who'll give me a hand—and remove it!

Not that any old hand-loss will do it: witness the *Star Wars* films, in which Darth Vader and Luke Skywalker take turns hacking off each others' manual extremities with their light sabers. A quick flash of electric red or blue followed by the briefest glimpses of the lost hands flying away? Uh-uh, sorry, no way, that doesn't cut it (pun most definitely intended). Where's the feeling? The emotional punch that makes you sit up and take notice? Something's missing here, but exactly what? That's what I'm here to find out.

The ideal place to begin this investigation is a listing of what I've found to be the greatest hand-loss sequences in cinema history. But before I begin, there's something I feel compelled to acknowledge. Yes, I have seen *Demonoid* (a/k/a *Macabra*, filmed in 1980, released in 1982). This endearing little effort features scene after scene of people being possessed with a desire to remove their left hands and utilizing such methods as slamming them in car doors, letting trains run over them, and forcing doctors to do it for them at gunpoint! That it doesn't make the top five is more or less due to the rather lackluster material in between the de-handings. If this doesn't sound fair, bear in mind that the best hand loss scenes are capable of carrying entire movies! Nevertheless, *Demonoid* rates an affectionate sixth in my book.

And now...REMO D'S LIST OF THE FIVE GREATEST HAND LOSS SCENES IN FILM HISTORY! In chronological order, they are:

1. DAUGHTER OF HORROR (1953)

The classic set-up. The dead man won't let go of the incriminating piece of jewelry, so...thwack! Doesn't stop there, though—the psychologically tormented heroine still can't get the hand to let go, so she picks it up and takes it with her! But when the demons of her mind seem to be catching up, she doesn't want to be seen with it...so, when she passes a blind flower girl, she drops the hand in her basket! Unforgettable.

2. ANDY WARHOL'S FRANKENSTEIN (1974)

Everyone remembers (or has at least heard of) the grand finale of this one, in which Udo Kier delivers a soul-searching monologue for a full minute or so after being impaled on a giant spear...but the prelude to this is every bit as outrageous. Failing to control his monster, the Baron tries to protect himself behind an iron gate. The monster reaches the gate simultaneously, and slams it shut on the Baron's hand! With his wrist gushing like the Revi Fountain, the panic-stricken Baron retrieves his hand and tries to force it back on—just by squeezing! When it becomes clear that this isn't going to work, he turns on his captive (Joe Dallesandro), hanging from the ceiling. The Baron viciously throws the hand at him, screaming "It's all your fault!" It's moments like this that can bring tears to your eyes.

3. THE HAND (1981)

Well, of course. Not that this qualifies on the basis of the subject matter alone. Director Oliver Stone sets this one up with an awe-inspiring moment in which Michael Caine, shaking his fist outside the window of his car, abruptly encounters another vehicle going the other way—and passing too close for comfort. The result is noisy, splashy, and simply wonderful.

4. DOCTOR BUTCHER, M.D. (1982)

Down to basics here. The opening sequence (of the film proper, not the tacked-on title scenes) closely follows a mysterious man in black paying a late-night visit to the morgue. He knows what he wants, and it's a hand*—no more, no less. We get to watch, up close and personal, as his blade slices through the donor's wrist, while the soundtrack begins with the clean squeak of the first few strokes and gradually develops through the ka-chunk-ka-chunk-ka-chunk of the "hard parts" and the final, satisfying snap of completion. The mystery man holds his trophy up for all to see, and then carefully* *places it in a plastic Baggie. This scene was obviously meant as a message for George Lucas—a message reading "This is how it's done."*

5. VIDEODROME (1983)
This David Cronenberg masterpiece has more intelligence and food for thought per frame than almost anything else you can name. But it also features the scene in which Max Renn (James Woods) opens up his abdomen to receive a living, breathing videocassette from his treacherous partner Harlan (Peter Dvorsk). Things get a bit sticky when Harlan attempts to remove his hand from said opening. The result makes it look as if Max had a Veg-O-Matic installed in his guts, along with an armory, as Harlan comes away with a ticking time bomb fused to his shredded stump (all together, now…"a hand grenade!") Okay, so it's a video hallucination, but it sure doesn't play that way on screen. "See you in Pittsburgh!"

Well, that's the top five—mine, anyway. But we've got lots more to explore. Let's see how long we can keep this column going. You have a favorite "hand" scene. I know you do. Think about it. Remember it. Write it down. And...hand it to Remo!

SHAUN HUTSON

THE SECRET OF HIS EXCESS!

by John Martin

With thanks to CREEPING UNKNOWN editor Nick Cairns for his assistance.

"This is 'ow you get slung out of a posh hotel" proclaims Shaun Hutson, stuffing salad up his nose. Conversation has turned to the point in SLUGS, the novel of monstrous mollusk mayhem that kick-started his notorious career into life, where a character's head explodes in a hotel restaurant after his reckless consumption of a lettuce-leaf impregnated with slug eggs. Apologizing for his inability to re-enact that magic moment, Shaun is doing the next best thing. Our immaculately tuxedoed and begowned fellow diners in this particular posh Manchester hotel are valiantly confining their attention to their own plates (British reserve, you see). But no doubt if they were aware of the books with which the leather-jacketed, bullet-belted dude with the shades over his eyes and the celery up his nose has made his name ("And that name is 'Sick Bastard' "), including SPAWN (which pits an escaped axe-murderer against a psychotic burns victim under the telepathic control of runaway vampire abortions), VICTIMS (in which a baby gets micro-waved) and ASSASSIN (in which a zombie hit-man ejaculates maggots into the mouth of the hapless hooker who's blowing him), they'd be trampling each other underfoot in their haste to get to the exit.

The Beast of Bletchley is smaller than you expect, but energetic and muscular, his bulging biceps attributable to long hours playing the drums (though Hutson himself offers an altogether more implausible and obscene explanation for this physical attribute). His twin passions are Heavy Metal music (he's a fully paid-up Iron Maiden groupie) and Liverpool F.C. soccer team ("My criteria for working are these... as long as Liverpool have got a full squad of fit players, there's plenty of money coming in, I'm healthy and my family's healthy, that's it, I'm happy!") and it's actually a bit of a struggle diverting him from these subjects to any discussion of his work. When you do manage it, he frequently interrupts to protest that the conversation is "getting too deep", Hutson, though an

Hutson rocks...hard.

"Reading one of my books is like going to a heavy rock gig...there's the same relentless feeling..."

excellent, entertaining companion, is a difficult interview. That's because he dreads being labeled as "pretentious", which is the charge he lays at the door of so many of his contemporaries, his scorn for whom is matched only by the amount of self-deprecating barbs he aims at himself, which fail to disguise his fierce pride in his craft. The upshot of these contradictions is that Hutson remains scandalously under-exposed for one with such outspoken views (not to mention healthy sales figures).

Hutson is a particularly neglected figure in America, (despite the stalwart flag-waving of my esteemed DEEP RED editor on his behalf), chiefly known as the man whose novel formed the basis of Juan Piquer Simon's woeful SLUGS - THE MOVIE. Since his move from the defunct W.H. Allen to Sphere in Britain, a States-side push for his work is being planned, but when I spoke to him, he was mourning missed opportunities.

SH: Dorchester was publishing my stuff in the States, I stopped 'em with *Relics* because they were paying peanuts. The agent I used to have said that they were trying to buy *Relics*, so I said "Tell 'em to fuck off!"
JM: Does *Victims* represent the start of a new phase in your writing?
SH: Yeah, I agree with you on that, I'm not saying I consciously sat down and thought "I'm gonna go in a new direction", because I didn't do that. But there's only so much pleasure you can get out of writing about bloody slugs, for a start! You can put characters in a situation where they're being chased by slugs, but they're not going to have much trouble out-running them, are they? No more slugs! People are always bugging me to write *Slugs* III but I won't do it. Even if they offered half a million, I'd be very reluctant to do it. The second slugs book, *Breeding Ground*, represented the end of the first phase in my writing career.

JM: I feel that around the time of *Relics* you were getting into a bit of a rut with that "inhabitants of a small town go ape-shit due to ecological disaster, or black magic, or whatever" story-line, and that you got yourself out of that with *Victims*.

SH: *Spawn, Victims* in particular, *Relics* and *Shadows* are all meant to be more like Whodunnits. I mean, with *Spawn,* I haven't met anyone yet who had figured out who the killer was, which is nice... and also with *Relics*, I defy anyone to identify the murderer in that. I suppose to a certain extent the characters are just cannon fodder... slug fodder... microwave fodder in *Victims*! But *Victims* does take a different direction, and the one that comes out in hard-back in October over here, *Nemesis*, is totally different again. It's got the lowest body-count of anything I've ever done, but it's got a far heavier atmosphere, the most depressing book I've ever written.

JM: You're touchy about this one.

SH: I couldn't talk about it... still can't. Sounds like bull-shit, which I'm not fond of, as you know, but it's true.

JM: Did writing it get something out of your system?

SH: When I finished it I knew it was either the best thing I'd ever done or the biggest load of crap I'd ever done. I suspected the former, but I wasn't sure. Then my editors rang up and said it was far better than anything they'd seen in the last five years, not just from me but from anyone else... and I thought "fuckin' 'ell!" But for *Monolith* (now out in Britain and retitled *Renegades - JM*). I've got to get back into the state of mind I was in before I wrote *Nemesis*, which was very personal, a lot of things that happened in that happened to me... the character in it is me, which is why I don't wanna talk about it. The new hard-back, *Assassin* is the quickest paced thing I've ever done, out of control, there's no way of stopping it. I was wasted when I finished it. I write so fast, I'd like to think that breathlessness conveys itself in the written word. I feel that reading one of my books is like going to a heavy rock gig, there's the same relentless feeling to both of them. When somebody finishes one of my books they should be drained and exhausted, just as they would be after a great rock concert. They should go "Whew! That was great!"

JM: Do you rattle this stuff off in a frenzy?

SH: I sit down and think "Oh Christ! Another day of this! Why did I ever give up that job at McDonalds?" (Laughs) No, actually, I sit there every day in my office, which is the spare bedroom, for tax reasons,

"I sent it to the editors and they said, 'The only way we're going to get it through is to cut out all of the blasphemy and change the orifices...' "

and I work 9-4, five days a week. I spend 2 or 3 months researching every book, which is why I can write them so quickly. I've got all my notes laid out and I've got my cast list in front of me, in case someone's scar changes position from under the left eye to under the right eye during the course of the book, what colour hair they've got, what sort of car they've got. Cars are the most difficult thing for me because I don't drive. I was once writing a 150 m.p.h. car-chase between a Chevette and a Capri, and someone said to me, "You can't do that in a Capri!" *Slugs* took 25 days, *Breeding Ground* was 18, the novelization of *The Terminator* only took 10, *Shadows*, at 48 days was the longest, and that included re-writes. The most I ever do is two drafts: The first is done quickly and I send it to the editor and he tells me what's wrong with it, then I put it right. That's it! I can't work any other way. I work at such a high emotional pitch that I can't sustain interest in anything for longer than two months at a time. Holidays are rare.

"Clive Barker called me irresponsible after I told him about *Chainsaw Terror*. I actually managed to shut him up for a couple of seconds, which is no mean feat."

JM: In *Spawn* you've got the escaped axe murderer, plus the psychotic burns victim, not to mention the telepathic vampire abortions, (Hutson laughs) and there's no way it should work, but it does, and you say that the story is based on real life events!

SH: Yeah, my inspiration for that one came from a newspaper story about a German hospital porter who couldn't bring himself to burn abortions, so he buried them in a shallow grave behind the hospital. But it was a difficult book to research, trying to get doctors and nurses to talk about abortions. I got quite friendly with a porter at the local hospital and he told me what they do with things like that.
Victims was very difficult too, they very nearly didn't let me into Scotland Yard's Black Museum. I'd gone down looking very smart, I actually found a tie somewhere to put on...

JM: Did it give you any good ideas for *Victims*?

SH: The only idea it gave me was that I wasn't gonna be able to use it in the bloody book, because the original idea for *Victims* was that there was going to be someone taking exhibits from the Black Museum and using them in murders. But once I got there and saw how impossible it was to get stuff out, the Black Museum became redundant. But it got me in there to have a good look around, which is what I really wanted. I like to keep at least one part of my stories rooted in reality, it gives the reader something to hold onto. The horror may be in my imagination, but the basis of it is in fact. For instance, there are, believe it or not, three species of flesh-eating-slugs in this country. There

"I'm hated by 99% of the horror authors because I don't give a shit about their self-congratulatory, back slapping scene."

wasn't actually much research to do for *Slugs* and *Breeding Ground*, because all I had to do was sit down and read what it is that slugs do. Obviously something like *Shadows* involved a lot more research –I learned to read tarot cards for that one. And the disease porphyria, as described in *Erebus*, actually affects one person in every 10,000.

JM: What about ideas that come from the reality of your own life?

SH: There are three people in *Breeding Ground*, that die horribly, who are real people. Two of them were guys that burgled our flat. There are very few people that I truly detest, apart from Thatcher, who I loathe with a passion, but I suppose I did use *Breeding Ground* as a revenge novel. The only way someone usually gets into one of my books is if they ask, they want to be a victim, and I think six or seven of the people in *Victims* are real people. My inspiration for that book was the song *Gary Gilmore's Eyes* by the Adverts. I know the guy who wrote the lyrics to that. And there are a lot of in-jokes in *Victims*, as there is in all my work, there are plenty of jokes in there, if you can spot 'em.

Someone once described something I'd written as the ultimate in black comedy. There's nothing wrong with that, you know that from watching bloody horror films. If there's no natural safety valve in a horror film or a horror book, then the audience tends to laugh in all the wrong places. *The Exorcist*, there was no safety valve in that, so the place where everyone laughed was where the girl threw up all over the priest. Now I don't find that particularly funny. *Jaws* is the example I use: The shark's head appears, and everyone goes "Waaah!!" and then Roy Scheider says, "I think we're gonna need a bigger boat," and everyone cracks up laughing. If you're gonna spend four pages describing something, then the readers are going to nod out. They need something to lighten it up, poor bastards! But my stuff is obviously very strong, too... it's been cut — it usually is — everything I've ever written has had stuff taken out somewhere.

JM: Any notable passages that you can remember?

SH: Well, there's a very long necrophilia sequence in *Shadows* which was trimmed. I just went into a lot more detail than I needed to, probably because I was quite enjoying it. (Laughs) Actually I'm really worried about a guy who keeps writing to me. He lives opposite a graveyard, and every time a woman gets buried in there, he writes to me to tell me what he's going to do to her.

JM: Is it true that you censored yourself on *Relics*?

SH: No, I didn't, what happened was that the black mass sequences had blasphemy in them as well as all the nasty business with goats and stuff. One black mass sequence in particular was about eight pages long, really bad, really over the top, even I was disgusted when I was writing it. So I sent it in to the editors and they said, "the only way we're going to get it through is to cut out all the blasphemy and change the orifices", because it was really bad. The baby eating sequence in *Shadows* was heavily cut, too.

JM: I've heard rumours that copies of the un-cut *Chainsaw Terror* manuscript are changing hands at £75 a throw in Birmingham.

SH: That's right, and I don't see a bloody penny of it! That's a mate of mine, and I use the term loosely, doing that. *Chainsaw Terror* is the only one of my pseudonymous novels that I'll own up to. What happened with that one was, I did a novelisation of *The Terminator* for W. H. Allen...I won't do novelisations as a rule, but I would have killed to do the one for *Scarface*. Anyway, they tried to get the rights for me to do a novelisation of *The Texas Chainsaw Massacre*. The rights were too expensive, so instead they said to me, "Just do us the most over-the-top novel, featuring chainsaws, that you can do." I did it in 25 days, sent it in, and two days later I got a phone call saying, "We're going to have to cut it, because we didn't think anyone could go quite as far over the top as you've gone!" W.H. Smith, the biggest chain in the country, still banned it anyway, simply because it featured the word "chainsaw" in the title, which meant we had to scrap plans for two sequels, *Chainsaw Blood-Bath* and *Chainsaw Slaughter*. (Laughs) *Chainsaw Terror* has been re-issued under the title *Come the Night*, and they want to put my name on it, but I won't let them unless they re-instate the cuts.

It was on account of all that that Clive Barker called me irresponsible. I actually managed to shut him up for a couple of seconds, which is no mean feat. It was on a panel discussion and question and answer thing and someone asked me if I'd ever had anything cut and I said yeah, *Chainsaw Terror*. They asked me to tell them what was cut, and I did. It was a scene where a woman gets nailed to a work-bench, gets her nipples cut off and is then raped with a chainsaw. Ol' Clive was speechless after that.

JM: So how serious is all this animosity between you and the likes of Clive Barker and Ramsey Campbell?

SH: It's not, not at all. Campbell knows what I've said, and I know what he's said. The next time we meet I'll say, "Alright!" And Clive Barker can jet off to America to make 86 films before the end of the year, good luck to him, just don't ask me to watch any of 'em.

JM: So you all get on OK when you meet up for panels, or whatever?

SH: No, I hate their guts! (Laughs) The whole point is that I'm hated by 99% of the horror authors, because I don't give a shit about their self-congratulatory, backslapping scene, with the sole, and very notable, exception of James Herbert, because he's got exactly the same attitude about the business as I have. It used to irritate me when people said I was ripping him off. We're from different generations. This might give you some idea of the age gap: they were passing *The Rats* around in the playground when I was at school, it was considered pretty hot stuff then. I mean there was what...eight years between *Rats* and *Slugs*. Guy N. Smith had already done all the ripping off that was going to be done. I mean, the shout-line for *Night of the Crabs* was, if I remember correctly, "In the tradition of *The Rats*"... they forgot to add "Except that this is crap!" That was the book that made me think maybe I could get horror published. I mean it was so very bad that it would give anyone hope.
But all that animosity stuff started with the others, not me. I love it when they have a go at me, but they've got to expect to get some back. Some people can dish it out but they can't take it, and if someone calls me irresponsible, especially if I'm sitting right next to them, I'm not gonna ignore it. But I've reached the point where I'm completely impervious to criticism. You walk a fine line between ego and self-belief in this business, and it's very difficult to know where to draw the line between the two, I don't think I'm a big-headed bastard, but I knew from the beginning that I'm good at what I do, because a hell of a lot of people buy my books. I don't need Kim Newman to say, "This man is a godawful writer", which is what he said after reading *Relics.* I think anyone who walks around in a three-piece suit with a watch-chain and a fedora hat is a terminal arse-hole, quite honestly.

JM: Ramsey Campbell did a review of *Breeding Ground* in which he said basically: "This is the second novel Hutson has written about slugs. The only problem with that is that slugs can't do much except be disgusting. Then again, much the same could be said for Hutson."

SH: (Laughing) I haven't heard that one before, that's good. But you know, what good is a brilliant review if you only sell 20,000 paperbacks? The public are the most discerning critics. Herbert's got the right idea, that it's all about entertainment. I think if someone pays good money for a book, the least you can do is entertain them.

JM: Is it true that even *you* were grossed out by NEKROMANTIK?

SH: Yeah, I saw it alright, I just couldn't believe it. I sat there like (adopts wide-eyed, slack-jawed expression), I'm not kidding! About three-quarters of the way through I nudged my wife, who was sleeping, and said, "This is a seriously dodgey movie!" Then somebody said to me afterwards, "Do you want to meet the director?" and I said, "No fuckin' way!" That film really turned me over.

"I saw *Nekromantik* and afterwards somebody said, 'Do you want to meet the director?' and I said, 'No fuckin' way!' "

The master of pulse-pounding, head- banging horror

"The chief enemy of creativity is 'good taste' "

Pablo Picasso

"Every mind-bending, horrifying, nauseating detail"

a character in SLUGS

A long-running controversy in the field of horror fiction has centred on the relative merits of understated, suggestive horror, which leaves it to the reader's imagination to fill in the gaps (the "what you don't see is scarier than what you do see" school) and the balls-to-the-wall, spare-the-reader-nothing shock tactics exposed by successive generations of young turks, most recently by certain American authors aboard the non-starting "Splatterpunk" bandwagon. Britain's Shaun Hutson leaves his devoted readership and the critics he so loves to bait in no doubt as to which side of the ideological divide he resides on. In evidence, consider the following passage from his 1988 novel *Victims*:

"The baby's body began to shudder violently as its skin finally turned a livid red. Its mouth opened as if it were screaming for help, but all that came forth was a foaming flux of dark-brown fluid and bubbling puss which gushed from its throbbing orifices as if it had been some gigantic boil squeezed and milked by invisible fingers. There was a loud and nausating plop as the entire body burst like a corpulent balloon, the whole figure exploding in a reeking, liquescent welter of corruption. The steaming mess splattered the insides of the oven..."

Or again, some...er, full-blown horror from *Assassin* (also 1988):

"Nikki's eyes bulged madly in their sockets as she felt her mouth fill to bursting point. Her cheeks swelled as she struggled to retain the ejaculation but then she realized that her mouth was filled not with fluid but with dozens of tiny objects. Objects which were moving. Twisting and turning on her tongue. She sat back as the pressure on her neck was released, her mouth opening wide.

The maggots poured from it in a sickly white torrent and, as she looked down, she saw that the penis was still jerking, still spurting, propelling the white monstrosities from the gland in a thick fountain. Some had already found their way down her throat despite the vomit which now rushed from her stomach and gushed from her mouth, carrying with it hordes of the parasites."

Beginning to get the picture? Hutson himself puts it like this: "Horror with a capital 'H' is what I do best". Few who've sampled his work would disagree. Having identified the most terrifying, universal fears (e.g. about fire, eye damage, bereavement, loss of control, and for the safety of our children, the wholesomeness of the food we eat, etc.) Hutson grabs his reader by the scruff of the neck and slaps them down in front of him; ruthlessly, relentlessly forcing him to endure them, always with the greatest possible degree of realism. A stickler for accuracy, Hutson takes his cue from one of his cinematic idols, Sam Peckinpah, never letting anyone die beautifully. But the traumatizing effects of this confrontational approach are generally mitigated by a wicked line in black humour and sense of knowingness that finds its counterpart in the author's own self-deprecating personality. Although Hutson once jokingly expressed an ambition to have someone die of shock while reading one of his books, the reader is just as likely to die laughing, but whether kicking in or tickling ribs, Hutson is always out to *entertain* the reader, and has little time for what he sees as the pretension of some of his contemporaries.

Ever the iconoclastic"Bad Boy of Horror", Hutson scorns the horror "in-crowd", feeling himself to have more of an affinity with the world of Heavy Metal, where he is revered as a cult figure. "I feel that reading my books is like going to a heavy rock gig," he has said, "There's the same relentless feeling to both of them. I'd like to think that when somebody finishes one of my books they'll be drained and exhausted, just as they would be after a great rock concert. They should go 'Whew! That was great!' " The music is frequently invoked in the pages of his novels, and lyrics from it can be found jostling for position with the likes of R.D. Laing, Shelley, Shakespeare and Tennyson, even quotations from the Bible.

As well as a whole host of mostly pseudonymous Westerns, war novels, film novelizations, etc., this prolific writer has managed to produce 10 major, best-selling horror novels in less than a decade.

By John Martin

JM: You must have some horror stories to tell about your own involvement in the movies, specifically in Juan Piquer Simon's *Slugs — The Movie.*

SH: I remember saying in an interview once, "I'm not interested in what they do with my book on the screen. Is it true to my artistic vision? I don't give a shit! As long as they give me huge amount of cash, they can make a comedy out of it if they like." Then that Simon bloke comes along and takes me at my fuckin' word! I believe two members of the cast walked out and some of the crew were tempted, when the stage-hands started throwing shovel-loads of live slugs around the set. There's going to be a sequel, which was tentatively titled *Slugs 2 — The Plague*, but now it's back to *Breeding Ground.* They asked me if I'd like to be involved with the screenplay, but I thought, "fuck that!" because if it turns out to be a flop, I can stand back from it, whereas if people though it was brilliant, then I could say, "Well, of course it's brilliant, it's based on my brilliant book." If it was something like a film version of *Spawn*, say, or *Erebus*, I would be more interested. I'm not slagging *Slugs* off, because it's still my biggest seller, but I feel it's less representative of what I write than the likes of *Spawn*, *Erebus*, *Shadows* and my latest stuff. I would insist on scripting any screen adaptations of *Victims*, *Assassin* or *Nemesis.*

JM: If *Breeding Ground* happens, will it be another J.P. Simon movie?

SH: Probably, yeah, and again I will take no responsibi!ty for what might end up there on that screen. I just hope they include the scene on the toilet (laughing). They'll have to, or they'll lose the entire Freudian sub-text of the story, won't they?

JM: So which horror films do you like?

SH: I tend to rent more mainstream stuff, nine times out of ten. Present day horror films leave a lot to be desired, really. I still rate the early Hammer stuff, because they had *style.* What have you got nowadays? The *Friday the 13th* series is just an excuse for how many pubescent kids you can kill in an hour-and-a-half...dear me! It sounds like a contradiction, bearing in mind the way I write, but I go along with the old line about what you don't see being more scary than what you do see, and that's why *Alien* still scares the shit out of me, much more so than its over-rated sequel.

"...two members of the cast walked out and some of the crew were tempted when the stage-hands started throwing shovel-loads of live slugs around the set."

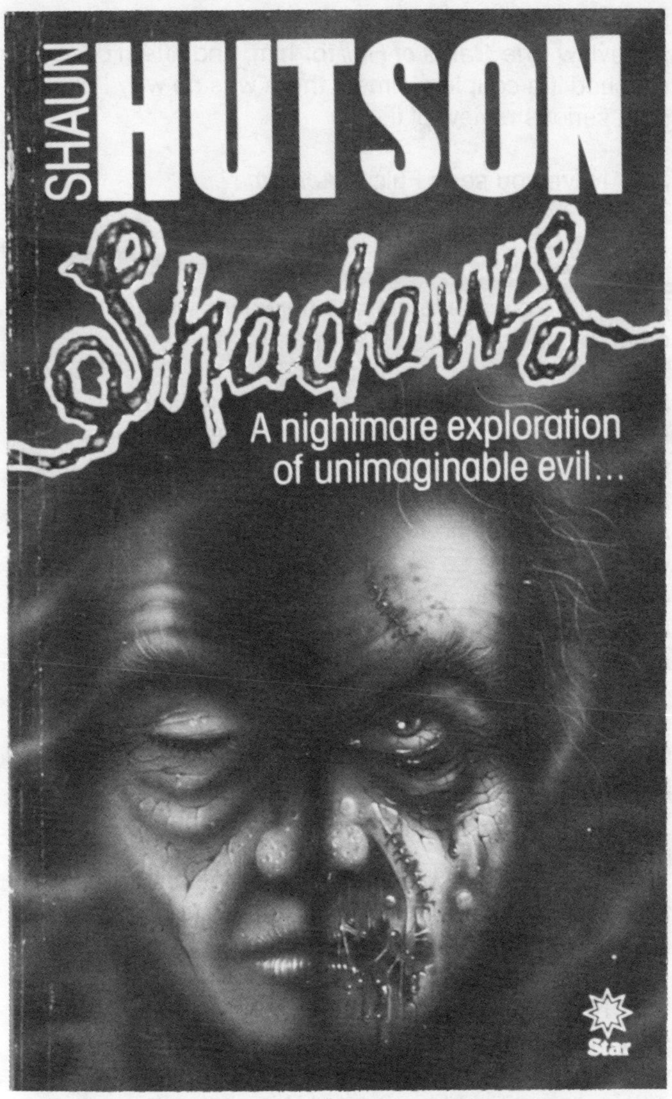

JM: I'm glad I'm not the only person on the planet who believes the original to be a far better film.

SH: *Aliens* for me was just *Rambo*-in-Outer-Space. The one thing that James Cameron did better than Ridley Scott was the old "camera prowling down dark corridors" bit. *Alien* could have done with some more of that, but to me it's up there with *Taxi Driver* and *The Wild Bunch*, the two greatest movies I ever saw. One of the reasons I don't watch much horror is that I wouldn't want to be subconsciously influenced... Actually, I would think the chances of me being influenced by someone like Lucio Fulci are pretty slim.

Some geezer who runs a fanzine recently asked me if I'd review *The Gates of Hell* for him, and after I'd watched it a couple of times, there was no way I could do a serious review of it.

JM: Have you seen Fulci's *Aenigma*?

SH: No.

JM: There's a scene in that one where a schoolgirl is eaten by slugs and snails.

SH: Bastards! I'll sue 'em! (Laughs) Another reason I'm not too keen on modern horror films, or novels for that matter, is that the writers keeping trotting out this tired old stuff that you just don't need. There's no reason that you should have some damsel in distress, who's only there so you can send the hero down some dark passageway to get her, y'know, which is why I always try and make the women a bit more powerful in my books than they are elsewhere in the genre. Y'know, in the interview I just did with *Penthouse*, the guy was saying that maybe I've had an influence on some off the young, up-and-coming talents...the only problem is, I don't see any of these up-and-coming talents. I mean, where are they?

JM: So we won't be seeing any glowing testimonials from Shaun Hutson on book-jackets for the forseeable future?

SH: No, I won't do endorsements. W. H. Allen have sent me copies of stuff to endorse, but I won't do it. I was sent a copy of Clive Barker's *Weaveworld* and the endorsement I sent back was "This shag-pile saga is totally shagged out." They didn't use it, funnily enough. I can't do that stuff, because I ain't gonna sell my fans out. Every horror novel you pick up these days has something saying, "This is the finest novel I've read since last week — Stephen King." Herbert has done it a couple of times, but he tends not to. Stephen King is a different proposition, though, isn't he, because he's an American...yanks fall for shit like that.

JM: What will you be doing in ten years time?

SH: I sincerely hope that I won't be doing anything different, just making loads of money out of what I write. I would hope by then that all of my books will have been turned into films, preferably decent ones, although I won't care, as long as they've paid me enough. I'll have a crack at anything there's a market for. If there's enough money to be made, I'll have a go. I've been toying with the idea of writing a children's horror novel...what could be more frightening than some of those fairy stories? Hansel and Gretel could be updated to modern day New York, with kids taken three blocks away from their home and abandoned. But the goriest stuff of all is bloody Shakespeare!

JM: Your U.K. fans are extremely supportive...do you enjoy meeting them at conventions?

SH: When I turn up, people look at me and say "If that's what a writer looks like, there must be hope for all of us." When they write to me they get a letter back, which they wouldn't from most authors, but I reply to all my mail. They get a letter from a guy who seems quite reasonable, who took the time to write back. That's the least I can do...it makes me seem more normal.

THE STRANGE CASE OF RUGGERO DEODATO

From Cannibals to Compromise in 10 Easy Years

by Chas. Balun

It seems as though the world can never quite forgive Italian director Ruggero Deodato for making *Cannibal Holocaust* (1979). Though arguably The Greatest Cannibal Movie Ever Made, its sullied reputation as a ferociously vile and uncompromisingly bleak nihilistic epic remains intact to this day. And, judging by Deodato's recent cinematic output, he has been paying some pretty heavy-duty penance in return for his sins.

If films like *Atlantis Interceptors* (1983), *The Barbarians* (1986), or *Dial Help* (1989) are any indication of his future direction, it wouldn't be all that surprising to see a new Deodato opus pop-up someday as a squeaky-clean, prime-time TV Movie of the Week. Deodato has come a l-o-n-g way, to be sure; but all too often, recent efforts appear to be cinematic apologies for the "crimes" of his past.

It could well be that Deodato has mellowed with age and is quite willing to compromise in favor of steady work, bigger budgets, better actors and wider distribution. Though both *Phantom of Death* (1988) and *Dial Help* retain some of Deodato's muscular, aggressive directorial flair, it is quite clear that he has begun a new chapter in his filmmaking career. Gone is the mean-spirited, shocking brutality, relentless misanthropy, and world-without-hope scenarios of his previous efforts; but in their stead, we have insipid storylines, scenery-chewing, name-brand actors and flashy, but empty, hi-tech camera noodlings.

Perhaps on some professional and economic level Deodato's career has flourished, but the genre has suffered because such a mightily talented, independent voice has been stifled.

Though *Cannibal Holocaust* is all-deserving of its notorious reputation, it remains a work of unparalleled power and vision. It rises above its simplistic, exploitation origins and presents a harrowing, multi-faceted adventure that mercilessly probes ever deeper into man's propensity for violence and self-destruction. As spectacularly pandering as the film becomes at times, there always remains an unassailable element of truth and a persistence of vision that is almost impossible to dismiss.

Deodato may have made the Ultimate Jungle Chunkblower with *Cannibal Holocaust*, but beneath the frothing blood and steaming guts lies a film that could be safely regarded as the *Apocalypse Now* of the subgenre. But just as Francis Ford

Coppola turned from the hellish nightmare of Col. Kurtz' jungle inferno to the cheery, neon-lit playground world of *One From the Heart*, so has Deodato forsaken his own heart of darkness for...*Atlantis Interceptors* and *The Barbarians*?

Perhaps both filmmakers are heeding the gentle admonishment leveled at seekers of the unknowable by Friedrich Nietzsche, "Be careful not to stare too long into the abyss, for it will begin to stare back."

In fact, Deodato continued his explorations of the untilled fecundity of the human jungle for several years after *Cannibal Holocaust* with both *Cut and Run* (1984) (*Inferno in diretta / Straight to Hell*) and *House on the Edge of the Park* (1984) marking the apparent end of his Primal Scream Period. After that, films bearing his name could scarcely be distinguished from the plethora of other wimpy genre offerings that flooded the marketplace in the mid-80's. Deodato still maintained an occasionally quirky, rebellious point-of-view, but by the time *Dial Help* arrived on these shores, it was quite clear that the holy fire had departed.

Although it was periodically reported that Deodato was considering a return to the "Green Inferno" with a proposed sequel *Cannibal Holocaust 2*, it now appears that the only film bearing that moniker will be the deceptively retitled Mario Giriazzo jungle-girl romp *White Slave* (1984).

For now, as a genre force, Deodato must be considered as missing-in-action. It is a loss worth mourning, too. Despite the fact that Deodato was often lumped together with other Italian opportunists like Bruno Mattei (*Night of the Zombies*), Umberto Lenzi (*Cannibal Ferox*), Joe D'Amato (*Trap Them and Kill Them* and 3,000 other titles), and Sergio Martino (*Island of the Mutations / Screamers*), it was quite obvious from the start that Deodato was no hack director. His cinematic roots lay not so much with the cheap thrill/fast-buck school of filmmaking popularized by his contemporaries, but rather with the classical approach espoused by his early mentor, the prolific and highly regarded Italian maestro Roberto Rossellini (*Germany Year Zero* (1947), *Ways of Love* (1948), *The Rise of Louis XIV* (1966)). Deodato's cinema verite´ technique used so effectively in *Cannibal Holocaust* is, in fact, a natural outgrowth of Rossellini's revolutionary neorealist style employed in such early works as *Open City* (1945), *Germany Year Zero*, and *Paisan* (1946).

Rossellini's raw, newsreel-like films showing European cities smoldering in the embers of World War II initially shocked audiences unaccustomed to such frank and forthright portrayals of man's bestial impulses. *Open City* (*Roma Citta aperta*) is generally credited as the first neorealist work of this period for its documentarylike tale of the Gestapo tracking down, torturing, and killing various members of the Communist resistance. Based on true events, the film used actual locations and employed various nonprofessional actors in order to maintain its punishing, naturalistic tone.

Rossellini was a prodigious talent, directing for the stage and opera, as well as for film and Italian TV and working right up to his death at age 71 in 1977. (Rossellini is also remembered for his scandalous affair with Swedish born-actress Ingrid Bergman, a liaison that produced a son and twin daughters, one of whom is Isabella Rossellini of *Blue Velvet* fame.)

After his tenure with Rossellini, Deodato's directorial career began unspectacularly with such films as *Gungula*, a tepid, mediocre jungle girl thriller that showed little of the powerful, assured style he showcased shortly thereafter with *The Last Cannibal World* (1976) (*Ultimo Mondo Cannibale, The Last Survivor, Jungle Holocaust*). Supposedly based on a true account of an oil company expedition that discovers a stone age tribe living in isolation on Mindanao Island, *The Last Cannibal World* is a riveting, compelling adventure tale that established Deodato as a talent to be reckoned with. Co-starring Massimo Foschi, along with Ivan Rassimov and Me Me Lay (who both appeared in Umberto Lenzi's earlier *Deep River Savages*), *Cannibal World* provides an early blueprint for the real holocaust to come. Despite being an adventure/thriller more closely akin to Cornel Wilde's *Naked Prey* (1967), Deodato unflinchingly presents ritualistic animal atrocity footage, cannibalism and other scenes of barbarity that quickly set this film apart from others in the subgenre. A high-water mark (of sorts) for graphic on-screen mutilation occurs near the climax when Me Me Lay is split open from crotch to sternum and her guts are scooped out and replaced by burning hot coals for aiding and abetting in the escape of the white interloper. (Umberto Lenzi shamelessly cribs this scene for inclusion in his own *Eaten Alive by the Cannibals / Emerald Jungle* (1980).) Lay's shocking evisceration gives fair warning of Deodato's nascent filmic credo—the no mercy / no prisoners motif that will be taken to extremes in *Cannibal Holocaust*.

Teaming up again with *Cannibal World* screenwriter Gianfranco Clerici (who also wrote *House on the Edge of the Park*), Deodato set out to knock the subgenre on its ear by making a film that actually attempts to condemn the exploitation of Third World cultures. Deodato painted himself into a corner here because *Cannibal Holocaust* remains a sensationalistic geek show whose moral message has a distinctly flat, tinny sound. The ambiguity of this cockeyed bit of moral posturing is neatly summed up at the climax when, after viewing atrocity-laden footage of a doomed Amazonian expedition, the central character mutters, "I wonder who the *real* cannibals are."

Come on, Ruggero. *They're* the painted and muddied, grunting little savages who've just ripped apart the entire cast and wolfed down their guts! Cannibalism as metaphor cannot work in a film that so gleefully wallows in violence and brutality while simultaneously casting judgment on other filmmakers whose actions appear no less reprehensible than Deodato's. While Deodato films another movie crew killing animals on-screen, did

he not kill them just as dead as his fictional counterparts? It's hard to think of Deodato and his crew as morally superior beings after watching 90 minutes of actual animal slaughter, repellent gang rapes, graphic castrations, and rampant, gratuitous nudity.

Many critics of the film have apparently missed the "message" of *Cannibal Holocaust* and still see only the vile, barbaric exploitation of the natives, the animals, and the audience.

Deodato further complicates matters by including sequences that are awfully hard to dismiss as special effects trickery and moviemaking "magic." The documentary-like footage of the fictional film shown in the New York screening room as *The Last Road to Hell* contains scenes of bloody battles, murders, and mass executions that look suspiciously real. Even some of the special effects sequences have been called into question. In the scene where the film crew finds a native girl impaled from ass to mouth on a huge stake, several conflicting accounts have been offered in explanation. Some say the girl is merely sitting on a small, hidden bicycle seat with a balsa wood prop in her mouth; while others respond in an elliptical fashion that further obfuscates the issue. Lamberto Bava, who was part of Deodato's crew at the time, reportedly refused to be on set for the sequence and has maintained a stoic silence about what really happened.

The film ignited a storm of controversy upon its release— legal action was threatened, prints were destroyed in a fire of suspicious origin, and many countries refused to show it at all. Still to this day, some dozen years after its initial appearance, *Cannibal Holocaust* is generally seen in one of two ways: either on illegal bootlegged cassettes or on an optically-censored Japanese import laser disc that renders the film nearly unwatchable.

Though several proposed sequels had been announced, then abandoned (*Cannibal Fury, Cannibal Holocaust 2, Voodoo Revenge*), Deodato made only one return trip to the jungles in the following decade. *Cut and Run* (1984) is a sometimes rousing adventure / thriller that eschews cannibalism in favor of action, dope cults and renegade Green Berets. Though many audiences felt *Cut and Run* to be remarkably restrained for a Deodato film, the folks who chanced upon the alternative, Italian-language version, *Inferno in diretta* were given a prime shot of the ol' ultraviolence in numerous scenes re-filmed for other foreign markets. *Cut and Run* is not an edited or censored version of *Inferno in diretta*, but rather an alternative print of the film that was tailored specifically for the U.S. and U.K. marketplace.

Inferno in diretta is actually the shorter of the two films, but nearly every scene of violence has been expanded upon. There is gore galore in the various graphic stabbings, throat slittings, decapitations, and eviscerations, but they're mere appetizers for Deodato's stunning piece de resistance— Vlado's (John Steiner's) ultra-explicit death by booby trap. The man is ensnared in a

primitive spring-laid tree trap that, when accidentally activated by a would-be rescuer, rips its quarry in half. No details are spared and the sequence ends with a close shot showing a vulture gnoshing on the guts of the ruined corpse.

Though this sequence probably stands at the apex of Deodato's post-*Holocaust* chunkblowing, *The House on the Edge of the Park* (1984) showcases yet another side of Deodato's formidable arsenal of fright. Deodato turns his sights from one jungle to another and proves that lost in the cities with the likes of David (*Last House on the Left*) Hess and John (*Cannibal Ferox*) Morghen can be just as harrowing as sharing a box lunch with Amazonian headhunters. No one in the genre can raise the hair on the back of your neck faster than David Hess can, with or without the straight razor he employs in *House on the Edge of the Park*. (He can also be seen doing the Hess thing in *Hitch Hike* (1977), co-starring with Franco Nero.)

Deodato maintains a pervasive atmosphere of seething tension and mounting suspense as Hess and Morghen torment and humiliate a group of snooty rich folk who've brought the pair home with them as the night's entertainment. Though Morghen is little more than a cipher — his character being both socially and mentally retarded — Hess is drop-dead scary.

For a film that begins with a brutal rape and strangulation over the opening credits, *House on the Edge of the Park* ends with a particularly lightweight credibility-straining coda. At the film's climax, Hess is handily dispatched without much fuss by the wimpy yuppiefolk who've just spent the last hour cowering in pants-wetting horror. Using a "twist" ending that hits a patentedly false note,

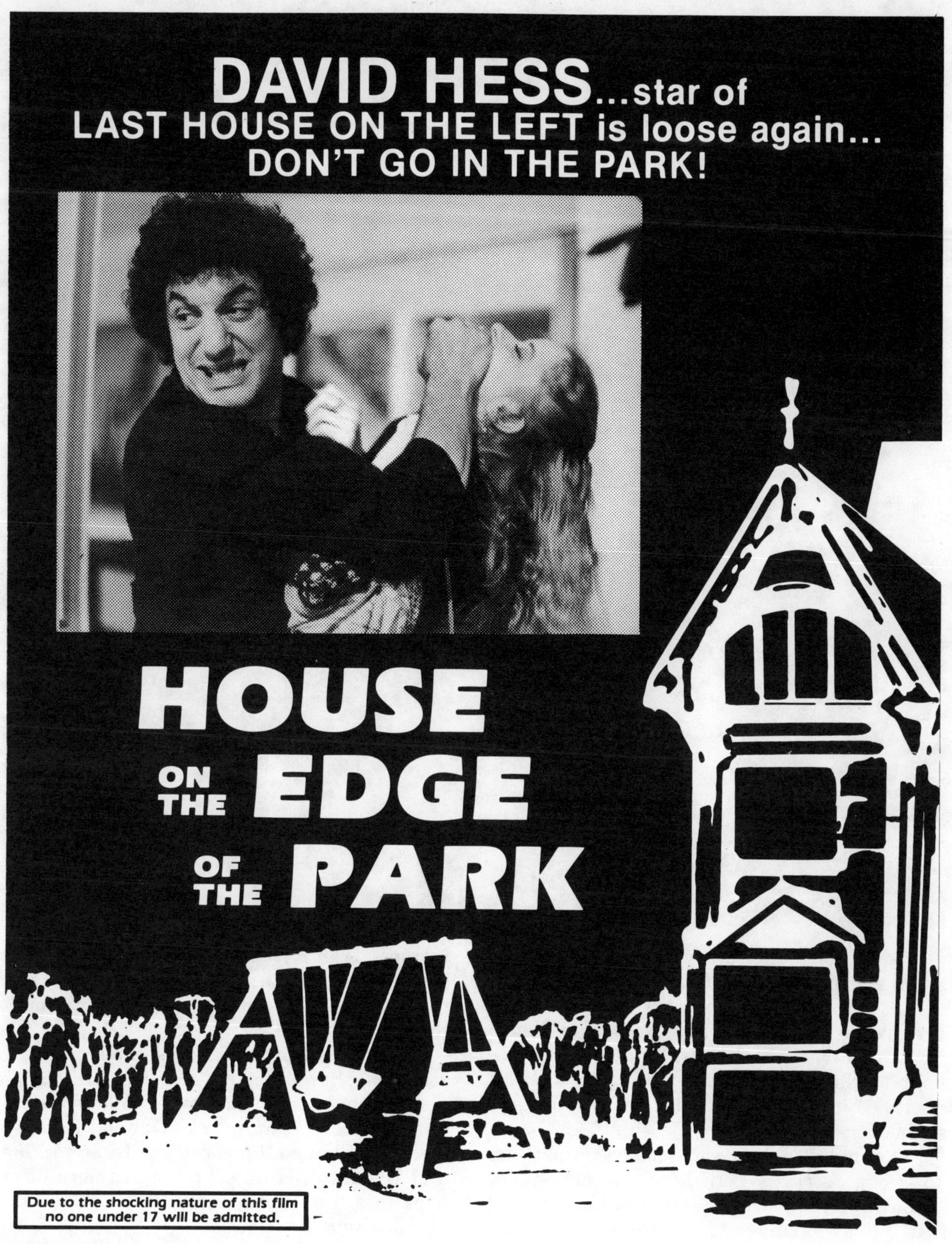

Hess ends up shot to death and floating in a pool because the sprout-eating yupfucks had really been just "playing along" all night and were just using Hess and Company instead of the other way around.

Up until the final denouement, though, the film crackles with a perverse power and testicle-retracting ghastliness that only a Deodato or a Hess can generate.

Would you trust this man with your nipple ?

Except for the unsatisfying final movement, *House on the Edge of the Park* remains a vital "home invasion" entry, joining such films as William Wyler's excellent *The Desperate Hours* (1955), Wes Craven's *Last House on the Left* (1972), and John McNaughton's *Henry: Portrait of a Serial Killer* (1986) in the "Hell Comes to Your House" Sweepstakes.

The mid 80's, however, seemed to mark an end to Deodato's Nasty Period and his subsequent work shows little of the vehemence and cynical brutality that earmarked earlier efforts. It's actually quite hard to envision Deodato becoming involved with a project like *Camping del terrore* (1986) (aka *Body Count*), especially in light of the fact that this lame slasher clone came so many years after the slice-n'-dice subgenre had already bled itself to death. Perhaps its only real distinction lies with seeing a laid-back, graying-at-the-temples David Hess essay a role in which he's not a drooling maniac. Ivan Rassimov, Mimsy (*Four Flies on Grey Velvet*) Farmer, and Charles Napier (speaking fluent Italian) round out a cast that simply goes through the paces.

There's plenty of kids, motorcycles, aerobic routines, shower scenes and bare breasts, though, along with yet another masked killer suffering from yet another traumatic childhood incident. On occasion, Claudio Simonetti's pulsing, rocking score and Deodato's slinky, probing camera offer brief hope in a film that's, sadly, still a good half dozen years behind the times.

It's hard to know what to think of Deodato's foray into the sword-n'-sandal arena, but *The Barbarians* (1986) is still lots more fun than John Milius' fascistic, chest-pounding braggadocio in *Conan the Barbarian*. The Barbarian Brothers, a twin set of musclebound Mr. Universe types, play the titular heroes and, contrary to expectations, deliver performances of unexpected warmth and

John Morghen about to be blown...away.

wittiness. With tongues firmly in cheek, Deodato and the B-boys make this film far more enjoyable than it has any right to be.

With both *Phantom of Death* (1987) (*Un delitto poco commune*) and *Dial Help,* Deodato makes a peripheral return to the genre, although each film can also be viewed as a suspense/thriller with splatter.

Phantom of Death again features a screenplay by frequent collaborator Gianfranco Clerici, a name-brand cast, good production values, colorful Italian locations, and a decent score by Pino (*The Howling*) Dinaggio, but, sadly enough, it still doesn't amount to much. On the other hand, Deodato should be summarily congratulated for providing continuing employment for the Strother Martin of Splatter—Giovanni Lombardo Radice (aka John Morghen). Despite the shortcomings of the film itself, Deodato has chosen a supremely inspired role for the Man of a Thousand Wounds—that of a priest who hears Michael York's tortured confession. York is a superstar classical pianist who is stricken with a devastating disease that causes rapid, premature aging as well as prolonged fits of homicidal rage.

The slickly paced inspired opening montage features scenes of a piano recital cross-cut with some pretty funky ninja sword play that briefly buoy one's hopes until the plot creaks into action and spoils it all.

Donald Pleasence co-stars and plays virtually the same role he's walked through in the last several *Halloween* movies. He wrings his hands, furrows his brow, gnashes his teeth and wobbles into the streets whining about evil and just how nasty this whole psycho-killer business has really become.

Deodato frequently manages to overcome the inert plot and spittle-spewing hysterics of Pleasence by staging several flashy, Argento-like

murder sequences that really click. When York's mistress is killed by a spear, majestic fountains of arterial spray erupt as she tumbles ever-so-slowly through a glittering shower of splintering glass in a scene reminiscent of Argentokills in *Suspiria, Deep Red, Tenebrae* and *Phenomena*. The film works best when Deodato allows his camera a free, unfettered reign. The serpentine tracking shots, artsy angles, and fluid crane maneuverings show that Deodato can, indeed, mount a very arresting visual package, despite the paucity of material.

Dial Help could have worked, but it would probably have had to have been a comedy. Anytime you're dealing with a possessed telephone line that kills tropical fish, strangles one women while making another wear kinky, black lingerie and spike heel boots in the bath then you've got to be mighty judicious with your material — and Deodato isn't. It's played as a full-tilt thriller, complete with a gag reflexive theme song (*Don't Answer the Phone*), a malevolent pay phone that splatters customers with disgorged coins, and smoky, surreal rooms filled with mysterious pigeons and lethal ceiling fans.

There's even a professor who delivers a straight-faced lecture on "unidentified love / hate energies" that circulate throughout the universe and seduce the ones who release them. A perfect example of which, one might guess, is the sequence in which a beautiful model is shown writhing on the floor in her underwear, tightly bound and then sexually aroused by a naughty phone that blow dries her hair and offers up an uninterrupted stream of titillating chatter. It's a scene without parallel in the Deodato oeuvre, to be sure.

So what can you say about a director who goes from garroting and skinning live crocodiles on screen to seducing leggy ingenues with possessed telephones? Jungle viruses and debilitating head injuries aside, Deodato appears to be healthy and cautiously revaluating his career. Perhaps in maturity, Deodato no longer craves the notoriety he generated with his cannibal epics and is content with further exploration of his craft without regard to genre. But those who remember the feverish intensity, uncompromising subject matter, and sense of kinetic recklessness exhibited in his earlier works are now, no doubt, perplexed by this kinder, gentler Ruggero Deodato.

The progressive decline in the later films of such other former firebrands and enfant terribles as Tobe Hooper, Wes Craven, John Carpenter and Sean Cunningham is a bitter lesson to which most genre fanciers have become accustomed.

If Deodato's next picture turns out to be the USA cable premiere of *Three Men and a Barbarian*, then it's probably time to switch the channel...for good.

GO FOR THE

Stephen R. Bissette

GROSS-OUT

"So: terror on the top, horror below it, and lowest of all, the gag reflex of revulsion . . . I recognize terror as the finest emotion (used to almost quintessential effect in Robert Wise's film The Haunting, *where, as in* "The Monkey's Paw", *we are never allowed to see what is behind the door), and so I will try to terrorize the reader. But if I find I cannot terrify him/her, I will try to horrify; and if I find I cannot horrify, I'll go for the gross-out. I'm not proud."*

—Stephen King,
Danse Macabre, 1981

Though I wouldn't have argued the point a decade ago, it seems to me that, given the state of the horror film in the '80's, one could chart the evolution of the genre via its 'gross-out quotient.' While doing so necessarily excludes the refined *frissons* of the acknowledged horror film classics, from *The Cabinet of Dr. Caligari* and *Nosferatu* to *Curse of the Demon* and *The Shining*, it does allow us to trace the roots of the 'modern horror film' and its feisty contenders for the crown: *Night of the Living Dead, The Texas Chainsaw Massacre, Re-Animator*, and their moist-'n'-meaty kin.

Though by no means definitive, this article will indeed try to trace the evolution of 'the gross-out'. Of all the arts, the cinema (by its very nature) seems the best suited to explore and exploit the mass audience's visceral involvement with violence. The cinema's plasticity of motion, time, and illusion of space and reality, coupled with the narrative potential of the medium, allows for a more emotionally immediate and involving exploration/exploitation of violence than afforded by all the other arts: theatre, music, sculpture, drawing and painting, comics, etc. In fact, films depend upon a fusion and synthesis of all these art forms to create its illusions. For example, consider what goes into just one horrific moment of (to choose a random example) *Evil Dead 2*. The staging and lighting of the scene for filming are theatrical constructs, the makeup effects highly detailed and fully animated sculptures, the direction of the sequence is usually storyboarded (á la comics), the final motion picture enhanced by the musical score, etc. The combination of these elements can, when well executed (and especially within the context of a well-told horror story), illicit a physical 'gut reaction' from an audience.

In this manner, the modern horror film speaks to its audience on a more primal, *physical* level than the older films usually did. They communicate, if you will, on a 'body' level; and while many critics and film scholars argue this level of communication is indicative of a reprehensible regression in the genre, I feel it is in fact the evolution of a different cinematic 'language.' No better, no worse, simply different, and as such a language that must be studied and understood.

The horror film may have become quite fluent in the language of the 'gross-out', but it is by no means the only genre to use it. Many key films in the history of the medium use (and hence contributed to) the 'gross-out' vocabulary: the Babylonian warrior sliced in two with a single stroke in *Intolerance* (1916), the horrifying Odessa Steps sequence in *Potemkin* (1925), the Union soldier shotgunned in the face in *Gone with the Wind* ('39), the torture of the underground resistance leader in *Open City* ('45), the ground-

FIENDISH IS THE WORD FOR IT!
NOT FOR THE EYES AND EARS OF ANYONE UNDER 16 YEARS!
COLOR ME BLOOD RED
IN DEVASTATING COLOR BIZARRE!
SEE IT AT YOUR OWN RISK!
IF "NIGHT OF THE LIVING DEAD" FRIGHTENS YOU TO DEATH YOU ARE COVERED FOR...... $50,000
A $50,000 POLICY covering death from heart attack for anyone in the audience during a performance of "NIGHT OF THE LIVING DEAD" for this special engagement only has been obtained through a leading International Insurance Company in London.
THEY WON'T STAY DEAD
An IMAGE TEN Production
NIGHT OF THE LIVING DEAD
They keep coming back in a bloodthirsty lust for HUMAN FLESH!...
Pits the dead against the living in a struggle for survival!
STARRING
JUDITH O'DEA · DUANE JONES
JUDITH RIDLEY · KEITH WAYNE
SPECIAL "FRIGHT BREAK"
There will be a special "FRIGHT BREAK" during the showing of William Castle's "Homicidal." All those too timid to take the climax will be welcomed to the COWARD'S CORNER!
THE STORY OF A PSYCHOTIC KILLER!
WILLIAM CASTLE'S
HOMICIDAL
ALIVE... WITHOUT A BODY... FED BY AN UNSPEAKABLE HORROR FROM HELL!
THE BRAIN THAT WOULDN'T DIE
STARRING
HERB EVERS · VIRGINIA LEITH
SCREENPLAY BY JOSEPH GREEN
DIRECTED BY JOSEPH GREEN
PRODUCED BY REX CARLTON
AN AMERICAN INTERNATIONAL RELEASE

breaking climaxes to *Bonnie and Clyde* ('67) and *The Wild Bunch* ('69), etc. Graphic violence is often central to the prison films, westerns, boxing movies, sword-'n'-sandal potboilers; war films, from *Le Croix de Bois / Wooden Crosses* ('31, in which a man is blown to shreds before our eyes by a direct hit) to *Attack!* ('56, wherein Jack Palance loses his arm under the treads of an enemy tank, and staggers back to command post with bloody tatters dangling from the stump) were often more harrowing than their horror contemporaries. Samurai bloodfests were ushered (gushered?) in by Akira Kurosawa's opening to *Yojimbo* ('62) and its sequel *Sanjuro* ('63), with its showdown's astounding geyser of blood at its conclusion; by the time of the *Kozure Ohkami / Lone Wolf* series, ('72-'73), the inventive gore had reached hallucinatory extremes. For American mainstream audiences, the mayhem came to a head in the winter of 1971:the major studio Christmas releases included *Dirty Harry, Straw Dogs, A Clockwork Orange, The Devils*, Polanski's *Macbeth*...bloodbaths all, paving the way for the acceptance and phenomenal success of *Jaws* and *The Exorcist* late in the '70's.

It is, of course, absurd to divorce these sequences from the context of the films, and in chronicling the 'gross-out' one is occasionally reduced to simply listing isolated bits of mayhem. Nevertheless, these vital threads are worth following, and for the purposes of this article, we must focus on the horror films; we must also end at the birth of the 'new horror film' with *Night of the Living Dead* (1968), at which point the floodgates were burst open. A flood...of blood. Bon Appetit!

SILENT SCREAMS (1893-1930)

For all intents and purposes, it started in 1893 with Thomas Edison (the inventor of the light bulb, natch) and one of his Kinetoscopes, *The Execution of Mary, Queen of Scots*. In less than a minute, turn-of-the-century thrillseekers could see what the live theatre never showed them: " . . . Mary approaches the chopping block. She kneels, the headsman swings his ax—and the audience is rewarded with the edifying spectacle of Mary's head rolling in the dust! But the gruesome bit of action continues on the screen without interruption."—(Arthur Knight, *The Liveliest Art*, 1957)

French film pioneer Louis Lumiere utilized a similarly simple substitution effect for *Charcuterie Mechanique / The Mechanical Butcher* (1895), as a whole pig is fed into one end of a machine and processed meat products (sausages, ham, etc.) grind out the other. International imitations followed: British George Smith's *Making Sausages* (1897), the American *The Sausage Machine* (1897), Edison's *Fun in a Butcher Shop* (1901), with the process reversed in Edwin S. Porter's *Dog Factory* (1904), wherein sausages and hotdogs are processed into live pet dogs! So ended the screen's first 'gore' cycle, with silly effects that were later revived for Ted V. Mikel's notorious *The Corpse Grinders* ('71). French magician Georges Melies would pioneer film fantasy with a more sophisticated bag of cinematic tricks, and though his intent and effect was almost always comedic in nature, his films featured many gruesome moments. *The Man with the Rubber Head* (1902) inflates a lively severed head until it explodes; *The Melomaniac* (1903) rips off heads (including his own) to string them like notes across telegraph wires, performing "God Save the King"; *The Terrible Turkish Executioner* (1904) lops off three criminals' heads with a single sweep of his scimitar, only to have the heads rejoin their bodies and hack the executioner into three frantic sections!

More gruesome effects figure in Melies' *Les Rayons Roentgen /A Novice at X-Rays* (1897), wherein an X-rayed patient's skeleton steps out of his body and his now-limp flesh sloughs off onto the floor, or *The Cook in Trouble* (1904), who plunges into a stewpot and simmers into broth, leaving only his wet clothing. A hideous ogre hacks up a little boy and devours him in *La Cuisine de L'Ogre / In the Bogie Man's Cave* (1908), a shock repeated in Melies' last masterpiece, *Conquest of the North Pole* (1912), as the Snow Giant (an impressively gigantic marionette) emerges from the ice flows to swallow one of the explorers whole (only to later vomit back up, alive and well). Rooted in historical reality rather than fantasy, Melies' *Humanity Through the Ages* (1908) catalogs war, crime, and death through the ages.

Italian spectacles of the period were similarly grim. While *L'Inferno* (1909) provided an often grisly (in medium and long shot) tour of Hell itself, another Italian short of this period (1910, title unknown: I saw it in a 1978 television documentary, *The Amazing Years of Cinema: The Monsters*, hosted by Douglas Fairbanks Jr.) went to shocking extremes to dramatize the tortures of the Inquisition. Scarlet, hand-colored tinting effects enhance the flames which burn the victims alive, as well as the spattering blood on a victim who is lashed to a spinning wheel and rolled into a bed of spikes! This gory short anticipates the entire 'torture' subgenre, from *Witchcraft Through the Ages* ('22) and *The Devils* ('71) to the nadir of *Mark of the Devil* ('69), *Cannibal Holocaust* ('79), and the *Ilsa* series ('74-'77).

Edison's 1910 *Frankenstein* showed the monster born (or rather 'baked') via alchemy, with gobs of wet flesh simmering onto the skelton using the same techniques (printed in *reverse*) later used for the decompositions of *Horror of Dracula* and *The Evil Dead*. Maurice Tourneur's *Le Systeme du Docteur Goudron et du Professeur Plume / The Lunatics* (1912) lifted its Poe adaptation from the French theatre of Grand Guignol, wherein the asylum director 'cures' insanity by cutting out an eye and slicing the throat. He bolts into a chamber, and emerges with bloodied hands, while the blood that seeps out from under the door arouses the inmates. Abel Gance's *J'Accuse* (1919) built to a shocking finale in which dead soldiers march on the living, "not a single one without a smashed face or body that dangled flesh" (George De Coulteray, *Sadism in the Movies*), many played by soldiers who would return to the World War I trenches and die after the filming.

The infamous *Haxan / Witchcraft Through the Ages* (1922) remains an exhilarating film when seen today. Director Benjamin Christensen's history of witchcraft and the persecutions is a rich blend of shocking dramatizations, black comedy, animation, and documentary, and many of its tableaus (the black mass, baby sacrifices, the Inquisition tortures) are vividly realized and still unnerving, brimming with Boschian demons, nudity, and blood. *Un Chien Andalou* ('28), a collaboration by Luis Bunuel and Salvador Dali, begins with a shot of a man holding a razor in one hand, and holding open a women's eye with the other. A cloud bisects the moon, and he slashes her eye open in an explicit closeup. It remains one of the cinema's most shocking images, and the film itself is an avant-garde classic and a seminal horror film in that it is the first film to dare assualt the audience: its gut-wrenching opening, the refusal to attach its barrage of dreamlike and nightmare (a severed hand, rotting donkey carcasses, ants streaming from a hole in the palm of a hand) to any coherent narrative...on every level, the film attacks the viewer's perceptions and preconceptions.

Antonin Artaud, the creator of the Theatre of Cruelty, tried to go Bunuel one better, and wrote a screenplay entitled *The Revolt of the Butcher* (1930), wherein "eroticism, savagery, blood lust, a thirst for violence, an obsession with horror, collapse of moral values, social hypocrisy, lies, perjury, sadism, depravity, etc. have been made as explicit as possible" (Artaud's introduction to *The Revolt of the Butcher*, 1930). The screenplay was never filmed.

Less brutal in its intent, but no less provocative to its contemporary audiences, was Jean Cocteau's sound film *Le Sang d'un Poete / The Blood of a Poet* (1930), a hypnotically dreamlike avant-garde film. Though Cocteau's approach is sensuously gentle compared to the assault staged by Bunuel and Dali, the poet's passage through the Hotel Des Folies Dramatiques is punctuated by a bloody suicide (his own, from which he reawakens), a boy killed by an iceball, choking on his own blood, and the poet's final (genuine?) suicide. Cocteau would mirror the poet's death even more graphically in his later *Le Testament d'Orphee / The Testament of Orpheus* ('59), in which a poet (played by Cocteau himself) is transfixed by a spear.

BLOOD AND THUNDER: (1930-1950)

The mainstream horror (and crime) films of the early sound era often delivered the goods, especially in America, where Depression audiences were in need of whatever cheap thrills they could find, and Hollywood was eager to deliver them. The relaxation of the Motion Picture Production code allowed the horrors of the early '30's to sharpen their edge. Even low-budget fare like *White Zombie* ('32) had its highlights: the undead sugar-cane worker falling into the cane-grinding works, the bullet holes in the chest of an attacking zombie. Depression audiences saw *King Kong* ('35) greedily chew and crush his human victims (in footage that remained unseen for a generation), and dispose of a Tyrannosaurus Rex by gorily breaking its jaws and neck. But they didn't see the fate of the sailors thrown into the chasm by Kong . . . the animated sequences of giant spiders and lizards dining on the screaming victims was considered too gruesome by the studio, and were trimmed before its release. The classic 1931 *Frankenstein* lost the sequence of Karloff's monster throwing the little girl into the drink, and the shot of him impaling his tormentor (Dwight Frye) on a hook. The censor's scissors also reportedly clipped the climax of Tod Browning's *Freaks* ('32), as the circus freaks emasculate (indicated by the character's screams going falsetto) the villainous Hercules the Strong Man in the murk of mud and rain.

Similar in tone, and just as grim, was the excellent *Island of Lost Souls* ('32), with its own climax of vengeful primitive surgery inflicted upon the howling Dr. Moreau (Charles Laughton) by the manimals he had carved out of living flesh and medical technology in 'The House of Pain'. The hero and audience are given a brief glimpse of the good doctor at work midway through the film, and it is a suitably chilling sight. And there was more:

Bela Lugosi's bleeding of the prostitute (Arlene Francis) on a rack in *Murder of the Rue Morgue* (1932), and the discovery of the old woman's body crammed up the chimney in the same film...the megalomaniacal Count Zaroff's trophy room of mounted and pickled human heads in *The Most Dangerous Game* (1932)...Boris Karloff, back from the dead and carving symbols into his own chest as an offering to Anubis in *The Ghoul* ('33)...the peasant army's death by molten metal, crushing, and (in a particularly rude split-second) smashed between a falling ladder and the Notre Dame Cathedral's walls as *The Hunchback of Notre Dame* ('39) defends his beloved church and Esmerelda against them. Perhaps the most graphic of the early sound horrors to emerge from the major studios was Paramount's *Murders in the Zoo* (1933). Betwixt the obligatory mystery padding and unfunny comedy relief, villain Lionel Atwill dispatched his victims with sadistic glee. From its genuinely horrible opening, as Atwill leaves his wife's lover to die in the jungles of India after having sewn his lips shut, to its rousing finale, with Atwill (in closeup) crushed to death in the coils of a murderous serpent, *Murders in the Zoo* is a neglected masterpiece that still packs a wallop.

There are also moments that foreshadow more graphic future horrors. The disturbing shots of melting human figurines in *Mystery of the Wax Museum* ('34) and the discreetly presented final decay of *The Mummy* ('32) point to the graphic meltdowns to come, while *Dr. X* ('32) unveiled its cannibalistic 'Full Moon Murderer' in an electronic fusion of flesh and (as the grotesque killer chants its name) 'synthetic flesh' that is curiously echoed fifty years later in Cronenberg's cry of "Long Live the New Flesh!" in *Videodrome* (1982).

While there was no shortage of classic grossouts in the mainstream horrors, the real meat-and-potatoes typically lurked in the occasional imports, underground films, and especially the exploitation films, whose non-Code approved fare was more often that not their greatest source of income. Usually relegated to roadshow exhibitions (proper theatres wouldn't show such films, you know) were films like *Savage Gold* ('33) and *Maniac* ('34). *Savage Gold* is a seminal 'Goona Goona' jungle gore film, filmed in Ecuador by Commander George M. Dyott, a famed Royal Geographic explorer of the era.

Dwain Esper's notorious primitive *Maniac* ('34) spices its murky plot and photography, hideous overacting, and Poe pastiches with a sequence in which the mad doctor finds a black cat chowing down on a heart he's about to transplant. Furious, he gouges the cat's eye out and swallows it ("not unlike an oyster ... or a grape! But the gleam is gone!" he declares).

From Europe came Abel Gance's remake of *J'Accuse* ('37, released in the US in truncated form as *That They May Live* ('39)), which Wiliam K. Everson calls "still one of the most horrific films ever made". Again a passionate antiwar statement, in which a desperate scientist raises the dead (killed in past wars) to frighten the living into ending all wars, the film also stands as a curious precedent to George Romero's *Night/Dawn/Day of the Dead* (particularly the latter). Gance's walking dead were memorable: "Gance secured the cooperation of a league of French War veterans, all of them maimed and disfigured, sometimes into grotesque faces that far outdid the work of the studio makeup departments, and he used the most tragic — and repellent — of these faces as the ones to demand audience attention as they march at the head of dead legions." (Everson, *More Classics of the Horror Film*, 1986)

The 1940's were tame by comparison; the Code rule was strictly enforced by the censors during the war years, and it is doubtful the most fantastic of horror films could compete with the all-too-reals that emerged in the wake of the war, the concentration camps, and Hiroshima. Unable and unwilling to dwell on more visceral effects, the horror films went for lots of thunder and minimal blood. Even the transformation films, typified by *The Wolfman* ('41), *The Cat People* ('42), and Universal's *Paula the Ape Woman* trilogy ('43-'45), chose not to exploit the physical agonies of their werewolves/cats/apes as they change. . . in *The Cat People*, the shape-shifting remains deliberately (and, in this case, effectively) out of sight.

Surprisingly, Val Lewton provided two of the decade's grisliest *frissons*...surprising because Lewton's name is synonymous with the masterful use of understatement to evoke horror. Admittedly, both sequences simply punctuate subtler passages: the famous prologue to *The Leopard Man* ('43), as a young girl's screams and pounding at her stern mother's door are suddenly cut off, and the thick blood seeps under the door; and the fleeting but gory closeup during the climax of the noirish *The Ghost Ship* (also '43), as a blade is twisted into the mad captain's belly.

In *The Beast with Five Fingers* ('46), an ambulatory severed hand that scuttles around like a spider, plays the piano, and is out to strangle Lorre. The disembodied hand (with its clean-cut stump in plain view) is genuinely nightmarish, and the abuse it suffers (impaled, cooked, burned in the fireplace, etc.) easily makes it the '40's ultimate Hollywood grotesque.

More direct and brutally felt was Georges Franju's documentary from France, *Le Sang des Betes / The Blood of the Beasts* ('49). In harrowing contrast to Lumiere's comedic *The Mechanical Butcher* (1895), Franju takes us into the Parisian slaughterhouses and presents an unflinchingly vivid portrait of live animals being professionally reduced to meat.

THEY COULDN'T ESCAPE THE TERROR!
THEY COULDN'T BELIEVE THEIR EYES!
AND NEITHER WILL YOU!
"The Beast From 20,000 Fathoms"
It's alive!
The King of Prehistoric Sea-Giants raging up from ages past to tear a city apart!
Suggested by the SATURDAY EVENING POST story by RAY BRADBURY
WARNER BROS.' THRILL-PICTURE YOU'VE BEEN HEARING ABOUT ON TV AND RADIO!
STARRING PAUL CHRISTIAN · PAULA RAYMOND · CECIL KELLAWAY
KENNETH TOBEY · JACK PENNICK
Screen Play by LOU MORHEIM and FRED FREIBERGER
Photography by Jack Russell, A.S.C. · Associate Producer BERNARD W. BURTON
Technical Effects Created by RAY HARRYHAUSEN · Music by David Buttolph
Produced by HAL CHESTER and JACK DIETZ · Directed by EUGENE LOURIE · Distributed by WARNER BROS.
WB

NOT FOR THE SQUEAMISH (1950-1968)

With the coming of the 1950's films—particularly horror and science fiction films—began to depict more graphic mayhem as a matter of course. That the decade began with movies willing to expose and linger over society's underbelly (such as Bunuel's *Los Olvidados / The Young and the Damned* (1950) and Jean Yves Bigras' *La Petite Aurore, L'Enfant Martyre* (1952), vividly depicting the ravages of poverty and child abuse) had less to do with it than the birth and growth of the drive-in theatres in America, and the overwhelming success of television in the American homes. Simply put, filmmakers had to lure the audience out of the home by promising and delivering greater sensations, by showing on the theatre screens what could not be shown on the TV. Younger teenage audience flocked to and nurtured the drive-ins, whose screens were further challenged to show fare that was more vital, daring, sensational (and cheaper. . .and as we've heard from Stephen King at the beginning of this article, the 'gross-out' is the cheapest shot of all) than the proper indoor movie theatres would show. 3-D, CinemaScope, PanaVision, etc. were one way to lure audiences into the theatres...sexual situations, nudity, and more graphic horrors were another.

While the American Gothic horrors ushered in the '50's in the manner of the preceding decade, with *The Strange Door* ('51, wherein torture-loving Charles Laughton is crushed to death in a water-wheel, jamming the device that would squash the hero and heroine) and its like, the science fiction film stepped from the sterility of *Destination Moon* ('50) to the pulse-pounding confrontation with *The Thing (From Another World)* ('51). After the nerve-wracking buildup to the appearance of 'The Thing' at the doorway (Its hand is splintered by the slamming of the door), the throbbing blood-fed spores of the creature, and the climactic electrocution — not to mention the box-office success it earned—there was no looking back, only up ("Keep Watching the Skies!") as more bloodthirsty extraterrestrials rained down. *Invaders From Mars* ('53) power drilled mind control devices into the back of their hosts' tender necks, *It Conquered the World* ('56)) or tried to, anyway—using flying murderous parasites, while *Teenagers from Outer Space* ('59) ray-gunned their victims down to bare skeletons.

Most insidious, and gruesome, of the extraterrestrial invaders was the unknown entity possessing the hapless astronaut who returned from space during *The Quatermass Xperiment / The Creeping Unknown* ('55), Hammer Films' successful adaptation of Nigel Kneale's BBC television play. The gradual, grueling transformation of the astronaut (Richard Wordsworth), taking sustenance by absorbing his victims and partially taking on their form (i.e., he absorbs a cactus plant, and his arm and shoulder be come vegetal and thorny), even as the extraterrestrial presence asserts its amoebic form, touched a new, deep nerve in audiences. The empathic suspense created by depicting a pitiful man who is losing his humanity, eaten away and changed from within as if by a disease, unsettles the viewer on a decidedly uncomfortable, intimate level of biological revulsion. The sequel, *Quatermass II / Enemy from Space* ('57) pursues other concerns (though it's notable here for the grisly moment in which the alien-controlled workers block the high-pressure ventilation pipes with their own bodies, pulping themselves and filling the pipes with blood), but other films tried to touch the same nerve: *Night of the Blood Beast* ('58) featured an astronaut infected with the throbbing embryo of an alien lifeform growing inside of his body (the first monster birth imagery), the *First Man Into Space* ('59) returns encrusted with space shit and thirsting for human blood, while, most famous but least physically visceral of them all, Don Siegel's classic *Invasion of the Body Snatchers* ('56) had slime-popping vegetal pods from space supplanting sleeping humans with cold, emotionless replicas of the original person. Other terrestrial horrors also touched the same level of biological disease that *Quatermass Xperiment* explored: the wriggling, brain sucking 'thought-creatures' of *Fiend Without a Face* ('58), the early stages of transformation in *The Manster* ('62) as the reporter sprouts a blinking eye on his shoulder that soon grows into a monstrous head, the centipedal parasite that lives in our bodies and is awakened into murderous activity by fear in William Castle's *The Tingler* ('59), the outsized cancer cells that devour bone and leave the victims' shapeless flesh behind in Terence Fisher's *Island of Terror* ('66). All of them anticipate the primal bio-revulsion and monstrous birth imagery that would later be explored by David Lynch (*Eraserhead* ('76)) and David Cronenberg (*They Came from Within* ('74), *Rabid* ('77), *The Brood* ('79), etc.) and exploited by the likes of *Alien* ('79) and *The Manitou* ('78), among others.

Less risible monster flicks of the '50 s often punctuated and spiced their thrills with doses of gore. Monster feeding habits provided many such moments: Ray Harryhausen's stop-motion Rhedosaurus picking up a valiant (or stupid) New York policeman by the head and gulping him down in *The Beast from 20,000 Fathoms* ('53); James Whitmore pumped full of formic acid in the jaws of an outsized ant in *Them!* ('54); a giant bug gorily

BRIAN DONLEVY
Quatermass II
with SIDNEY JAMES
JOHN LONGDEN · BRYAN FORBES
VERA DAY · WILLIAM FRANKLYN
THE UNDERTAKER AND HIS PALS
A MACABRE STORY OF TWO MOTORCYCLE-RIDING, KNIFE-WIELDING, SHIV-SHAVING, EYE-GOUGING, ARM-TWISTING, CHAIN-LASHING, SCALPEL-FLASHING, ACID-THROWING, GUN-SHOOTING, BONE-BREAKING, PATHOLOGICAL NUTS AND THEIR PAL THE UNDERTAKER...
HOUSE OF GLAMOROUS MODELS BECOMES A TERROR HOUSE OF BLOOD!!
BLOOD and BLACK LACE
GUARANTEED! THE 8 GREATEST SHOCKS EVER FILMED!
A WOOLNER BROS. PRESENTATION
TECHNICOLOR®
starring CAMERON MITCHELL · EVA BARTOK
AND THE 30 MOST GLAMOROUS GIRLS IN THE WORLD!
Produced by Alfred Mirabel · Directed by MARIO BAVA
NO ONE PERMITTED
THE WIZARD OF GORE
The Fly
20th Century-Fox presents the last word in excitement–the last word in thrills!
"Once it was human... even as you and I!"
THE FLY with the head of a man..and the man with the head of THE FLY!
It's the terror-topper first introduced to the public in "Playboy" Magazine!
For your own good we won't let you see it alone... unless you sign a waiver in our lobby absolving the management for the unpredictable effects of "The Fly" on your nervous system!
$100 if you prove it can't happen!
Terror-COLOR by DE LUXE
CINEMASCOPE
AL HEDISON · PATRICIA OWENS
VINCENT PRICE · HERBERT MARSHALL
Produced and Directed by KURT NEUMANN
Screenplay by JAMES CLAVELL

munching on a man's face (in closeup) in *The Strange World of Planet X / Cosmic Monster* ('57); the withered husk of a blood-drained victim in *Earth vs. the Spider* ('58); *The Trollenberg Terror / The Crawling Eye* ('58) leaving behind headless victims after chowdown, as do the crustaceans of *Attack of the Crab Monsters* ('56) and *The Monster of Piedras Blancas* ('59); the gators in the pit feeding on the remains of Whit Bissell's victims (and, finally, himself) and *I Was a Teenage Frankenstein* ('58); the sickening bloodsucking sequences of *Attack of the Giant Leeches* and *The Beast of Haunted Cave* (both '59); *The Black Scorpion* ('59) and its kin lifting train wreck victims aloft in their huge claws and stinging them to death before eating them; the amoebic *The Blob* ('58) and *Caltiki, the Immortal Monster* ('59) consuming their victims whole (the latter film especially nasty for its shot of the flesh peeling off the partially-devoured hand of a host), another blob, *The H-Man* ('58), provided the most graphic science fiction human meltdowns of the decade, compliments of *Godzilla* creator/ FXman Eiji Tsuburaya.

Injury to the eye was common, properly kicked off by the archetypal blinding of the Cyclops Polyphemus in *Ulysses* ('55), which naturally inspired the blinding of the Cyclops in *The 7th Voyage of Sinbad* ('58), and the more graphic eyeball puncturing of *It Conquered the World* ('56), *The Cyclops* ('57), *Invasion of the Saucermen* ('57),*The Flesh and the Fiends / Mania* ('59), *Horrors of the Black Museum* ('59, with the infamous spiked binoculars of its opening sequence), *Atomic Submarine* ('60), *Angry Red Planet* ('62), and others, including Italian peblum like *The Son of Hercules vs. Medusa* ('62), *The Minotaur* ('61), etc. The giant chameleon that tries to devour James Mason during the climax of *Journey to the Center of the Earth* ('59) is rewarded with a spike pounded through the tongue, and the ambulatory brains-and-spinal columns of *Fiend Without a Face* ('58) are shot, pierced, and axed in the climactic welter of black-and-white gore that remains one of the 50's grisliest highlights. When *It Came from Beneath the Sea* ('55) and attacked San Francisco, Ray Harryhausen's animated giant octopus dropped its tentacles onto sidewalk pedestrians and smeared them on the tarmac, a grisly interaction of stop-motion animation and live action echoed in the Harryhausen Ymir of *20 Million Miles to Earth* ('57) battling an elephant and pushing it onto its hapless trainer, or the Harryhausen dragon of *The 7th Voyage of Sinbad* crushing the evil magician in its death throes. *The Incredible Shrinking Man* ('57) gores an attacking spider with a pin, and thick, dark ichor runs down the pin over his arm; *The Amazing Colossal Man* ('57) is stabbed in the ankle with a gigantic syringe, only to pull it out and throw it, like a dart, through one of the puny humans annoying him. A giant spider is impaled by a stalactite in *Journey to the 7th Planet* ('61) to the accompaniment of four gurgling sounds and a torrent of multicolored guts. *The Hideous Sun Demon* ('59) crushes a rat in his scaly talons in full, dripping view of the camera; the *Monster from Green Hell* ('58), a giant wasp, injects foamy white venom into a snake; *The She Creature* ('56) dispatches her victims with hooklike talons, and we see the remnants of one of her attacks, with bloodspattered walls and bodies; *The Killer Shrews* ('59) are also messy creatures, slobbering poisonous bile and blood and chewing up their victims horribly. The *Attack of the Crab Monsters* ('56) is surprisingly gory for its time, with severed hands and decapitated heads in the pincers of the ridiculous crustaceans; the head-toting *Monster of Piedras Blancas* ('59) spits an incredible gob of phlegm onto the heroine's chest, just as *Reptilicus* ('62) spurts acidic green saliva over Denmark (to no visible damage, another throwaway shoddy effect in one of the worst giant monster films ever made). Jacques Tourneur's *The Curse of the Demon* ('57) ends with the now-visible demon viciously clawing Niall McGinnis to death in a trainyard, an explicit moment in an otherwise masterfully understated classic of supernatural horror. The most horrifying of all the 50's monster movies was, arguably, *The Fly* ('58), an absurd science-fantasy concerning teleportation and mixed up atoms that create a man with a fly's head and hand: the color film opens with the discovery of his body, the head and hand mashed to bloody pulp under a metal press, and the later sequence when we see the scientist force his wife to commit the act (thereby killing him and destroying the evidence of his monstrous state) is powerful.

Rude as the 50's monster movies may have occasionally been, they paled beside the horror films that were their contemporaries. The first wave was innocuous enough: the tortures of *The Hunchback of Notre Dame* ('56), the (for the time) graphic beheading in *The Undead* ('56), the voodoo heart-removal in *The Disembodied* ('57), and especially the brain surgery in *The Black Sleep* ('56), as the scalpel cuts into the exposed brain and transparent fluid oozes from the slice. This moment of clinical gore heralded the surgical horrors to come the following year (just as the exploding bullet-wounds that stitch through the zombies in *The Creature with the Atom Brain* ('55) foreshadow the spurting color bullet wounds in Hammer's *Curse of the Werewolf* ('61) and the slow motion gunshot gore of *Bonnie & Clyde* ('67) and *The Wild Bunch* ('69), effects which are de rigueur today). The film that

SEE outerspace monster tear huge elephants apart!
SEE space-beast defy modern weapons!
SEE space-beast battle a billion volts of electricity!
SPACE CREATURE RUNS AMOK ON EARTH!
20 MILLION MILES TO EARTH
starring
WILLIAM HOPPER • JOAN TAYLOR
Screen Play by BOB WILLIAMS and CHRISTOPHER KNOPF
Story by CHARLOTT KNIGHT • Technical Effects Created by RAY HARRYHAUSEN
Produced by CHARLES H. SCHNEER • Directed by NATHAN JURAN
A MORNINGSIDE PRODUCTION • A COLUMBIA PICTURE

kicked down the doors was Hammer's *The Curse of Frankenstein* ('57), a vibrant, violent full-color reinterpretation of the Mary Shelley classic that seethed at the civility and the repressed sexuality of the Victorian setting to show, with almost forensic detail, the organs, limbs, and surgery that went into the creation of the Monster.

Clinical blood and gore characterized *I Was a Teenage Frankenstein* ('58, leavened with some welcome deliberate humor: Whit Bissell to his monster: "Speak up! You've got a civil tongue...I know, I sewed it in myself!"), *Frankenstein 1970* ('58, with graphic heart transplants and a jar full of eyeballs shattering on the floor), *Blood of the Vampire* ('58, despite the title a surgical horror film), *Corridors of Blood* ('58), *Dr. Blood's Coffin* ('60), etc. A Frankenstein variation on H.G. Well's The Island of Dr. Moreau shot in the Phillipines, *Terror is a Man* ('59), lent its pitiful, surgically created cat-man a genuine depth of feeling and dignity that balances the film's gimmick of an audio-visual warning system before the film's few gory scenes; the film was rereleased in the 60's as *Blood Creature*, making it forefather of the 'Blood Island' trilogy, *Brides of Blood* ('68), *Mad Doctor of Blood Island* ('68), and *Beast of Blood* ('69), crudely meshing sex, gore, and the tacky 'Chlorophyll Man'. Edward L. Cahn's *The Four Skulls of Jonathan Drake* ('59) carried the surgical motifs into the realm of voodoo, with a Jivaro curse leading to some nasty sequences of (offscreen) beheading and (onscreen) lip-stitching, skinning, and head-shrinking.

Hammer's other major international success, Terence Fisher's *Horror of Dracula* ('58), again brought consummate filmmaking skills, production values, and performances into a full-color, physically rousing reinterpretation of Bram Stoker's famous novel. As with *Curse of Frankenstein*, the drama (here supernatural in nature) is enhanced rather than overwhelmed by the Grand Guignol highlights: the graphic staking of the vampires, the bloodied fangs and slavering blood-drinking, and especially the remarkable climactic disintegration of Dracula (Christopher Lee) in sunlight. *The Return of Dracula* ('58), a fine, atmospheric American variation, had indeed also shown the bloody staking of a female vampire (in black and white), and Dracula (Francis Lederer) being impaled upon a splintered mine support and dissolving into a skeleton.

Hammer's success with their new versions of Frankenstein and Dracula had them quickly mounting remakes of other horror classics, spiced with the trademark Grand Guignol: *The Mummy* ('59, with a gory tongue removal and graphic piercing, puncturing, and gunshot wounding of the Mummy), *The Phantom of the Opera* ('62, with a gratuitous eye gouging), *The Brides of Dracula* ('60, with Cushing's Van Helsing cauterizing the vampire's bite with a red-hot iron, an effect repeated in *Kiss of the Vampire*), *The Curse of the Werewolf* ('61, with the already noted bloody gunshot effect and an athletic werewolf slobbering blood), *Kiss of the Vampire* ('62, climactic attack of bats which chew the vampire coven to death), *Curse of the Mummy's Tomb* ('63, energetic hand lopping and spurting stumps), *Dracula, Prince of Darkness* ('65, a shocking throat slashing to revive Dracula), and more.

Hammer imitators hoped to emulate their success, though it wasn't until Roger Corman and AIP began their series of loose Edgar Allan Poe adaptations that Hammer's crown as the 'Kings of Horror' was threatened. Robert S. Baker and Monty Berman, two British producers were first on the bandwagon with four films that were filmed with more explicit gore and nudity for export versions (a practice that was often mistakenly attributed to Hammer in the pages of Famous Monsters of Filmland magazine). First was a *Quatermass* imitation, *The Trollenberg Terror / The Crawling Eye* ('58), followed by Hammer Gothic/Grand Guignol variations, *The Blood of the Vampire* ('58, scripted by Hammer writer Jimmy Sangster), *Jack The Ripper* ('58, switching from black and white to color for its final scene as the Ripper is crushed by an elevator, and gloriously scarlet founts of gore seethe up from the floor), and best of all, *The Flesh and the Fiends / Mania* ('59).

Even grislier and more memorable were the Anglo Amalgamated trio of horror films which gleefully wore their sadism on their sleeve: *Horrors of the Black Museum* ('59), *Circus of Horrors* ('59), and Michael Powell's classic *Peeping Tom* ('60).

Of the three, *Horrors of the Black Museum* is the crudest revelling in vulgar, lip-smacking mayhem committed by hammy Michael Gough and his young assistant: the infamous trick binoculars that impale a woman's eyes, an old woman's neck pierced by murderous ice tongs, a sultry prostitute guillotined in her own bed, etc. *Circus of Horrors* was a better made film though no less sensationalistic: while its plot (fugitive plastic surgeon manages a circus of criminals whose faces he has altered) allowed for another procession of brutal deaths, the surgeon (Anton Diffring) is so obsessed — and aroused — by disfigured women that the film flirts with sexual sadism to considerable effect, carrying an erotic charge its lewd predecessor never even approaches. The most intelligent and disturbing of the trilogy, *Peeping Tom*, is also the least violent; however, its uncompromising portrait of a young photographer

(Carl Boehm) driven to murder women and photograph their death throes so outraged the British press that the film ended the distinguished career of its director, Michael Powell.

While the primal, violent imagery of Ingmar Bergman's *The Virgin Spring* ('59, wherein a father brutally kills the men who raped and killed his daughter; the 'source' for *Last House on the Left*, ('72)) and Akira Kurosawa's *Throne of Blood* ('57, a rendition of Macbeth that ends with Toshiro Mifune transfixed and bristling with countless arrows) must be acknowledged, a French film by the director of *Le Sang des Betes / The Blood of the Beasts* ('49) brought the decade to a close with the most graphic, distressing footage of the 50's. Georges Franju's *Les Yeux Sans Visage /Eyes Without a Face* ('59, released in the U.S. under the exploitation title *The Horror Chamber of Dr. Faustus* on a double-bill with *The Manster*!) tells its mad-scientist tale with a fusion of poetic elegance and glacial cruelty that is spellbinding. *Eyes Without a Face* spawned a number of near remakes: *Corruption* ('67), *Blood Rose* ('71), *Mansion of the Doomed* ('75, grafting eyes instead of skin), *Faceless* ('88), etc., but none of them hold a candle to Franju's achievement, save to exceed the gore quotient to negligible effect. Jesus Franco's variation, *Gritos en la Noche / The Awful Dr. Orloff* ('62), shifted the surgical horror into the realm of sadoerotica with its blend of surgery, sex, nudity and bondage; Franco's own sequels seem tame in comparison, though the best of his later work (*The Diabolical Dr. Z* ('65), *Venus in Furs* ('69), *Les Avaleuses / Erotikill / The Loves of Irina*, ('73), etc.) displays a progressive obsession with sex and horror. The surgical horrors continued: *The Brain That Wouldn't Die* ('59/'62); *The Virgin of Nuremburg / Horror Castle* ('63), mixing color Italian gothicism with a disfigured madman whose features were flayed off by Nazi surgeons (in a graphic monochromatic flashback), and including a horrific torture scene in which a rat in a cage is strapped over a woman's face; *The Murder Clinic / Revenge of the Living Dead* ('66); John Frankenheimer's brilliant *Seconds* ('66), with a brief but painfully vivid detailing of the facial plastic surgery that changes middle-aged John Randolph into Rock Hudson.

The key transitional 50's SF - 60's gore films were *The Brain That Wouldn't Die* ('59/'62) and *The Flesh Eaters* ('62/'64), both of which were made before Herschell Gordon Lewis unleashed *Blood Feast*('63) on an unprepared nation, and both of which are in black and white, denying their status as seminal 'gore' films. *The Brain That Wouldn't Die* is patently absurd and tabloid-sleazy SF, as a doctor keeps his lover's severed head alive in his lab (an image repeated to chilling effect in *The Frozen Dead*, ('66)) only to have her telepathically urge the hideous monster-in the-closet (the result of the doctor's previous grafting experiments) to murder. The creature rips off the lab assistant's deformed arm in an excessively gory sequence, which is topped when the monster bursts out of his closet and attacks the doctor, biting a chunk of flesh out of his throat and holding it up to the camera to gloat over it before throwing it aside (at which point we are further treated to a shot of the quivering gobbet throbbing on the floor; all of this footage is, alas, trimmed from the commercially available videocassette). *The Horror of Party Beach* ('63, directed by Del Tenney in tandem with a mystery-gore thriller *The Curse of the Living Corpse*, which became its co-feature) turned its silly toxic waste spawned sea monsters against beach babes and pajama party girls with surprisingly bloody results (again, all of which is trimmed from the commercially available videocassette), but it was outdone by *The Flesh Eaters* (which, again, loses its most graphic footage in its commercially available videocassette). *The Flesh Eaters* is the 'missing link' between the 50's creature features (like *The Blob*) and the 60's splatter films (like *Blood Feast*): a group of vacationers and their pilot are marooned on an isolated island surrounded by microscopic-flesh-eater infested waters, which are in fact the creation of the mysterious German Scientist (Martin Kosleck) who lives on the isle, as an extension of his World War II Nazi biowarfare experimentation. Until the climax (electricity causes the tiny organisms to coalesce into a single cyclopean crustacean, which the hero kills in proper 50's monster movie fashion), the movie's highlights are more and more graphic scenes of the 'flesheaters' at work: ocean spray consumes the captain of an approaching rescue ship; a beatnik is slipped a flesh-eater Mickey by the doctor, and eaten from within, catching his spilling intestines in his hands; and finally, the doctor is thrown into the surf, and lurches onto the beach in agony as his skin dissolves, until he fires a bullet into his own eye.

Four films that were released in 1960 paved the way for the new (and grislier) wave of horror films. Alfred Hitchcock's *Psycho* provided the definitive model for the psychological-splatter thriller, with its iconic phallic murder weapon (the knife that carves Janet Leigh up in the shower, which would make way for the profusion of knives, hatchets, and chainsaws to follow). Mario Bava's *La Maschera del Demonio / Black Sunday* went Hammer's *Horror of Dracula* one step further, presenting the physical manifestations of metaphysical forces with grueling detail and

explosive visceral impact. Nobuo Nakagawa's *Jigoku / Hell*, an allegorical morality play whose central movement brings its characters through a truly horrific vision of hell in a nightmarish blend of sex, mutilation, and death that would inspire a wave of Japanese horrors that are reportedly more extreme than any of the Western fare. Roger Corman's first Edgar Allan Poe adaptation for AIP, *The Fall of the House of Usher*, was not itself delivering any gross-outs whatsoever, but must be mentioned as its subsequent Poe spinoffs (from Corman, AIP, and imitators) challenged Hammer's exclusive claim on the Gothic Grand Guignol school of horror. Though these films and their successors appeared and evolved together, they must be separated for discussion, leading up to the year 1968, when the modern horror film (which fully incorporated the 'gross-out' as one of its most vital dramatic and esthetic devices) was born.

Eerie, irrational, and oddly sensuous netherworlds were the province of the European horror films in the 60's, with Mario Bava's *La Maschera del Demonio / Black Sunday* ('60) breaking the turf with a stylish and terrifying black and white tale of resurrected witches and vampires seeking a foothold by feeding on their own descendants 200 years after they were tortured and entombed. In the potent opening, we see Asa branded and a Mask of Satan, its interior lined with spikes, hammered onto her face; 200 years later, the Mask is removed, her skin still smooth but ravaged by the spikes and covered with scuttling insects. As the dripping blood settles into one of her empty sockets and revives her, we see the orbs swell and bubble in the sockets until her glowering eyes emerge; a vampire's head is burned, in horrible closeup, in a fireplace, while another is staked through the eye; Asa's vampiric identity is revealed when her robe is pulled back to reveal her rotted, skeletal chest. The catalog of 'gross-outs' become a powerful and expressive narrative tool in Bava's vision, embellishing, rather than at odds with, his telling of a powerful supernatural horror tale.

Many of *Black Sunday*'s devices became part of Bava's vocabulary (i.e., the revelation of Asa's decayed chest is repeated verbatim to unveil one of the undead astronauts' true condition in *Planet of the Vampires*, ('65)), and his subsequent films continued to mesh the ethereal and the corporeally horrific with considerable (and occasionally brilliant) effect, despite cripplingly low budgets and slapdash screenplays. His best films of this period, which include the sadomasochistic Gothic classic *La Frusta e Il Corpo / The Whip and the Body / What:* ('63), the first true giallo *Sei Donne Per L'Assassino / Blood and Black Lace* ('64), and the evocative *Operazione Paura / Kill, Baby,*

Kill / Curse of the Living Dead ('66), abandoned *Black Sunday*'s monochromatic look to embrace a lush, sensuous use of color.

In America, the catalyst for an entirely contemporary approach to the horror film came from Alfred Hitchcock's *Psycho*. Volumes have been written on the film, so I'll spare you my two-cents' worth; suffice to say the filmmakers who followed in Hitchcock's path were incapable of matching his dazzling artistry, and so merely emulated the film's most sensational elements: the kinetically edited shower murder, the stairway murder, and the mother fixation/sexual identity reversal of the shock ending. Where Hitchcock's horrifying murder makes us feel the stabbing blade without actually showing the knife entering bleeding flesh (an emotionally effective ploy repeated by Tobe Hooper for most of *Texas Chainsaw Massacre* fourteen years later), his imitators went for gore-spattered, explicit murders: William Castle's *Homicidal* ('61) opens with a bloodgushing stabbing during a bogus wedding, and Castle's *I Saw What You Did* ('65) encores the *Psycho* shower murder with gory bluntness, while *Straitjacket* ('64) opens Castle's arsenal to use axes for the brutal murders. Axes, hatchets, and cleavers were also the preferred executioner's tools in Francis Ford Coppola's *Dementia 13* ('63), *Night Must Fall* ('64, a remake of the 1937 chiller that replaces the original's creepy suggestive horror with the 60's sledgehammer brutality), *The Thrill Killers / The Maniacs Are Loose* ('65), Robert Aldrich's *Hush, Hush , Sweet Charlotte* ('65), and *Chamber of Horrors* ('66) .

The most repulsive of all horror films to emerge in the wake of *Psycho* came out of Florida from two men who had established their reputations in the black and white 'nudie' films, producer David Friedman and director Herschell Gordon Lewis. Having little money at their disposal, and in desperate need of an attraction to compete with the mainstream films, they chose to produce what Hollywood and even the hungriest low-budget distributors had not: a no-holds-barred, full color 'gore' film, *Blood Feast* ('63). With a vapid script (that flirts with, but never actually depicts, cannibalism), shoddy actors, abysmal music, and functional photography, all that *Blood Feast* had going for it was the repellent, blood-drenched gory tableaus of murder, dismemberment, tongue-removal, brains pulled out, etc. The camera dwells lovingly over the butchery; nothing like it had ever been seen in American theatres, and the brisk box office (especially in the rural Southern states) assured there would be more. The 'Splatter' film was born, wherein the gory violence was the sole raison d'être, and H.G. Lewis and Friedman put more money and a better story together to make *2000 Maniacs* ('64). The colorful mayhem (including a cannibal barbecue with an arm on a spit) was just as gruesome, the plot more engaging, but the authorities were laying in wait: *Blood Feast* snuck by them, but *2000 Maniacs* had difficulty playing theatrically in some locales. As a result, it wasn't as successful as its predecessor, but still turned a healthy profit. Friedman and Lewis parted ways with their third gore film, *Color Me Blood Red* ('64), separately continuing to exploit the splatter genre they had pioneered: Lewis made *A Taste of Blood* ('67), *The Gruesome Twosome* ('67), *The Wizard of Gore* ('70), and *The Gore Gore Girls* ('72), while Friedman would produce *Ilsa, She-Wolf of the SS* ('74) under a pseudonym. Imitations soon followed, with directors like Andy Milligan and films like *The Undertaker and his Pals* ('67), and directors like John Waters (*Pink Flamingos*, ('72), etc.) and Frank Henenlotter (*Basket Case*, ('81)) would cite Lewis as an influence, but the mainstream films soon incorporated graphic violence into its vocabulary. If *Bonnie & Clyde* ('67) and *The Wild Bunch* ('69) could deliver gory effects along with excellent storytelling and filmmaking, performed by Hollywood's finest, why see a 'splatter' horror film made on a shoestring budget? Crime films, biker flicks, and especially westerns (with Giulio Questi's *Django, Kill* ('67), Ralph Nelson's *Soldier Blue* ('70), Don Medford's *The Hunting Party* ('71), and Joaquin Marchent's *Cut-Throats Nine* ('73), being the most graphic, along with Sam Peckinpah's oeuvre) would, for a time, eclipse the horror film's exclusive claim on the 'splatter' genre. The 'gross-out', after all, is merely a dramatic device; it would take an essential transformation from within the genre to reestablish its values and priorities, and reaffirm its need, as a genre, to break taboos and shock audiences anew with a clarity and power unlike that of any other genre of film or literature.

THE BIRTH OF THE MODERN HORROR FILM: 1968

1968 was a seminal year for Western (especially American) culture; it is not surprising, then, that it also represented an important shifting of gears for the horror film. Culturally, politically, and artistically, revolution and transmutation was the order of the day; if the horror genre were to address the unconsciousness, the underbelly, the dark side of its audience, it would have to do so with a vengeance. The change came with a handful of aggressive, subversive films that used the traditions of the genre to strip it raw, exposing vital, angry nerves. If graphic violence were de rigueur, then that device too, would have to be turned on its head, the audience's nose rubbed in it, their eyes opened anew to the power of the illusory violence they had grown numb to. There were three seminal horror films in 1968, each of which clearly marked the birth of the modern horror film: *Rosemary's Baby*, *The Witchfinder General / The Conquerer Worm*, and *Night of the Living Dead*. The first, Roman Polanski's successful adaptation of Ira Levin's bestseller, marked the first major Hollywood horror film in decades; commercially, it brought the genre out of the ghetto of the low-to-medium budget strait jacket, though its subversive content is masked by its guise of respectability. Its production and popular success assured the economic growth of the genre, leading to the future box office hits based on bestsellers (*The Exorcist, Jaws*).

Rosemary's Baby also indelibly launced the archetypal 'demon child' into the popular pantheon of the horror genre: while the youth of America embraced the rebirth of the starchild in Stanley Kubrick's *2001: A Space Odyssey* (also '68), another older, massive audience embraced the dread of the rebirth of the Antichrist. The crest of that wave carried far into the 70's, with the likes of *The Exorcist*, ('73), *The Omen* ('76), etc. and the nonreligious organic spawning of the monster children in *Eraserhead, It's Alive* ('74), *Alien* ('79), etc.

However, Michael Reeves' *The Witchfinder General / The Conquerer Worm* (which I will hereafter refer to by its original British title) and George Romero's *Night of the Living Dead* are of the greater importance to this article; *Rosemary's Baby*'s horrors are ideological and religious in nature. Though Polanski does make us feel Rosemary's (Mia Farrow) physical revulsion and distress at her situation, it is not sustained at the body level; even for female viewers, the fear is for the infant's nature and safety, and the horror at how satanic forces may have used Rosemary sexually, rather than the "body fear" generated by, say, David Cronenberg's birth imagery in *The Brood* ('79) or *The Fly* ('86). Reeves and Romero, however, orchestrate the use of violence — extremely graphic, strongly felt violence — to reach their audiences at a truly physical, gut level. It is a deliberate, carefully controlled use of the language I have traced at such length throughout this article: the 'gross-out' as a dramatic device in the hands of an artist, a storyteller, who provokes a profound shock or deeply felt sense of revulsion within the audience to make a point. *The Witchfinder General* and *Night of the Living Dead* represent the first calculated, sustained use of the language; not to belittle the mastery with which Terence Fisher, Georges Franju, or Mario Bava spoke the language in the previous decade, but the impact of Reeves and Romero's films had an immediate and clearly

visible effect on every horror film (and those of other genres as well) to follow.

Hence, the birth of the Modern Horror Film.

Both *The Witchfinder General* and *Night of the Living Dead* were treated with critical disdain, and were at the time easily ignored by the critics: they were after all, just drive-in fodder. However, both were widely seen, as drive-ins and neighborhood theatres were still a viable outlet, and given a year or two could no longer be ignored as the shockwaves they generated were felt internationally.

The Witchfinder General was an extension of Reeves' disturbing meditations on violence. Set during the British civil war, the young hero's (Ian Ogilvy) hatred for the authoritarian fanatic Witchfinder General (Vincent Price giving a genuine performance) is fanned into violence when Price tortures his fiance´ Sara (Hilary Dwyer) and executes her father, a priest. Vowing vengeance, Ogilvy tracks Price to a tower where he is torturing Sara, only to be captured and bound, forced to watch his lover's agony until he will confess to the crime of witchcraft. Reeves has shown us a country wracked with pain, death, and decay, with Price institutionalizing the most brutal tortures and executions (depicted in almost unbearable detail) for his own profit and sick pleasure; given the emotions the film has roused in us, and the Witchfinder's role as the focus of our, as well as Ogilvy's, rage, Ogilvy's final escape from bondage and his attacking Price with an axe would, traditionally, be presented as a justifiable moment of release and revenge. Instead, Ogilvy's hacking away at the prone, twitching Price provides no vicarious release: when his friend shoots Price in the head to put an end to his misery, Ogilvy turns on him like an animal, screaming "You took him away from me!" as Sara, unable to bear her lover's descent into bestial violence after the horrors she had already been subjected to, begins to scream in madness.

Despite the period setting (rooted in the Hammer tradition), Reeves had captured the climate of the times with frightening immediacy, depicting a society whose morality and values have been so frayed that it can no longer contain the violence it has made even more explosive by forcibly repressing it. When it explodes at the end of *The Witchfinder General*, there is no right or wrong, only madness. Tragically, it was Reeves last film; a short time after, Reeves died at 25 years of age. Happily, George Romero is still with us, and his remarkable body of work shows that although *Night of the Living Dead* was a communal effort, it was no fluke, and Romer's vision since remains consistent with that so fully realized in his first film.

Night of the Living Dead borrows its imagery and story structure from many previous horror films. Romero and writer John Russo admit readily their debt to Richard Matheson's *I Am Legend*, while the unstoppable army of walking dead recall the pasty-faced undead from *The Cabinet of Dr. Caligari* (1919) *J'Accuse* (1919 and 1937), *White Zombie*, (1932) *Return of Dr. X*, (1937) *Strangler of the Swamp* (1940), *Invisible Invaders* (1959), *The Last Man on Earth* (1962), *Carnival of Souls* (1962), and *Plague of the Zombies* (1966), while the story has structural blueprints in *The Killer Shrews* ('59) and especially Alfred Hitchcock's *The Birds* ('63). I've deliberately avoided mention of *The Birds* until this point (it was, for its time, quite a harrowing and grisly film, with the bird attacks and particularly Tippi Hedren's grueling ordeal in the attic being unusually graphic for a major studio release) because its link with Romero's film is so strong. As in *The Birds*, the walking dead attacks are never explained: it is almost as if they were a force of nature, an elemental force without motive or reason. Comparison of the two films is telling: Romero mirrors Hitchcock's dynamics, pacing, and rhythms carefully, and even specifics of imagery (the farmer with his eyes pecked out/the body at the top of the stairs; the beaks coming through the windows and doors/the arms bursting in through the windows and doors) reverberate clearly. Ultimately, though, Hitchcock harbors hope for his put-upon band of characters, as the birds mysteriously call a truce and allow them to escape (to what?), and the entire film has the undercurrent of a black joke. Romero, however, is deadly serious (though the film is not humorless): there is no shelter, no respite from the desperate life and death struggle, and in the end it seems there is no hope... Ben survives only to die, meaninglessly. Just as *The Witchfinder General* draws from the Hammer tradition that was, during the 50's, a progressive movement, Romero finds bedrock in Hitchcock's *Psycho* and *The Birds*, the clear forefathers of the Modern American horror film.

[Thanks to Tim Lucas, Bill Kelley, Michael Price, Dennis Daniel and 'The Things From Another World', Tim Ferrante, Chas Balun, and Stan Wiater for their knowing and unknowing assistance.]

THE MONSTER LIVES IN A GLASS CAGE

BY CHAS. BALUN

I am not often truly shocked, left numb nor slack-jawed by very many films. In most cases, when it does occur, it usually results in a flurry of frenzied writing in an attempt at catharsis and a chance to make the prose fuel the purge. On only a handful of occasions have I ever felt that I *had* to write about the experience. It was a way of coming to terms with something that had shaken, not stirred, the very foundations of sentient thought.

These were movies that melted the paint off the walls of your mind and made you want to fumigate for brain parasites. Films that spread plague to the house of horror. These were films that looked you straight in the eye and then ripped your spine out your ass. I wrote about them because there seemed to be no other way to bring the demons to the light. Something in each of these films got under my skin and burrowed down deep in the marrow. They worked their way up to my skull and stayed there until words could be conjured to combat their black magic.

Besides being the *only* film to come close to making me blow my Oreos, *Cannibal Holocaust* was also the first of the bunch to force my hand into the arena of confessional journalism. But all too often, one's reactions to certain films reveal deep-seated fears, paranoias and hang-ups in the viewer that, in most instances, one would not want trumpeted in the nation's press. Sometimes, however, there is no choice.

I watched *In A Glass Cage* in *three* installments, like a mini series of an epic Nazi pedophilic nightmare that was just too intense to be taken full strength. Contrary to prurient expectations, the film is by no means an exploitation vehicle of any kind. Despite the smarmy subject matter, *In A Glass Cage* plays more like an earnest, albeit particularly twisted, art house film.

Actually, finding an audience for *Glass Cage* has proven unusually problematic. It doesn't seem to fit in anywhere. It did play at an East Coast gay and lesbian film festival, but even "special-interest" audiences were no doubt just as ill-prepared for *Glass Cage's* jolting, soul-wracking sucker punch as were their 42nd Street counterparts.

This is not entertainment. This is a sobering, heartbreaking descent into a world filled with obsessive cruelty, medical dementia and sexual perversion. One might expect as much from a film that begins with a sequence showing a trussed and naked, badly beaten young boy being photographed, kissed on the face, then clubbed to death by a 2x4. The perpetrator then sails off the roof as we cut to opening credits over cheery Nazi death camp photographs. No punches are pulled. This film starts telegraphing its moves right away and you'd best buckle down, snuff the reefer and get yourself ready.

Besides sharing common historical roots, *In A Glass Cage* remains a light year away from such leering, contemptible Nazi torture films as *S.S. Hell Camp* (*Nazi Holocaust*), *Ilsa: She Wolf of the S.S.*, or *Love Camp 7*. *In A Glass Cage* is a film about torture–physical, mental and spiritual–but there is no titillation, no excitement in the prospect.

After the heavy-duty, black-and-white slide show of Nazi crematoriums, mass graves and attending legions of hollow-eyed walking corpses, *In A Glass Cage* formally opens with the man in an iron lung (the "Cage" of the title) as a result of his pre-credit suicide leap.

(I must confess...it's really depressing writing and recalling this experience. I feel spiritually scarred in some place that can't be reached by even the most fervent prayer. This film is not merely about the evil and seditious nature of just one Nazi doctor. Nothing so prosaic here. All of humankind is on trial and the verdict rendered causes shudders down the spine.)

The paralyzed man's family hires a male nurse to provide the requisite around-the-clock care and thus begins an evil alliance that eventually climaxes with one of the most unspeakable acts of death bed perversion ever seen in a *major* feature. And, make no mistake about it. *In A Glass Cage's* production values are impeccable. The photography is lush and surreal, the direction assured and the acting is dead on. Some serious money was spent here.

After the newly-hired attendant fails to administer an injection properly, it becomes quite clear that his motivations were other than conscientious patient care. Apparently, the young man was willing to do or say anything just to be close to his Nazi mentor-idol. He takes great delight in reading from the doctor's personal atrocity journals, which only serve to whet his appetites, both sexual *and* violent, for the real thing. Reading about the death throes of pre-adolescents caught in cardiac arrest after lethal gas injections invokes quite a rise from the student which, in turn, leads to several scenes of some seriously bent self-abuse.

Forget *Nekromantik's* notorious stiff-dick suicide. This film literally comes on your face. And it ain't pretty.

Aping his mentor's actions, the youthful acolyte is soon kidnapping kids from town and then killing them in the precise way the paralyzed doctor did it during the halcyon days of the Holocaust. Nothing too graphic nor explicit (except for one gory throat slitting) is shown, and mercifully, no child is ever shown totally unclothed nor engaged in any simulated sex act. All scenes of that nature are suggested, but not seen in any detail whatsoever. Thank God for small favors.

(Though the film is in Spanish (with English subtitles), it appears a disclaimer of sorts follows the credits and assures its nervous viewers that no children were harmed in any way nor exposed to anything of a sexual nature.)

The escalating violence and dementia soon envelop the entire household as the sadistic student holds the entire family hostage and begins a questionable relationship with the Doctor's young daughter.

The Doctor is clearly at odds with himself throughout the film; and, though he doesn't necessarily condone the violence of his most apt pupil, he is powerless to interfere. He witnesses the killings with the detached and dispassionate vision of one who has murdered for a living.

A key to the real identity of the young assistant is withheld until the finale when a revelation connects the image seen earlier in a photograph with its flesh-and-blood counterpart. The climax, both literally and figuratively, involves an act of lethal oral copulation that brings the whole twisted mess full circle.

One man's evil has infected an entire family, maybe an entire generation; and as the film ends, hope for future change appears as bleak as the grainy death camp photo montage seen under the opening credits. *In A Glass Cage* explores evil in many forms and finds our capacity for it to be endless. One violent or perverted act has the insidious power to influence far more lives than just those of the perpetrator and his victim.

In A Glass Cage, with its relentlessly pessimistic view of human nature and man's propensity for monstrosity, seems to effectively negate what many scholars and scribes have concluded about our endless flirtation with the dark side. Nathaniel Hawthorne proclaimed in *Twice Told Tales* (1937) that "there is no such thing in man's nature as a settled and full resolve either for good or evil, except at the very moment of execution." That proves patently false in the demented world of *In A Glass Cage*.

Instead, this powerful, fearless and vexatious film better reinforces Shakespeare's oft-quoted line from Julius Caesar: "The evil that men do lives after them; the good is often interred with their bones."

With *In A Glass Cage*, evil not only lives, it triumphs.

"STALKING SPLATTER'S SACRED COWS"

by Dennis Daniel

This piece is about truth. My own personal truth. The truth the way I see it. Many will disagree. Fine. I don't claim to be a know-it-all about the horror genre. I'm a fan, just like you. If there's one thing I can't stand it's a critic. Yet, here I am about to be critical. But, it's my own criticism. I speak for no one else but myself. If there are any among you who agree with what I'm about to say, cool. Those that don't, cool too. Everybody's got a right to their own informed opinion. (Note: I said "informed." If you're a hopeless fan-boy who believes that the shit of the above genre-related peronalities doesn't stink...turn the page. Blind devotion is not my bag.)

> I'm sick and tired of hearing things from
> Uptight, short-sighted, narrow-minded
> hypocrites.
> All I want is the truth.
> Just gimme some truth."
>
> *From the song "Gimme Some Truth"*
> *by John Lennon.*

Many of my *DEEP RED* brethren are no doubt familiar with a column I wrote way back in issue #l entitled "Whatever Happened To Tobe Hooper, or Tobe Or Not Tobe." The article allowed me the chance to exorcise some of the demons that were plaguing me regarding the films of Hooper, especially the three turkeys he made for Cannon. It was my first genre-related published piece and, since I had no previous reputation to be watchful of, I laid the nerves bare, as I saw it, on how progressively awful his films had become. It was after seeing *Texas Chainsaw Massacre II* that I truly had my first taste of bile regarding the "fall from grace" of my horror genre heroes. I remember entering the theatre, tingling with

excitement! "Imagine...Tobe Hooper and Tom Savini! Together! This is going to be amazing!" Of course, we know the results. I was so pissed off that I wrote the article that very evening! (By the way, Hooper's *Invaders From Mars* is the only movie in my history of going to the theatre that I actually fell asleep watching.)

Since *Chainsaw II*, Hooper has done very little, if anything of note. His *Spontaneous Combustion*, as far as I can tell, never received a theatrical release and went straight to video (I haven't bothered seeing it.) He also directed a TV movie (I forget which one and couldn't be bothered looking it up. I'm not doing heavy research for this piece, it's all from the gut. Period.) The point is...Tobe is still considered one of the giants of the genre by many. Why? Because his first genre offering, *Texas Chainsaw Massacre*, is so *fucking* good, that's why! I'm not going to take that away from him. But damn it, I feel duped!! I want more! Is there anything wrong with that?

When it comes to Tobe Hooper, I've heard my share of stories and excuses being made for him. Everything from drug problems to studio interference has been linked with his filmic demise. Some of it may be true, some may not. All that matters in the end is the final product with his name on it. Look, I don't wish the guy any ill will. From what I've heard from many pople who have worked for him, he's a terrific-cigar-chomping-real cool-upstanding-hang-out-with-ya kinda guy. I just wish he'd make another good movie. There's still time.

My own personal Tobe Hooper debacle was the first time in my horror movie-loving career that I began to smell a rat. Could it be that all these "name brand" horror film directors were just making films on reputation alone and quite possibly might have (shudder) no real lasting talent? Was it all just press release bullshit?

Another person who enjoys a large following of blind hero worshippers is Wes Craven. Okay...I know...he created Freddy Krueger and *A Nightmare on Elm Street* is a bonafide classic; but what else is there? (The sequels, both with and without Craven's involvement, where tremendous moneymakers, but as far as being rewatchable classics, they can all lick my ass! They made a star out of Robert Englund, but come on...this guy is no true horror star! Boris Karloff, Bela Lugosi, Lon Chaney, Christopher Lee, Peter Cushing, Vincent Price...*these* are horror stars! These guys show diversity! All Englund does is hide under make-up playing glorified slashers. Big fucking deal.) *Last House on the Left*? Sure, it broke a lot of taboos and was daring for it's time, but I don't cuddle up to the VCR to watch it. The same goes for *The Hills Have Eyes*. Ground-breaking..yes! The work of a director finding himself..yes! A film to base a reputation on? No. I'm sure Wes feels the same way! *The Serpent and the Rainbow* is a really fun film too, but it's also a very polished Hollywood-type product that ruins itself by having a contrived *Raiders of the Lost Ark*-type ending. I don't know about you, but that ending really killed the film for me. The whole film sets itself up as being realistic. A story about "real" zombies. Hot damn! It was even based on a true story; the book by Wade Davis. Once again, I'm not saying it was a bad movie. But, considering the reputation Wes Craven has in the genre, it's not the film he should lay his hat on. If films like *The Hills Have Eyes 2, Deadly Friend* and *Shocker* are any indication of what Wes Craven is really all about; we're in big trouble.

Again, with Craven, you have a situation where many outside entities are being blamed for the poor quality of the products bearing his name. It hurts even more because you know Craven is good! Some of the *Twilight Zone* episodes he directed were the best of the new series ("Wordplay" being my favorite).

Another director who's currently on my personal skid row is John Carpenter. Here's a man with practically nothing but crappy movies on his roster. And yet, he's also the man who brought us one of the greatest horror films of all time. A film so revered by this humble writer that I count it as one of my favorite films, regardless of genre. John Carpenter's *The Thing* is glorious! (And the new letterboxed laserdisc is a wonder to behold.) But good God...those turkey's! *The Fog, Prince of Darkness, They Live, Christine*...yeech! Oh sure, he's done critically praised films like *Starman*. Many critics like *Halloween* and consider it a ground breaker (which it is). I even dig *Escape From New York*. *Big Trouble in Little China* was a noble attempt but it hurts my head to watch it. The fact is, John has yet to really deliver the goods since *The Thing*. What's John's excuse? He's had artistic freedom. What gives?

What gives, I believe, is that these fellows are fed up with horror. Yes. They want to try something new; but *we* won't let them.

The director that falls right in line with that kind of thinking is George Romero. If ever there was a director linked with the genre, it's George. But, think about it: what has George really done besides the Living Dead trilogy and *Martin* that has any real lasting value? When we think of George Romero, we think zombies! And hey...there's nothing wrong with that! If all George ever did was *Night of the Living Dead, Dawn of the Dead* and *Day of the Dead*, he'd have done plenty! The trouble is, he has done more than that and most of it doesn't stand the test of time. Films like *Knightriders*, *Creepshow* and *Monkey Shines* certainly have their moments, but they're really just two star diversions. *Creepshow* is the kind of film you watch on a boring Sunday afternoon, when the VCR is broken and it's running on some local station. But oh,those zombie films! Nobody does them better (although Lucio Fulci certainly tries his best).

Romero is currently working on the screen adaption of Stephen King's *The Dark Half*. Sounds promising, but....

Stuart Gordon. Whatever happened to him? Bad business deals, mostly. Movie companies going belly up and leaving his projects in limbo (which really blows dead dogs because some of the announced projects like Lovecraft's "The Shadow Over Innsmouth" have mouth-watering possibilities). When it comes to "films that might have been," Stuart is the director of choice. That's all well and good but let's quickly examine the films Stuart did make. *Re-Animator*? Well, I think we all feel that it's *the* horror film of the eighties. Chas. has written at length, many times, about the importance of this film and I agree without question. However, I don't believe Stuart conjured the same kind of magic with *From Beyond* and *Dolls*, noble attempts that they may be. I'm finding more and more that I judge a films greatness by the amount of times I'm willing to view it or, if I'm into owning a copy of it. The jury is still out on Stuart (I'm still waiting to see *Robotjox)*. Let's hope he enters the genre again soon. (Too bad he didn't get to direct *Honey, I Shrunk the Kids*...he'd be writing his own ticket by now.) As with Romero, if Stuart is only remembered for *Re-Animator*, that would still be quite a feather in his cap.

Now we come to the genre-related personality that has caused blood in my stool. I'm speaking about the so-called "future of horror," Clive Barker. Talk about being duped! Through the years I've heard stories about this man that you wouldn't believe! Here's my Clive Barker scenario in a nutshell: It took Clive many years to write the *Books of Blood* (which, I might add, deserve their excellent reputation. They are truly magnificent short stories). He has been riding the crest of their popularity ever since. I've never found any of his novels engaging (maybe it's because he hasn't had years to write them). They all seem quite overblown. The short story, in my opinion, is Clive's domain. Then came Clive's directorial film debut *Hellraiser*, an interesting, original vision that, although confusing at times, was a much needed breath of fresh genre air. I loved it. Still do. (The sequel wasn't so hot. It had a lot of gory stuff and some real striking imagery, but it missed the boat overall.) The short story it's based on "The Hell Bound Heart" is also excellent. In fact, I'll go so far as saying that "Pinhead" and the Cenobites are the most striking original monsters to come to the screen in decades!

And that's it for Clive.

The Books of Blood and *Hellraiser*.

Future of horror. Yeah, right.

Clive Barker embodies the quintessential example of a man who was made by the media. The hype about Barker was, and still is, unrelenting. Through it all, he's become a very rich man. Do you realize how many spin-offs, comics, biographies, sequels and other assorted projects Clive has in the can? Most of it is complete, total crap! (The only one I've enjoyed is the "Clive Barker's Hellraiser" comic from Epic.)

How about that *Nightbreed*, huh? For the love of God, there's no excuse on earth for *Nightbreed*! What a mangled mess of a movie that was! Remember the hype surrounding *that* puppy before it came out? There were *Nightbreed* monsters on the cover of every horror mag there was (many of which have since gone out of business). I remember reading an editorial in *Fangoria* about how Clive was boned by the studio and it was *their* fault that *Nightbreed* was so rancid. It was full of the typical whining about lack of proper promotion and other various studio interferences that led to the downfall of *Nightbreed*. Maybe some of it was true but ...come on! Even if they promoted it as better than the Second Coming it it still would have been a bad film. *Nightbreed* is a crazy, mixed up clunker!

Stick to the Cenobites Clive.

Now we come to the film that sort of wraps this whole thing up — the remake of *Night of the Living Dead*. If ever a film had promise, it was this one. All of the original creators were involved and Tom Savini, a good buddy of them all, would direct.

From it's initial announcement, many a horror fan scratched his head and said, "Huh? A remake? Why?" The reason became clear very early on — money. George Romero, John Russo, Russell Stiener and Image Ten all got fucked the first time around with the copyright on the original. Doing a remake would set everything right and put the ball back in their court. Fine. Let's knock everyone's dicks in the dirt and create another masterpiece..whattya say guys? Let's make a film that speaks for the nineties just as the original spoke for it's time, okay?

No such luck.

The remake of *Night of the Living Dead* will not stand the test of time. It will not be remembered. It will fade away and vanish. It just kills me that a film with so much talent behind it..proven talent...turned out to be so dull.

The production was plagued by problems and contractual obligations (an R rated picture had to be delivered). Everything from financing to personal problems of various individuals involved lead to the remake's downfall. How do I know? *I was there*. Thanks to the good graces of make-up/FX masters Everett Burrell and John Vulich (with an okay from Tom Savini), I was given the once-in-a-lifetime chance of becoming a flesh-eater in a Romero zombie film. They even allowed me to bring along my partner Steve Morrison and my buddy Gahan Wilson (who has a great scene with a torch). Once more, I got to eat flesh! (I'm in the truck explosion scene.) They were all wonderful to us! The attitude on the set was very cheery and fun. But...you hear things, know what I mean? Things come down through the grapevine. It can't be helped. Still, I didn't expect it to be as bad as it was. The rushes looked great! Frankly, I was shocked that it turned out the way it did. I feel like such a shit telling you this because everyone was so kind to me.

But, what am I supposed to do? Lie? The remake turned out to be unnecessary.

So, there you have it. A group of individuals with reputations that far exceed the realities of what they've done. Every one of them has created one or more classics; but they've got just as many, if not more, dogs in their kennel. Does that really matter? After all, they're all human, right? Mistakes can be made.

Sorry, I don't buy it.

Look at somebody like Alfred Hitchcock. Here's a man who worked in the Studio system for practically his entire career. Nearly every one of his films is a classic. In other words, he earned his reputation as a genius and proved it time and time again.

Most of these guys have been hyped to us in magazines. We read press release-type articles about their films before they come out, get all hot and sweaty, go to see them, and end up projectile-vomiting at the putrid product. Now I know it's tough for filmmakers these days, but how long are we going to make excuses? Goddamn it, I'm paying good, hard-earned money to walk into a theatre and see their work. I don't like getting ram-rodded up the bunghole.

I've actually lost my love of current horror. It's true. I'd rather watch the old classics. I'm tired of the hype and bullshit I read. I was suckered in for too fucking long. I don't even buy horror mags anymore. What are they going to write about? I even sold my entire collection of *Fangoria*. Think I'm a dick? Of all the films and events they've covered, how many are worth picking up and re-reading again? What am I going to read about? *Chud*? *Dead Heat*? *Prophecy*? *Amityville III*? Forget it! These days, I stick to fanzines. At least they tell the truth.

Still...I haven't lost all hope. I'm just reading the labels more carefully.

NEKROMANTIK

Corpse-Banging as High Art

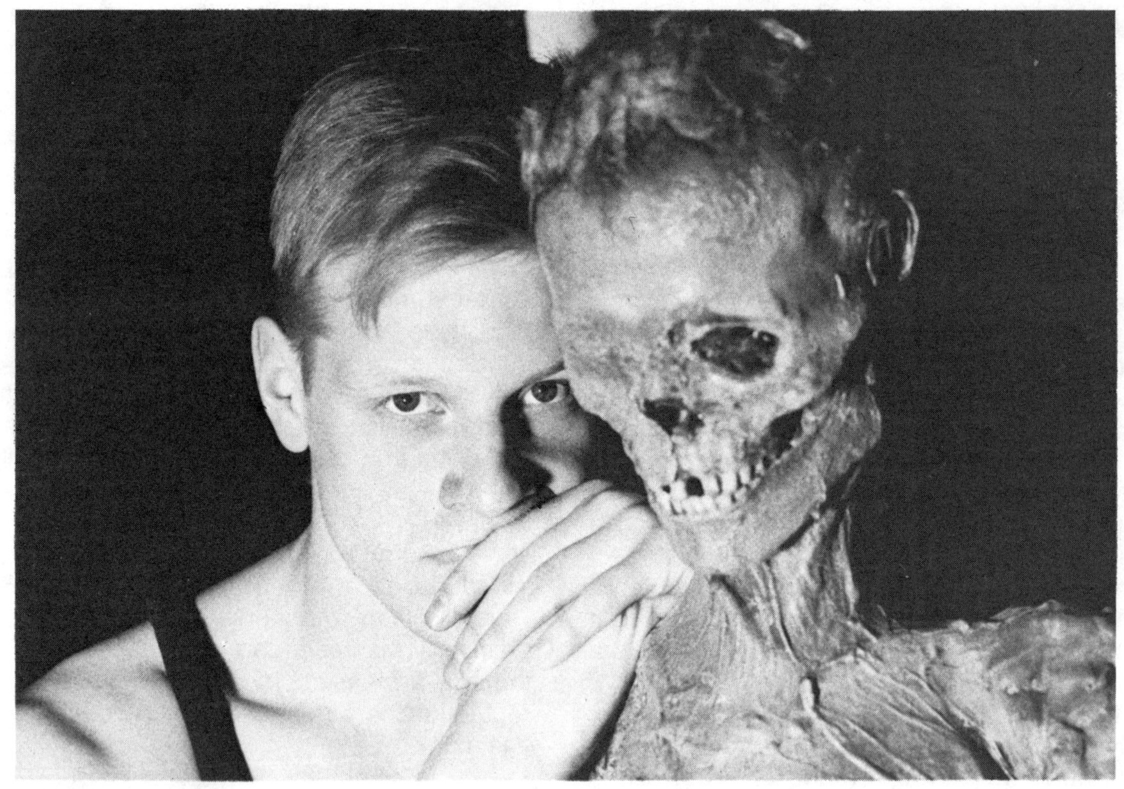

AN INTERVIEW WITH JORG BUTTGEREIT

By John Martin

The following interview was conducted at the second *Black Sunday* (Britain's premiere event of its kind) film festival in Manchester, which featured screenings of Jorg Butgereit's *Nekromantik* (the heart-warming story of a boy, a girl, a dead body and a broomhandle) and *Hot Love* (boy meets girl, boy loses girl, boy rapes girl and kills himself, girl gives birth to baby, baby mutates into boy's zombie and kills girl).

As for Jorg, whom I described in *The Deep Red Horror Handbook* as a "strange Aryan boy whose career threatens, rather than promises, to develop along wildly anarchic lines", the following encounter gave me no reason to reconsider that assessment.

JM Jorg, this is the second screening that *Nekromantik* has had in Britain. Has *Hot Love* ever been shown here before?

"...I wanna have this poster with the woman and the corpse, kind of like *Gone With the Wind...*"

Director Buttgereit and dead pal.

JB No, It's an earlier one but it's just getting some attention because of some kind of success of *Nekromantik.*

JM Where else have you shown *Nekromantik*, and what sort of response has it received?

JB It's been shown two or three times, I think, in the USA, one time in Britain, the second time was here, and yet it's more a kind of warm response in these kind of countries, you know? In Germany it's more like "Vot's that?!? He's trying to..." what's the word? "...put a bad light on our children!" and so on, I'm a black sheep in Germany, you know?

JM Did you bring *The Todeskins*?

JB No, it's a little bit different with this one because I just finished it and it's not like *Nekromantik* because I just wanted to make a film like nobody expected, so the people got really confused when I showed it first in Berlin, you know, they don't know what to think. The critics are...they don't know what it is or what kind of film it is. Some people have said it's going to be a hit in about 10 years or so, it's gonna be a cult movie, but now it's too early, but I don't know. What is so difficult is that there's a lot of talking in it. There are some new kind of jokes that I told. The whole film is not going very well, you know, it's some kind of work to watch it. It's very fast at the start, then it goes very slow, then cut, it's over...it's very strange. I like it very much but the people are getting confused. It's made of seven different parts, and between the parts there's a rotting corpse. There are very strange relationships between all these things. They are fitting very strangely together.

"The last really good horror film I saw was *Dead Ringers*...and it wasn't even a horror film."

JM But the imagery is not as extreme, as strong, as with *Nekromantik*, for instance.

JB No, no with *Nekromantik* we tried to do something to let people know that someone – me – is making films and we make this poster with a corpse and the woman in the way Roger Corman used to do it: "OK, great poster, now we have to do the film".

JM Did the poster really come first?

JB No, not really, but it's a long way to go if I'm doing a film. It takes about a year. For *Nekromantik* we didn't pay anyone. Everyone worked for free, including me, so it took a whole year and during this year I found an artist and told him, 'Yeah, I wanna have this poster with the woman and the corpse, kind of like *Gone with the Wind* ', you know, and with the new one it was a new poster. We tried to do a film poster that no one can think about what kind of film it is. I think it's the same with the trailer. You've seen the trailer, but still you don't know what the movie is about. Strange.

JM Is it true that you've put out a comic version of *Nekromantik* in Germany?

JB I didn't, but a friend of mine did.

JM You've got a small franchise turning out records, T-shirts, etc.

JB Oh yeah, but we used to make all the merchandise things for ourselves, so it's not a real business thing, it's more a kind of joke. So we made a picture soundtrack of *Nekromantik* and it sold out! We just made 500 copies and made it in picture disc with two different sides and lots of music on it so you can hardly hear the music because it's so (makes scratchy noises) but it's cool.

JM Did you have any cases of British customs confiscating *Nekromantik*?

JB Yeah, about four times.

JM Did they ever get back to you and say "Stop sending these disgusting films"?

JB No, they just sent a message to the guy I wanted to send it to and they told him that they wanted to make a raid...is that the expression?...in his flat if he tried to do it again. So I stopped doing it. So it was a little bit exciting to go through customs with a copy now, but they were just a little bit worried about the title *Hot Love*, but I told them that it was not a porno movie.

JM What's German censorship like? At one time it was more liberal than in Britain, but now it seems just as bad, if not worse.

"I like the weird little ones like *Combat Shock*, *Eraserhead*, stuff like that."

JB Yeah, I think finally it is like no distributor is interested anymore in getting any films over to Germany because they cut all things out, and when they show just these bits of the film with lots of talking, nobody is interested anymore, so the whole thing is going right down the... whatever. So nobody is interested anymore in horror films because all the guys who wanted to see horror movies had all the films on video before that stopped in Germany. There's just no market for that now, they damaged it by themselves.

JM Did you have any trouble with *Nekromantik* in your home country?

JB No, not yet! (Laughs) It's strange. They had some parts of *Nekromantik* on the TV in Germany and nothing happened.

Nekromantik blew alot of minds.

JM But you had problems in a town called Bielelfeld, I believe.

JB They showed *Nekromantik* but they refused to show *Hot Love* because it's, y'know, "against women". I make little tours through West Germany with my Super-8 films, showing them and introducing them. And that was during *Hot Love*. I made a *Hot Love* "World Tour" through West Germany. After Bielelfeld, the staff rung me up one year later and told me that the people from Bielelfeld wanted to see the movies again. They wanted to have a party and so on, and I said OK, you can book me and the films and it's OK, and then came this letter where they wrote to me and said, "We want to play all the films but we do not want *Hot Love* because that's against women."

JM So here's your chance to set the record straight Jorg. Are you "against women"?

JB No!

JM I didn't think so. There's a credit at the start of *Hot Love* for somebody named "Freudenstein". Was this a real person named Freudstein, or is that an hommage to Lucio Fulci?

JB No, that was just a sort of name for a guy who did the lights. He also did the *Nekromantik* poster later and he also did the *Hot Love* poster. I sent some to this cinema, but they've gone away, so I can't show you them. They're on someone's wall somewhere!

JM I also noticed that you used the soundtracks of some Fulci movies for the horror film that Daktari Lorenz goes to see in *Nekromantik*.

JB Yeah, it's just that we wanted to have a real film soundtrack for it, to let the people know outside that there's a film going on, and it just happened that we chose that.

JM Are you a Lucio Fulci fan?

JB Not at all. I have to say that I'm not into horror films anymore, because there's nothing new in them...they're so boring! The last really good horror film I saw was perhaps *Dead Ringers* and it wasn't a real horror film, so it's kind of new horror films that I like, different ones, the weird little ones, like *Combat Shock, Eraserhead*, stuff like that. I never liked mainstream kinda stuff, y'know, just because you know what's coming in advance. Nothing's exciting anymore.

JM Was the baby transformation scene at the end of *Hot Love* intended as a tribute to *Eraserhead*?

JB No, but that's what people ask. It's just a baby. It's a very different thing. It's a funny movie and it's in colour, it's just...I have no intention to do a tribute, but it's OK if that's what people think.

JM What about *Horror Heaven*, a film that hasn't been seen over here?

JB That's one of my earliest. I think it was done before *Hot Love*. It's another Super-8 movie, so it's about 30 minutes. Just a very short movie...remakes of *The Mummy* and *Frankenstein* and *Godzilla*, all of these kind of things just to make history, y'know, very fast.

JM Have you seen *Porno-Zilla*?

JB Not yet, but I've heard about it. I'm a big fan of Godzilla movies, I used to see them all at the local cinemas. That's my background. So *Horror Heaven* is just a joke. That's why when *Nekromantik* came out people got confused, because the films I was doing weren't funny anymore. It's the same now, one critic said: "After *Hot Love* he shocked us with *Nekromantik*, with a serious picture, and now he's getting more serious and it's a very heavy, important movie", or something like that. But Jorg Buttgereit is not going to make it easy for his audience, so all the people stay away from the movies because they are like hard work.

JM Another film you've worked on that nobody has seen over here is *Jesus – The Movie*. Can you tell us something about that?

JB Yeah, that's a project from a guy in Germany. He asked a lot of different people, famous underground people, if they would

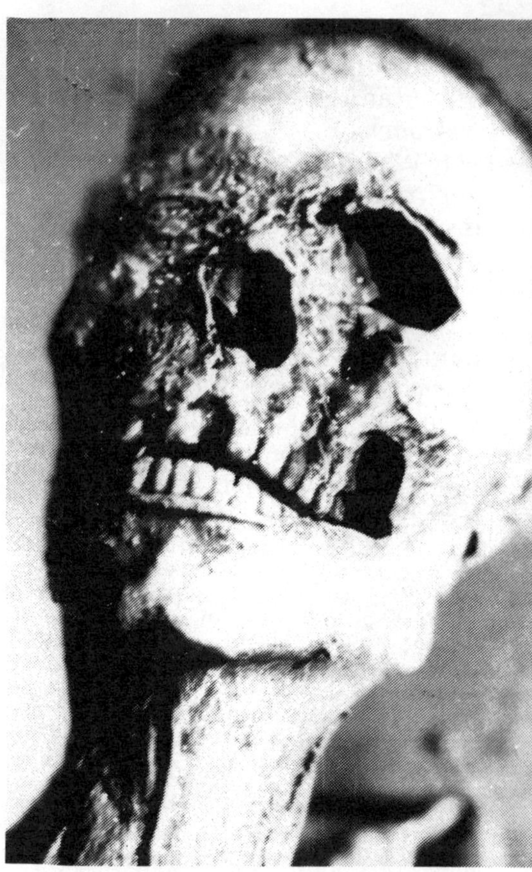

"There's nothing new in horror films any-more...they're so boring!"

each make a little part of the whole Jesus story, and he played Jesus in every one. He asked me if I would do a part and of course I wanted to do the things with the nails on the cross (mimes hammering nails in). It's just a one-day shoot, we just sat in a car with two pieces of wood. I grabbed Daktari, the main actor from *Nekromantik*, then we nailed him to the cross. That's it... the crucifixion scene, I don't know what it's called over here.

JM What kind of a guy is Daktari?

JB (Pulls face) A *strange* guy... the hard thing about him is that he didn't like *Nekromantik* and he doesn't like the new one and yeah, that's very hard, to shoot a film with an actor who thinks, "I don't like this". He told me that one day he

Nekromantik

wanted to do a big movie with machine guns and all that kind of stuff, but he doesn't like the movie at all because he thinks it was too arty and all this kind of stuff. But he provided the soundtrack for the new one so in some ways he must like it...I don't know.

JM Are there any other interesting young German filmmakers whose work we should be looking out for?

JB I don't think so.

JM So there's no kind of scene of filmmakers and artists in Berlin? You're pretty much on your own?

JB There used to be a real underground film scene, more kind of art films, and during this art period I used to make films that you could laugh about. All the people used to like that, so one day this guy came over and wanted me to make a little film for the TV, but I couldn't come up with a story-line because I had no idea how to do a storyline for TV. Then I just asked him to pay for my film and *Nekromantik* came out.

JM How have the lives of people in general and artists in particular been affected by the recent political upheavals in Germany?

JB Nothing! It's just an ordinary wall there.

JM Yeah, but it's gone now.

JB Yeah, but during the time of *Nekromantik* it hadn't gone. It's like at first it was funny for us, the people in West Berlin, it was no problem to go over to East Berlin, so it was an ordinary thing to do. Now all these people from East Berlin are coming over and filling the streets and we're getting a little bit tired of it now. So much for political history!

JM Did you go out onto the streets to film the events?

JB No, there were plenty of people to do that, I didn't have to. I am always trying to do things that nobody else is doing,

The Todeskins has just been released on video in Britain, after much deliberation by the British Board of Film Classification, by Headpress, a small distribution company run by Dave Flint, editor of the inestimable *Sheer Filth*, and fellow writers (and Daves) Kerekes and Slater. Headpress can be contacted at P. O. Box 160, Stockport, Cheshire, SK1 4ET, England. Jorg Buttgereit's new project is, brace yourselves, *Nekromantik* 2.

[Thanks to David Bryan, Malcolm Daglish, Andrew Featherstone and Pip Kennedy for their valued assistance.]

NASCHY 101

A User Friendly Guide

by Shane M. Dallman

The fact that you're reading this book indicates that you are already aware that we, as fans of horror, have passed the point where the shockers of Europe were largely ignored in favor of our homegrown product. Argento, the Bavas, Fulci, and even Deodato and D'Amato have received their due recognition in these pages and others. So why has it taken so long for Paul Naschy to get his share of credit in these parts? The man's been making horror films practically non-stop since 1967, functioning as star, screenwriter (as Jacinto Molina Alvarez, which is his real name), and as producer/director since the late 1970's. His reputation in Europe, especially in his native Spain, is assured, so what's holding him back here?

The answer is easier than you might think. Argento, Fulci, and the other well-knowns command the attention of their audiences by virtue of their visual flair above all else — from eye-popping camerawork to creative gore. Their characters and stories, though rarely less than interesting, are secondary, and have a better chance of surviving the dubbing jobs imposed on them en route to America. Though Naschy's films feature many striking, atmospheric sets in the flavor of Hammer's gothic thrillers, these are used to create a feeling of absorption and familiarity and do not induce the viewer to keep his eyes open for offbeat surprises. Naschy entered show business as a screenwriter — even his acting career was an afterthought — and the emphasis in his films is on the strength of the characters; in keeping the role of the actor important. The sloppy dubbing routinely given to his films in the States makes his old-fashioned monster movies seem unduly wordy — and a social satire like *Human Beasts* (1980) has no chance at all.

Getting into Naschy's work takes a bit of practice. It also takes getting hold of the uncensored video versions, as the television prints rarely add up to anything worth watching. If you're interested in getting started, here are some suggestions as to good starting points for the various tastes of various horror fans.

To destroy the Monster,
was to destroy the one she loved!!
Could she?
Could you?
DR. JEKYLL AND THE WEREWOLF

For those who enjoy Spanish horror primarily for the rich, moody atmosphere and aren't bothered by leisurely pacing, the adventures of Naschy's most famous character, werewolf Waldemar Daninsky, have a lot to offer. 1980's *The Craving* is a remake of (and improvement on) 1970's

The Werewolf vs. the Vampire Woman directed by Naschy / Molina himself. But the standout entry of the series is 1973's *Curse of the Devil*, directed by Carlos Aured. An ancient curse is visited on Waldemar in a quiet village after the accidental death by shooting of a young gypsy man "mistaken" for a wolf. The story is familiar, but the direction, sets, makeup effects and overall feel of the film are simply outstanding. This is also one of the few times in which the strength of the characters and the quality of the performances come through in spite of the English dubbing.

Those who enjoy that style of horror might also want to see Leon Klimovsky's *The Devil's Possessed* (1974). Despite the title, this is not a supernatural thriller, but a tale of medieval madness, torture dungeons, a devious alchemist and a peasant revolt, with more than a hint of Macbeth thrown in. If you don't go in expecting non-stop action, the look and feel of this film will slowly but surely win you over. The physical abilities of former weightlifter Naschy also come into play in some bouts of violent fencing.

There aren't too many Naschy films which emphasize pace and action over atmosphere and character, and those that do (such as 1969's *Assignment Terror*), though they can be fun to watch, don't really show Naschy at his best. Here are a couple, however, which qualify as decent "jumping-off" points. 1972's *Vengeance of the Zombies*, another work of Naschy's most frequent collaborator, Leon Klimovsky, has a mystery maniac utilizing voodoo rituals to amass a small army of pale-faced, black-robed zombie slave women. Naschy plays Krishna, an Indian mystic, and two other roles caught up in the goings-on along with the men of Scotland Yard. This campy bit of fun scores surprisingly high in the sex and violence departments, and it's all set to the bizarre, wacky jazz score of Juan Carlos Calderon (who also did the honors for 1973's *House of Psychotic Women*).

Night of the Howling Beast (1975) doesn't offer the Waldemar character much in the way of absorbing sets and gripping story-line, but doesn't give him much time to think about it either. This M.I. Bonns film whisks him off on a trip to Tibet, and puts him up against cannibal cave girls (responsible for the werewolf curse this time), an evil Khan and his goon squad, Wandessa (a torture chamber mistress probably intended as Spain's answer to Ilsa), and the legendary Yeti. After a few violent werewolf attacks, shootouts and tortures (one of which got this movie banned in Britain as a "Video Nasty"), Naschy has to battle his way out of the Khan's fortress, once again putting his duelling talents on display. It's not one of the best, but it's great disposable fun.

Lest the gorehounds think they're being neglected, let me now direct you back to 1972, which featured two of Naschy's most overtly horrific (and effective) works. Javier Guirre's *Hunchback of the Morgue* (aka *The Rue Morgue Massacres*) casts Naschy as the titular hunchback, a half-witted, put-upon, and occasionally vicious character who finds himself working for a mad scientist—providing him with human victims after being told his dead girlfriend will be brought back to life for him as a reward. The various murder scenes are hideously graphic, but the film's most infamous moment is a sickening scene, done mostly for real, in which Naschy sets fire to a group of rats which attack him when he discovers them busily eating his girlfriend's body. This film won Naschy a Best Actor trophy at the Paris Convention of Fantastic Cinema. (Point of interest: Naschy himself has a poor speaking voice and is dubbed even in Spain — this award only goes to show that there's more to good acting than the delivery of the lines!)

Horror Rises From the Tomb, another Carlos Aured film, has Naschy as an ancient, evil sorcerer and his modern-day descendant. The good Naschy takes a group of friends along on a trip to his ancestral home—and they arrive just in time to find themselves on the business end of a curse

handed down by the evil Naschy, who at this point in time would very much like to have his severed head returned to his body. Though it's not quite as graphic as *Hunchback of the Morgue*, this film packs more violence per square inch than any other Naschy film I've seen, including executions, garden tool murders, human sacrifices, and a show-stopping heart removal. There's also an impressive gathering of the walking dead. Aured, responsible for the above mentioned *Curse of the Devil*, is obviously a director with a lot of talent. His other two Naschy films were *The Mummy's Revenge* and *House of Psychotic Women*. The former is just a decent bit of fun — the latter is an effective, non-supernatural murder mystery with a misleading American title.

Depending on your personal taste or frame of mind at any given moment, each of the films described above can serve as a fine introduction to the films of Paul Naschy. If you enjoy them, there's a lot more to choose from. Barry Kaufman's Video Mania (Suite 129, 2520 N. Lincoln, Chicago, IL 60614) is an excellent source for those who don't have easy access to the Naschy line-up. Louis Paul's Blood Times Video (44 East 5th St. Brooklyn, NY 11218) offers adventurous thrillseekers a chance to see some of these films in their original Spanish language editions.

Naschy's 20-year plus body of work covers both ends of the spectrum and all points between in terms of quality, but ultimately offers something for everyone. And hey, nobody who's done this much for horror for this long deserves to be obscure anywhere. So let's get the ball rolling. If you like Naschy, tell two friends. And they'll tell two friends. And so on, and so on. And so on...

CHAS. BALUN'S
MONSTERFOLIO

Creature designed for Fred Olin Ray's Evil Toons —
a live action/animated feature film starring Dick Miller and David Carradine.

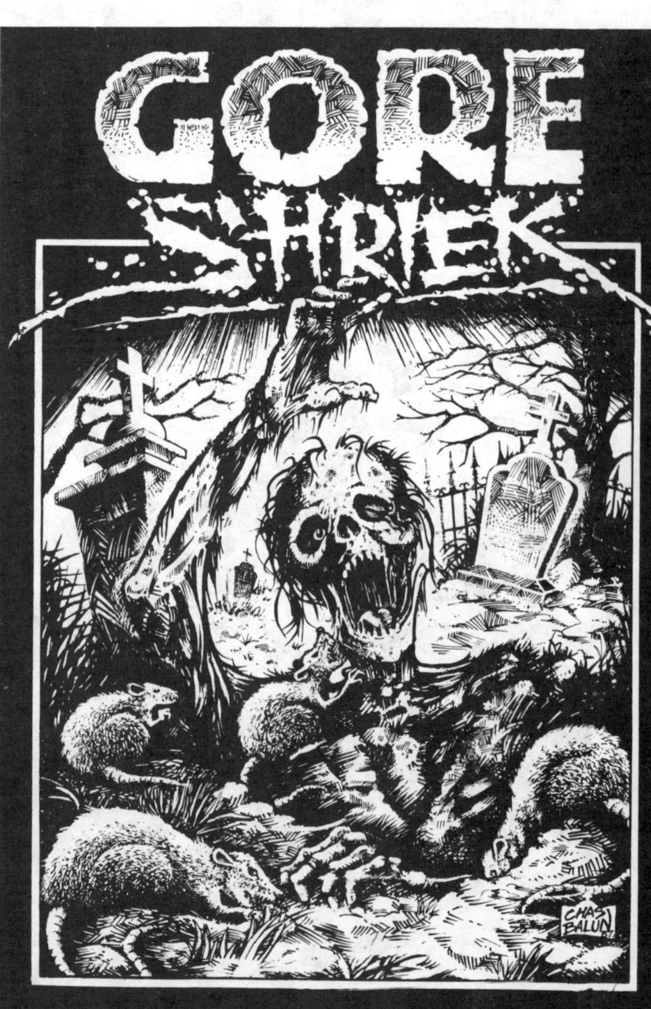

Gurch's Gallery

AAAAAAAHHHHHHHHHHHNNNNNNG
HONEY? WHAT ARE YOU DOIN'?
SCRITCHA SCRATCH
SCRITCH SCRITCHA
SCRITCHA SCRITCH
COM'ON BACK TO BED, LOVER. SHIT! I DON'T EVEN THINK YOU SLEPT LAST NIGHT, DID YOU?
WAS I THAT BAD?

Fantaco
WARNING: Contains disturbing material and is not intended for children!
GORE SHRIEK™
$2.50 No.2
Volume 2

Portrait Of A

JOHN McNAUGHTON

Serious Conspirator

Interview by John Martin

Deep Red thanks Graham Rae, Justin Stanley, and Andrew Featherstone for their valued assistance.

Henry: Portrait of a Serial Killer was one of the most harrowing genre films to emerge from the Eighties. It cut through a blizzard of cinematic shit pies and dickless sequels with the ease of acid through bologna. Besides igniting a flurry of controversy and heated hyperbole from all corners, *Henry* once again proved that budget bears little correlation to brilliance.

Writer/director John McNaughton and producer Steve Jones discuss *Henry*, *The Borrower*, and several new projects, including *The Last Words of Dutch Schultz* and *Carney Kill*.

DR: *Henry* ends with a real kick in the guts.

SJ: We didn't want to end by having Henry removed by the police, or put in jail or something, we didn't want to let anyone off the hook that way. Henry goes off into the distance, and he's the one person who's still out there, and we thought that would add more to the horror of the business.

JM: Well, again, the real Henry claimed to have murdered — was it 360 people? I forget — over a 7 - 9 year period in which the police pretty much never had any idea who this character was. I do find it a bit strange that people like Freddy are becoming mass heroes, but it's usually the bad guys who are the interesting characters to me, y'know.

DR: The critical consensus appears to be that Henry is so disturbing because the viewer is forced to identify with Henry.

JM: That's the idea.

DR: I found that you were dangling the idea that this guy could be redeemed all along, and then you snatched it away at the end, and ultimately I felt that he remained inaccessible.

SJ: I don't think there's any redemption...

JM: I think that all of us are capable; we're all connected to The Beast in some way or other and some of us are born or formed along our lines of developement in such an unfortunate way...again, I think the traditional way to deal with someone like Henry is to say "Look how bad this person is! He shouldn't have done it, he's bad and he should have just said no and not done this." I think that's kinda silly. I think there are those that are born so

Yeah, I killed my Mama...

malformed, maybe they get pressure put on their skulls when they are born or something, nobody knows...but there will be another Charles Manson, there will be another Henry Lee Lucas, somewhere, somehow. I think as long as there are human beings there are going to be disturbed ones who are somehow missing that mechanism that stops them, when their anger rises, from reaching out and slaughtering someone.
I do think Henry had a code. Some people have a problem with drugs and can't control themselves and it may even cause someone to die, it may cause someone in their family to die, it may cause them to lose control of an automobile. It may not, but that's something that's compulsive and they can't control, and in a person who's compulsive, uncontrollable behaviour happens to be incapability of stopping themselves from killing,...well, it's his problem, but I also think that we try and point out that there's a difference between him and Otis, who just *lets go*, totally, to The Beast. With Henry, it was like..."I can't help myself from doing *this*, but this, this and this are *wrong*!". We all have our rights and wrongs.

DR: So what was Henry's problem?

JM: We did a fair amount of research...oh, it was his mother, that whole thing about his mother, a line here and a line there were taken from actual quotes and woven into the dialogue, but y'know, I read Henry giving his life history to ten different reporters, printed in ten different newspapers, and the basis of the story was always the same but the details were always different. Henry was diagnosed as a pathological liar, so I don't think he knows himself exactly what he did. He has now recanted and says that he didn't murder anyone, including his mother, for whom he served a nine year jail sentence.

SJ: They have hard evidence on a few of his murders, which is why he's in jail. He claimed many more, in a lot of ways to get better treatment in jail — he just kept admitting to murders and police would come in from all over the United States and say, "Did you do this one?" and he said yeah, it just helped them out, cleaned their slates of unsolved murders, and so when he got up towards 400 murders he just recanted, and said no, I didn't do it.

JM: To me in many ways the more interesting story is what happened to Henry after he was captured, which we talked about doing as a picture, subtitled *Superstar of Crime*, because you take a man who's from such a deprived background, and 's so low on the social scale in every way, and now he's arrested for murder, and every time he starts opening his mouth and confessing to another one, he becomes more popular with the press and he also becomes the police's buddy because each police jurisdiction has a book of unsolved murders. So they just call Henry up and they say we'll blame it on him and cross it off the books and Henry went on TV, they were writing about him...

ST: He's got a phone in his cell...

JM: Right, they're flying him around the country, various police jurisdictions, and then he started making demands, y'know...I *must* have a fresh carton of Pall-Mall cigarettes, I must have a hot thermos of coffee, I won't eat hamburgers anymore, I must have steak, and I want a VCR in my cell at all times...so it's very strange that it was in many ways the best thing that ever happened to him.

DR: It's like the situation we have over here with the "Moors Murderers", who sexually tortured and killed children back in the sixties...for 25 years in jail they've been milking it for all it's worth, hinting that they might reveal the burial sites of some of the victims, and the media has turned them into...well, as you say, "superstars".

SJ: It keeps people off Death Row in the U.S. also, y'know, as long as they can come up with a new crime to solve every now and then, most of them get away with it.

DR: Given *Henry's* tie-in with real life events, is there any litigation going on at the moment?

JM: There was never anything. We did some legal research, very little, but enough to establish that what Henry can come after us for is basically defamation of character.

"I find that good people usually lead boring lives."

JM: I mean, he's convicted!

SJ: Our lawyers, in typical lawyer fashion, has preconceived ideas about what could happen, so we had to adjust to those things, that's why there's a disclaimer at the front of the thing.

JM: Right. In terms of our deal with Vestron, they were afraid of possible litigation.

SJ: You're talking about the victims' families.

DR: How did you feel about that? Were you concerned with the feelings of the bereaved?

JM: Well, because none of the killings in the film are based on the actual killings at all, no.

DR: You've talked about setting out to re-define horror in the most extreme way possible with *Henry*, and the documentary way that you did set about that task reminds me of *The Last House On The Left*, which was not a slaughter-fest, but instead focused sharply on a few ghastly events. Was that an important film for you?

JM: I didn't see it until it came out on video, and by that time I felt it was a little bit dated, but again it was the grittiness, the reality of it. The forest preserve scene, if you remember that, was very, very effective. I think the score aged very poorly. It really hurt the film for me, took my attention away and made me think how dated this music sounded on this picture.

DR: And there were ill-advised comic sequences that just should not have been in there.

JM: Yeah, again, to me, you have to be very careful. I mean, There's horror which is fantasy, where you can be comic, and it's great, but when you get into reality..we didn't have the money to make *Henry* horrible through special FX, so we made it horrifying by making it *real.* Pull the fantasy out and then you can't run from it, and when you do that, you have to be very careful about humour — it can't be gag-type humour, where they turn around and say a gag to the person next to them, to me that really takes you out of the story.

SJ: John's original idea was to do a documentary-style depiction of a week in the life of a serial killer. By staying with that idea of it being documentary-style, I think that's what made it as mean as it is. There's no frills — we didn"t have any money for any frills, but we used it to our advantage for once.

DR: So how would you compare and contrast that with the very flashy style they used in a film with a similar subject, Michael Mann's *Manhunter*?

JM: I can comment on that because I read the book, *Red Dragon*, about four times, thought it was the best mystery, thriller, psychological thriller, I dunno how to genrify it exactly. I thought that book was wonderful and I formulated the script in my mind and y'know, it's hard enough to make a film and I don't want to talk bad about other film-makers, but I didn't care for the film at all. I really think it was a TV treatment of an incredibly rich book. So I didn't care for it. I don't like *Silence of the Lambs* as a book as much as I like *Red Dragon*, because it focused more on the good person and I find the good people usually lead boring lives.

DR: I got the impression in your movie that Henry didn't even get off on what he was doing, he just *had* to do it.

JM: That probably came from Michael, the way he chose to play it. It was very, *very* low-key.

DR: How did you get all those glowing testimonials for *Henry* from Richard Pryor and others?

SJ: That was kinda second hand. We didn't have it in writing.

JM: We had it in writing from John Waters, who is a big fan of the picture and sent me a few postcards praising it and I sent him a few back. He seems like a great guy.

DR: He's been itching to play a serial killer for some time. Has he sounded you guys out about that?

JM: He's got a great face, a great look and I've loved his pictures, they're hilarious...more success to John Waters for what he's done.

DR: You got an amazing quote from Stuart Gordon.

JM: Steve worked with Stuart Gordon in The Organic Theatre, he did video stuff for two of their plays. The Organic Theatre is like, I dunno if you're familiar with The Living Theatre, they were like the wild men and women of the theatre in their era and Chicago theatre, which is incredibly wild and wonderful, and produces an incredible amount of excellent actors and actresses — The Organic Theatre was kind of like these wild dogs, y'know, they did the crazy stuff and Tom Towles came out of The Organic Theatre, as did Richard Fire, Joey Montaigne and a whole bunch of other people who've become famous and successful. They were quite a crew.

DR: Stuart Gordon said something along the lines of "Makes what I've acheived on far bigger budgets look pitiful".

SJ: Yeah, that's what he told me. Right after we got done with *Henry*, he saw one of the early cassettes and he said that for five times the budget they weren't getting as good movies out there and that we should be working immediately...and three years later, we finally get another job.

JM: *Henry's* original budget was $100,000, and it went over budget to the tune of about $111,000, but that was before it was blown up. With the blow-up, legal fees, etc., etc., I dunno what it is, but the finished product was $111,000. *The Borrower* was two million — it was easier for us to make a movie for $120,000 in Chicago than it was to make one for two million in Hollywood.

SJ: We had really dedicated people for *Henry.*

JM: Nobody looking over your shoulder and saying (whines) "Well, I dunno, shoot it from another angle, get a covering shot for that, do this, do that, etc., etc." When you work in an entertainment corporation, it's like working in the advertising business, you've got a lot of people looking over your shoulder — do this, do that, everything costs more, everything's more complicated.

Henry (Michael Rooker) and Becky (Tracy Arnold)

DR: Does all this make you reluctant to work the Hollywood system?

JM: N-o-o-o! I've already shot my mouth off and put my foot in it in print and I'm hoping not to do it again, because that's where the deals are made.

SJ: That's where the money is.

JM: $5 million to make a picture — try and raise it from your friends and neighbours and see how far you get!

SJ: On *Henry*, the fact that there was no money at all meant that the people that worked on it just wanted to do a good job. *The Borrower* was done more in the studio way of doing things, and the people who worked on it, that was their job and that was what they did week-by-week. It was not...

JM: ...a labour of love...

SJ: ...by any means. That meant some people were good at their job, like in any job, and some people were lousy at their job but would get another job and continue to work and earn their living and feed themselves and their families. On *Henry* there wasn't any money.

JM: Yeah, nobody fed their families on *Henry*, believe me.

SJ: Unless they had real small families.

JM: Like a family of gerbils or something.

DR: I was wondering if Michael Rooker, now that he's got some "respectable" credits under his belt, has tried to distance himself from *Henry*?

JM: No. Michael is in a kind of position where Hollywood is typing him a little bit in bad guy roles. But I don't know when Hollywood is going to get hip to the fact that he can be a very effective leading man, and today *Henry* is his only leading role.

SJ: He also turned up at the Telluride Film Festival in Colorado and basically made friends with the entire town and the entire film community. Y'know, they see him in this horrible picture and then they meet Michael Rooker, who's this gentle bear of a guy, and he did a great job.

"We did some legal research, very little, but enough to establish that the real Henry can come after us for, basically, defamation of character."

DR: What has happened with *The Borrower*?

SJ: *The Borrower* was a logistical nightmare — we started in Chicago, ended up doing it in L.A., there were three different regimes of executives quit before the picture got done, the company that we were doing the picture for went bankrupt...it's kind of a miracle that the picture ever got completed, and now it is, we just have to let it go until they finally decide to release it.

JM: In some ways, that turmoil and strife worked to our advantage, because all of the executive teams kept leaving, due to the collapsing nature of Atlantic Entertainment. Consequently we had no interference during post-production and editing, so it's pretty much untouched. I mean its director's cut is the cut that's going to go out, unless whoever buys it decides to recut it, which is certainly a possibility, given the history of the film, but so far, each time they would try and have us alter the film, they would leave the company within a week or so, and so it worked out in that respect, at any rate.

DR: But there were so many problems you came up against while you were making it...forest fires, earthquakes...

JM: It was not a blessed project!

SJ: We had a pretty big earthquake.

JM: There were a lot of problems. It was the first Hollywood project for both

> **"There is something about just delving into blood and guts, and revelling in it, that is...part of being human."**

of us and we really got...it was like waking up every morning and getting punched in the face until you went to bed at night, basically. Making that picture took about two years, start to finish. We were always skin-of-your-teeth-one-micron-ahead-of-disaster, and we managed to finish the picture. It's a totally different tone to *Henry*, and the more I've seen it, the more I'd have to call it a horror-comedy, although it's very tongue-in-cheek, not gag humour.

SJ: It's much more of a fantasy, also.

JM: Your right, much more of a traditional sci-fi fantasy.

SJ: More palatable to audiences in general while it's a fantasy. All these heads are ripped off, it's not like *Henry*...not as real.

JM: But again, Tommy Towles opens the picture, and Tommy's original training in Chicago was with the Second City Company. If you've ever seen *Saturday Night Live*, that's basically what Second City have been doing on stage for years — skit comedy. Tommy came out of this improvisational comedy school and he's quite a comic, quite a funny guy, and he's great in *The Borrower* and it's pretty funny, it's more of a rock 'n' roll movie for teenagers rather than something that makes you think, something that affects you very deeply.

DR: In the projects that you're working on now, which of those strands are you going to develope?

JM: We've got two or three things...we're hopefully about to conclude negotiations to buy a William Burroughs book called *The Last Words of Dutch Schultz*, Dutch Schultz being an American gangster of the 1930's, and I think that when we get back on Monday we're going to take a ride out to Lawrence, Kansas and talk to Mr. Burroughs. Unfortunately, Mr. Burroughs doesn't own the book. If he did, I think we would have made a deal months ago.

DR: That property's been around a long time, hasn't it? I seem to remember that at one time Keith Richards was going to play the part.

JM: I talked to a producer in L.A. and he said that Keith Richards had optioned it or has tried to option it or had talked about optioning it at one point, and at one point Elliot Gould was going to do it. Yes, it has been around for some time.
Richard Fire, who co-wrote *Henry*, and myself, have just finished a script last Friday, called *Step Right Up*, which is about a young man whose life falls apart and he joins a traveling carnival.

DR: This is from your own personal experience, isn't it?

JM: Yes, this is an autobiographical piece, and I just bought a book, optioned a book, called *Carney Kill*, which isn't horror, it's more of a noir/murder-mystery thing that takes place in a carnival in 1961, and there's a screenplay on that which is out.

DR: Can you tell us something about your experiences with carneys?

JM: They run games and have freaks and rides, crazy rides, so it's great fun , y'know, there are a lot of people in the carnival who are pretty disreputable, but that core of people I hung out with in the carnival that I traveled with were some of the most trustworthy and solid people in terms of people you could count on in a fix or a scrape. The rest of the world might not see them perhaps as the best of citizens but there were some really top-notch folks in the carnival I traveled with. I was running a game called the glass pitch. I was also taking pictures while I was in the carnival so I have a series of photographs of that which we are going to use in our next re-write of the script.

DR: Have you seen Jodorowsky's *Santa Sangre*, a film which is set in what I would imagine is a similar milieu?

JM: I didn't buy in, the way I did with *El Topo*. But someone always comes along in the horror genre with a new picture, a *Chainsaw Massacre* or a *Day of the Dead*, and blows it wide open again. I think it's like film in general, or literature, or the music business, there are landmark works that blow it open, then the imitators come and it kind of peters out for a while. I don't know what to think of horror now because the MPAA has so castrated the genre. Again, when I read *Texas Chainsaw Massacre 3*, which at one point I might have directed, *The Borrower* is like a fairy story compared to that, and it came to me about the time we were on about our fourth X-rating for *The Borrower*. Fortunately, *The Borrower* was not damaged badly by the MPAA, a little bit, but not badly. They were sort of lenient with us in a way.

DR: Is this because you personally sought out Richard Heffner, the Chairman of the MPAA?

JM: We had to, because we were in a bind, but he was pretty fair with us, in my opinion. But really, the *Texas Chainsaw 3* script, it's like, New Line have been in the business for a while now, and I couldn't see why they wanted to shoot it, because it was quite obvious that none of that stuff was going to get onto the screen, and this was indeed the case. I haven't seen it, but I've talked to the writers, and from what I understand, they've cut everything.

SJ: I think that technically, they can do anything now, as far as showing you anything, they can show you coming off realistically, bodies being ripped apart realistically, so it's time for the imagination to take over again and the stories to get a little better. Horror doesn't just come from seeing that kind of stuff. I think everyone's going to get immune to all this blood and gore. I think what's really horrifying is what's in your mind and what people do to each other, as opposed to what you see just splashed on the screen.

JM: Yeah, but I guess there is something about just delving into blood and guts, and revelling in it, that is...part of being a human being.

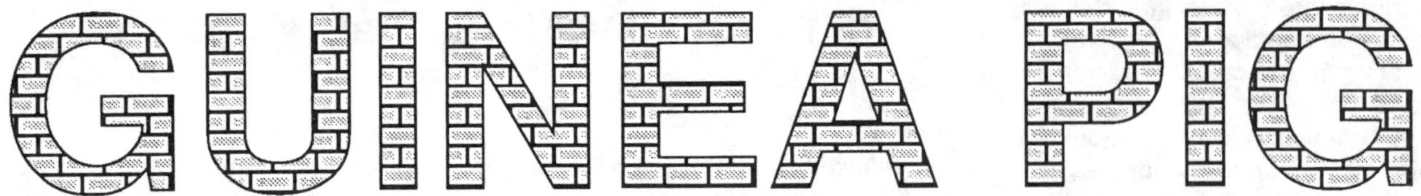

Cutting-Edge Splatter or Porno Gore?

By
Chas. Balun

"At worst, is not this an unjust world, full of nothing but beasts of prey, four-footed or two-footed?" *Thomas Carlyle, 1833*

It was inevitable. The genre has been flirting with the concept for decades, so *Guinea Pig* was a film destined to be made by someone, somewhere, somehow. In many ways, it is the climax in a cycle of thrill-kill mutilation epics, first popularized by Herschell Gordon Lewis' primal gore shriek *Blood Feast* (1963) and perpetuated through the years by films such as *Last House on the Left* (1972), *Snuff* (1976), *Last House on Dead End Street* (1977), and *Maniac* (1980).

Even mainstream films like Paul Shrader's *Hardcore* (1979) and John Frankenheimer's *52 Pick-Up* (1986) have alluded to the existence of actual "snuff" films purporting to show victims being tortured to death.

David Cronenberg's *Videodrome* (1983) addresses the issue forthright and comes up with answers as disturbing as they are compelling. The idea that a video signal sent from stations specializing in hardcore sadomasochistic death fantasies could irreparably warp the consciousness of the viewer is a chilling, paranoid, hyper-revisionist concept that Cronenberg exploits to the fullest.

In Joe D'Amato's sleazy *Emmanuelle in America*, a wealthy degenerate playboy shows painfully realistic black-and-white footage of graphic brutality in order to sexually excite partners apparently unable to be aroused by the "usual" fetishistic scenarios in which he specializes.

Snuff (aka *Slaughter*), Roberta and Michael Findlay's bungled attempt at capturing an audience with a pathological blood lust, is a complete wreck of a film, but serves as an ideal example of the hysteria generated by a film that crowed it was "too real to be simulated." No one who had seen the film was fooled, but that didn't stop protestors (some hired by the producers) from causing an impassioned outcry far outstripping the actual significance of both the film and the particular act in question.

Last House on Dead End Street (1977) is probably the most unswerving of the films dealing with the actual making of a "snuff" film, though both *Effects* (1980) and Larry Cohen's *Special Effects* (1983) make pivotal use of a similar theme. In fact, the ersatz surgery scene in *Last House on Dead End Street* showing a bound woman being dismembered and eviscerated is echoed again in a far more disturbing manner in *Guinea Pig*. Herein lies a critical, salient point. Despite *Last House's* admittedly vicious, degrading and sociopathic scenario, the film is still operating within the paradigms of accepted techniques of both storytelling and filmmaking. *Guinea Pig* dispenses with these cinematic accoutrements and simply, directly and unflinchingly presents a porno-style sensibility that provides us with nothing more than a man, a woman, and a bed. Only this time, *blood* is the body fluid of choice.

Though a good case may be made linking a film like *Guinea Pig* with its splatter movie past, another essential element must be considered in order to view it in a more contemporary perspective. As the horror genre has mutated and shape shifted in the past in order to satisfy its audiences' ever-changing tastes, so also has the entertainment industry in general and the news media in particular. Audiences that were justifiably shocked with the explicit butchery in Lewis' *Blood Feast* are no longer conned quite so easily.

The mondo-style films of the 60's and 70's have made way for their modern counterpart: the *Faces of Death* series; thrash videos featuring autopsies and speed metal; unedited war footage and live news reports that leave absolutely nothing to the imagination.

Though *Guinea Pig* packs an undeniably perverse visceral wallop, it still remains somewhat predictable because of its theatrical context. Such is not the case with completely unedited, live news footage that suddenly appears on your screen without the benefit of even a primitive establishing shot. *Guinea Pig*, because it was shot on professional quality video, may, in fact, even be mimicking the in-your-face style of the mondo video papparazzi.

Vile and unredeemable as *Guinea Pig* may be, it remains a deliberately staged, highly manipulative vehicle for a *simulated* ritual dismemberment and *not* an actual snuff film. Because it *is* just that, the viewer is provided with the necessary perspective in which to deal with the atrocities in his own particular manner.

One doesn't escape quite that easily when confronted by the suddenly live news broadcast that jump cuts to scenes of barbarity, cruelty and violence that *no* splatter film, regardless of era, has yet approached. Nothing, not *one* thing in even the most notorious splatter film, can match the unbridaled moral terror and visceral peristalsis inadvertently provided by CNN's live broadcast of disgraced politico R. "Bud" Dwyer inserting a .44 magnum revolver into his mouth during a press conference. What you witness next can only be described in terms *you* must wrench from your own heart of darkness. The live ultra-graphic on-screen suicide (subsequently circulated on various underground videos) of this unfortunately flawed and despairing human being unleashes a torrent of troubling and contradictory emotions in the viewer that *no* act of simulated violence is capable of under *any* circumstances.

The culpability of the media is not really the point here. No case is being made for censorship of any sort, but it is important to note the ever-increasing levels of violence in film, television and *real* life in order to more fully understand the breeding ground that spawned a film like *Guinea Pig*. The simple fact, and few politicians, policemen, judges *and* neighbors would care to disagree, is that *more* people are *exposed* to *more* violence than ever before in "civilized" history.

Perhaps we have always been (and always will be) a violence-prone species, but no one can deny that since the revolution in communications, a whole *helluva* lot more people *know* about it. They've been reading, watching, hearing and now tape recording it more frequently than at any other time since the first stone axe splintered its first human skull.

Though its real roots may lie with the primitive, misanthropic fury found in films like *Salo, 120 Days of Sodom*, the *Ilsa: She Wolf* series, *Maniac, Pieces,* and *Man Behind the Sun, Guinea Pig* owes at least a cursory nod to the Brave New World of televised assassinations, executions, famines, plane wrecks, serial murderers and global terrorists brought to us daily by the most complex web of communications ever known to man.

Thanks to that very same worldwide communications umbrella, a Japanese copycat killer was exposed on ABC-TV's "20/20" national newsmagazine and, once again, a key link was to be made between ultra-violent entertainment in film and human psychopathology. The killer was alleged to have an extensive collection of splatter videos, some amateurishly doctored to include inserts of his own taped adventures spliced right next to their cinematic counterpart. Now, this, indeed, is creepy stuff, further exacerbated by the discovery of *Guinea Pig,* the film alleged to have been the inspiration for the copycat murders.

Other films, specifically those in the *Friday the 13th* and *Halloween* series have been singled out in several capital cases as being influential to the murderer's state of mind, but rarely has the connection been as damning as it was in the case of *Guinea Pig*.

Though the films were subsequently banned in Japan, any one who has seen the notoriously violent, sexually perverted antics in such Japanese animated films as *The Wandering Kid, Supernatural Beast City, Demon Apocalypse* or *Vampire Hunter* is familiar with the Japanese way of dealing with taboo subjects. As shocking and disturbing as *Guinea Pig* truly is, there exists a tradition of ritualized brutality that extends far back into the bowels of Oriental culture, darkly illuminated at times by such novel concepts as Samurai warriors, hara-kiri, kamikaze pilots, death marches and the numerous exotic and lethal tortures visited upon the various invading armies throughout history.

Both the Japanese and the Chinese are no pikers when it comes to playing for keeps. Witness the hideous Eastern Asian tradition of Leng-Tch'e, a method of torture/execution dating back to the 17th century that involves the slow and deliberate cutting into pieces of a condemned criminal. In Georges Batailles' *The Terms of Eros*, a book detailing the relationship between violence and religious ritual, a particularly disturbing photograph bears mute testimony to the extreme levels of sadistic cruelty employed by the Emperor's executioners. A pathetic victim, bound in some manner of scaffolding, is being stripped of his appendages, nipples and skin by a completely unruffled stoic bunch of butchers because their Emperor has decreed that the condemned's original sentence of being burned alive was far *too* cruel!

Though this method of torture dates back to the Manchu Dynasty (1644-1911), the explicit sadism inherent in such acts is echoed in contemporary films like the sickening atrocity extravaganza *Man Behind the Sun*. Its modern parallels lie with the World War II Nazi death camp films, but the depths of cruelty and debauchery exhibited in *Man Behind the Sun* show the Japanese Imperial Army to be in a class by themselves. Autopsies are performed on living humans, others are contaminated by experimental chemical or viral strains, while some are thrown into decompression chambers until their ruined guts come sluicing out their asses.

Guinea Pig did not just appear from a cultural vacuum. It was most definitely not a virgin birth, so it is rather perplexing that modern-day Japanese society reacts with such fury over a 60-minute videotape. Pernicious and baleful as *Guinea Pig* may be, it has been seen and done before, and it joins the crowded ranks of films, books and songs that have been accused of everything from precipitating suicide and serial killing to teenage pregnancy and willful disobedience of posted highway speed limits. *Guinea Pig* is not without some degree of blame, of course, but still it is *not* the problem, but merely symptomatic of a far greater and complex one. Senseless violence and irrational behavior will simply *not* go away, irregardless of how often we vote, pray, fast, wish or legislate against it.

True, the film is a repellent, molar-grinding experience, but, alas, it's only a movie...only a movie. And a cheap one at that. One interior set, one pretty woman and a deranged quasi-Samurai psycho that makes Joe Spinell's *Maniac* look like Olivier's Henry V. The dialog is sparse, guttural and one-sided. The woman never says a word. Immediately after her abduction, she is drugged, bound and gagged and she stays that way for the entire film.

The camera almost tenderly and lovingly zooms, pans and glides throughout the boarded-up, gut-smeared Samurai slaughterhouse, pausing only long enough to steady itself for the next excruciating close-up of surgical dismemberment. Limbs are cut, sawed and chiseled apart, with not a detail being spared. With cum-shot clarity, every popping sinew, cracking bone and spurting artery is given its due. And, contrary to audience expectations, the "special effects" are of an unusually high caliber. Though it was rumored in some circles that actual corpses were mutilated during filming, there is not *one* scene of mayhem that couldn't have been effectively rendered by a journeyman FX artist. Even the one sequence in which you might expect them to use the *real* thing (in this case a *chicken*) employs such cuts and deceptive angles that the decapitation gag is exposed for what it is. Other FX, though, are terribly realistic, especially the scenes of dismemberment that involve not only scalpels, saws and huge knives, but also hammers and chisels.

It is not only the degree and frequency of the violence that is especially troubling, but the obsessively detailed, microscopic close-ups thrust in your face without respite for the entire ordeal. Porno gore, indeed.

Despite the fact that the woman is young, attractive and physically alluring, no attempt is ever made to exploit the sexual angle of the bondage sequences. No nudity is ever shown, nor suggested, as the woman is covered in white (then red) sheets the entire time. The Japanese exhibit a very prissy, schizoid attitude regarding sex and violence. While permitting the most vile and aggressive acts to be explicitly shown, they always insist upon optically censoring even the most harmless shots involving frontal nudity and/or pubic hair. The import Japanese laser disc cut of Ruggero Deodato's *Cannibal Holocaust* is rendered nearly unwatchable due to the omnipresence of the "traveling dots" that obscure much more than just a patch of pubic bush. Even at the climax of *Guinea Pig*, when the woman is sliced open with a scalpel and then eviscerated, the bloodied, looping lengths of intestine are strategically spilled so that they completely cover the terrible triangle.

Finally then, the woman, who has remained semi-conscious throughout, is finally beheaded in slow-motion. Blood geysers in fire-hose torrents as her dispatched head slams against the wall and splats to the floor. The mumbling, snaggle-toothed Samurai then retrieves the head, raises it to his lips, and with a wriggling tongue, licks the blood off the mouth. Then, an eye is popped out with a tablespoon and sucked on with lascivious abandon as soap opera style music swirls in the background.

You wanna barf. He wants a smoke.

Since the dialog is in Japanese without subtitles, the Occidental mind can only speculate just what is going through the man's head as he relaxes and puffs contentedly on the killing floor. The camera then wanders off, revealing a room decorated with death masks, jars full of pickled chicken heads and plucked eyeballs, an aquarium stocked with human hands and various decomposing body parts swarming with worms and maggots. It's all in your face. You can almost smell it. Then, the film ends like it began in true horror show style—

hand-held point-of-view shots of the next potential victim being stalked at the subway station.

Guinea Pig is a vilifiable cinematic experience, but curiously one well in touch with our times. It seems nigh impossible to feign indignation and abhorrence towards this type of film whilst all around us, flickering on our television sets, are shockumentary-style video images of the horrors of the real world: AIDS, famine, religious "holy wars," beaten and abused children, crack mercenaries, terrorist bombers, chemical weapons, environmental catastrophes and the latest designer-style serial killings.

Violence seems endemic to our particular species. We will remain at war, perhaps perpetually, both from within and without. The horrors of *Guinea Pig* echo the horrors of the human soul. Until we come to grips with that black-hearted abyss that lurks within, there will *always* be another battle to fight, another infidel to kill and another...*Guinea Pig*.

WHAT YOU WILL NOT FIND IN ANY OTHER BOOK

Recalling Some Favorite, Forgotten Horrors

by GREG GOODSELL

What other subject, save World War II, has been as exhaustively researched as the horror film? In search of different and exciting new angles for this cinema phenomenon, the student and fan has been deluged with treatises on the existential nature of the John Ashley / *Mad Doctor of Blood Island* series, the method favored by actress Rosie (*Don't Look in the Basement*, 1974, *Encounter with the Unknown*, 1974) Holotik, and the Jungian nature of director Charles B. Pierce (*Legend of Boggy Creek*, 1973, *The Town That Dreaded Sundown,* 1977). Approaches in some corners border on the absurd; who really cares about the forty seconds snipped from some prints of *The Horrible Dr. Hitchcock* (1962)?

Not too long ago, matinee fodder such as *I Was a Teenage Frankenstein* (1957) and *Hideous Sun Demon* (1962) was looked upon with scorn; today, nostalgia and the release of even far inferior films since then have elevated them to "semi-classic" status. When these yeoman hacks of yesteryear were grinding out features to fill theater screens, they probably didn't know that their films would be the subjects of research, completing their features in one-fifth the time it takes the contemporary student to compile painstakingly detailed production notes.

The renewed interest in "bad" or "camp" films flourished in the late Seventies and early Eighties, not due to the elusive nature of these films' appeal, but rather in reaction to what then constituted a "good" film. It makes infinitely more sense to watch *Robot Monster* (1953) eight or nine times than to view *Kramer Vs. Kramer* (1979) more than once.

Some attempt to place social significance on these films, *Plan Nine From Outer Space* (1959) is a thinly veiled disguised anti-nuclear parable, blah blah blah. "Hidden messages," like the stoned teenager playing his heavy metal records backwards for directives from Satan, are there for those who want them. A picture such as *A Dry White Season* (1989) with its major studio backing and name stars may say something about apartheid in South Africa. It can be argued that a trivial bit of softcore fluff produced in South Africa, *Snake Dancer* (1978), where the scenery resembles Las Vegas crossed with fairy tale villages, the lowliest slop chef drives a Mercedes, disco jungle chants with white voices are played, and the only black person we see is a raggedy, ever smiling streetside flower vendor — *says so much more*.

Still, a few worthwhile films escape the modern horror film scholar's pen. Some of these pictures have received attention, but only in passing. To the unitiated, there is no difference between a *Final Exam* (1981, stock-teen-kill-pic) and *Sleepaway Camp* (1983, bee-zare cross-breeding of John Waters with body count film as filtered through the sensibility of a jaundiced pervert). In spot-lighting these films, we run the risk of showing qualities that just may not be there. Film criticism is a subjective kind o' thing, independent of any set yardstick. We present this gallery for the reader's enjoyment. There are no "classics," per se, and for the genre's sake let's not hope our standards drop to the point where we regard them as such.

We make no claims about the following other than they stood out from the rest.

DRONING, CHEAP SYNTHESIZERS OF DOOM

The Redeemer (aka *Class Reunion Massacre*, 1977) is a sterling example, yielding new and different levels of care and complexity on it's third or fourth viewing. The largely negative critical reputation of the film (most curtly dismiss it as "irredeemable") misses the mark.

Characterized by a droning, cheap synthesizer score overly inspired by Jerry Goldman's Academy Award-winning work for *The Omen* (1976), *The Redeemer* begins with a beautifully composed shot of a country lake as a cloud passes over the sun. The placid surface of the lake is broken by the hand of a little boy, who walks, fully dressed to the shore. The ominous tyke hitches a ride with a bus headed towards a church.

The Redeemer cuts abruptly to a sleeping figure on a cot. A hand, later revealed to be the little boy's, is shown with an extra opposable thumb waving over the figure on the cot. The sleeping figure grows an identical extra appendage. What's going on?

Cut to a disguised man killing the crippled undertaker of a deserted high school. The little boy is seen preparing for church choir. Services begin, and a hellfire preacher (T. G. Finkbinder, the masked killer and "redeemer" of the title) launches into a sermon on the sins of the flesh intercut with the killer casting a death mask from the murdered janitor.

The viewer, now confused on how all these disparate elements are going to mesh together, is now introduced to the film's erstwhile "protagonists," i.e. assholes we don't mind seeing die creatively. The budget too low for the seven deadly sins, the preacher lashes out at six members of a high school graduating class, all typifying human failings; a grasping lawyer, a promiscous bimbo, a lesbian, a vengeful huntress, a conceited actor and a divorced glutton. Each character is given a terribly acted vignette to introduce them to the audience so that we may "hate" them. The six are invited to a high school reunion at the abandoned high school, where they quickly learn that they are the only attendees, cannot escape and are at the mercy of a disguised killer.

The Redeemer settles into a body count mode from here on in, but with a marked difference. The killer, "the Redeemer," is not your run-of-the-mill faceless killing machine. Witty, verbal, and always entertaining, he dons a different disguise for each murder; a hick hunter for the huntress, a murderous clown for the bimbo, a stylized melodrama villain for the actor, and a lawyer for the lawyer! A life-sized distorted Harlequin clown doll with a flame thrower and machete joins in the fun.

After dispatching the six, we return to the preacher, who we now recognize as the killer. There are a few more surrealistic episodes involving the boy before he returns to the lake, ending the film.

The fact that the Redeemer kills people who have character faults is a salient point in the production; to taste the Redeemer's wrath, you don't have to be part of some clandestine, long-ago murder or the tormentors of nerds like in the Jason or *Halloween* movies. You just have to be annoying. We don't know why the Redeemer has singled this insufferable six out. It's hinted that he's a former classmate, but he looks considerably older. Never revealed is the role of the little boy who gives the killer his extra digit, enabling him with supernatural powers. Is he from Satan (a subhead to the title, further capitalizing on *The Omen*, bills *The Redeemer* as "Son of Satan")? Or from the man upstairs, irritated with such flagrant disregard for His Will? For that matter, how many other conscienceless serial killers claim to be on a holy mission from God?

Director Constatine S. Gochis is to be commended for striving for a more complex than usual narrative style, lush, atmospheric photography and an overwhelming sense of mystery at what lies beyond the film's 84-minute running time. If *The Redeemer* makes the usually staid, undemanding fright flick fan bellow from his wing chair, *"But what does it ALL MEAN?"*, the film, in itself, is redeemed.

LET THE CARTOON BEGIN

One of the most devastatingly horrifying films of all time was this little ten-minute cartoon they used to show on educational television...

The International Tournee of Animation, hosted by actress Jean Marsh and shown in syndication on public television in the mid-Seventies, boasted a wide array of foreign and domestic animated films. On occasion, the program would revolve around a theme, and one time the theme was on things monstrous.

"Some animators approach the subject of monsters with humor," said Marsh. "Although this first feature is far from humorous. In fact, it resembles your worst nightmare, if anything else . . ."

The first feature in question was *Homo Augens*. Produced by Czechoslovakia's Zagreb Studios, *Homo Augens* is the most horrifying animated film, and one of the most horrifying films ever made, period. Viewed almost a decade ago, this writer still remembers it vividly.

In hard-edged, quasi-*Yellow Submarine* fashion using black, brown and yellow colors exclusively, *Augens* begins with a cartoon figure sleeping in a sparsely furnished bedroom. The figure is awakened by a noise outside his window. Looking out, he sees hordes of jubilant city dwellers pouring out of their monotonous skyscrapers to some point outside of town. The figure falls back into fitful slumber.

The next day, the figure begins to metamorphize into a werewolf-like monster. He kills a bystander and devours him. Growing larger, he devours a couple walking in an alley. Growing King Kong-size, the monster goes on a rampage until he falls ill. Staggering outside of the city, the beast collapses and dies on an expanse of desert.

The next morning, we see the people pouring out of their buildings as we saw at the beginning of the film. They swarm over the carcass of the monster, stripping him bare like a horde of hungry ants. The camera pans across the barren landscape where we see many more giant skeletons from previous monsters, ending with the hordes of people inside a giant cathedral constructed from out of one of the beast's ribcages, sending out unholy prayers for the next beast.

Words cannot describe the gut-bucket effect this cartoon has. Every aspect — color, music, animation and art utilized — is intended to direct a karate chop to the viewer's skull. In ten brief minutes, *Homo Augens* tells more about the relation society has towards its monsters than the entire *Chiller Theater* catalog combined. It's a good thing it's only ten minutes long. At thirty minutes, *Homo Augens* might very well have led to a mass suicide a lá Jonestown. Definitely a lethal little reward to those curious enough to investigate the benefits of public-supported television.

When I am asked what the most horrifying film I've ever seen is, I reply immediately "*Homo Augens*." Not many people know about it. Now you know.

U CAN'T TOUCH THIS

There is a sub-genre of horror film we shall call Eros and Thanatos, sex and death. Sexuality coupled with mortality, where your next kiss may be your last. Unsafe sex.

The vampire film is full of such connotations. Lesbian vampire films such as *The Vampire Lovers* (1972) to the snooty *The Hunger* (1982) makes the male heterosexual horror fan privvy to the onscreen activities of a provocative kind of creature. Clive Barker's *Hellraiser* (1987) has a strong sadomasochistic subtext. Certainly the appalling content of Cronenberg's *Dead Ringers* (1988) and David Lynch's *Blue Velvet* (1986) and *Wild at Heart* (1990) are made a bit more palatable with their scenes of arousing (if unnatural) eroticism.

Peter Greenaway's *The Cook, The Theif, His Wife and Her Lover* (1990) blurs the distinction between sex, food and death in painterly tableaus that combine all three. Bogus snuff videos that combine sex with mutilation are passed between the clammy hands of those who really desire it. One wonders where the ultimate combination of perversity and *frisson* in cinema took place...

In actuality, it took place in a film from a major studio at the hands of a budding director-star in the early Seventies. Paul Bartel's *Private Parts* (1973) is a sickeningly audacious debut, that in terms of kink plus terror has no equal.

Released by Metro Goldwyn Mayer, either in a sleep of reason or at the urgings of an equally perverse studio head (as the story is told), *Private Parts* never played widely due to its suggestive title (known variously as *Private Arts* and *Private Party* and dumped with nudie cheerleader pix) and unavailable on video, it's up to the conoisseur to seek it out by any means necessary. Those who do are amply rewarded.

Ann Ruymen plays Cheryl, an innocent waif stranded in Los Angeles who must stay with her dotty aunt at the King Edward Hotel, a once-stately lodge now presiding over a collection of misfits and wackos. Leather-clad priests, winos and degenerates are the Edward's clientele, and in time the innocent Cheryl succumbs to the hotel's allure by indulging her new found friends with acts of exhibitionism and voyeurism. She strikes up a budding romance with a handsome porno photographer by donning scanty underthings and allowing him to gaze at her through peepholes in the hotel's walls.

Unwholesome scenes of shock and degeneracy occur throughout, but the ultimate *coup de grace* happens in the last half hour. The photographer fills a crystal-clear love doll with water from a hose from a sink, as we see the limbs inflate on an unmade bed. The photographer pastes a photo of Cheryl's face on the doll's head. Cozying up to the polyurethane surrogate, he produces a velvet-lined box containing a needle and syringe (a clean needle, boys and girls—far from safe sex advocate Bartel to lead the impressionable youngsters who saw this with their apoplectic parents astray), draws blood from his arm—and stabs the doll in the crotch with it. The blood intermingles with the water, as the camera pans up to see the expression on the photo's face has changed to one of pain and horror.

By this time, the viewer is anxiously awaiting action from Jesse Helms. U Can't Touch This. If there is a more perverse or shocking scene in filmdom—I don't wanna see it.

Director Bartel's masterful hand never allows to make this scene or any others unwatchable. An assured hand behind the camera and a pervading sense of farce makes *Private Parts* all too accesible. Bartel would showcase extreme black humor in *Death Race 2000* (1975) and *Eating Raoul* (1982) before settling into the mainstream. Either way, *Private Parts* is a bizarre treat just as shocking today as when it was first semi-released.

Play with it.

20 POUNDS OF SHIT IN A 5-LB. BAG

How many of us out there will admit that we're into "sleaze"?

Sleaze. That special ingredient that sends us scurrying to the cinema's slimy underbelly. *Mondo* movies, *Ilsa, Harem Keeper of the Oil Shieks* (1976), and women-in-prison-with-skimpy-haltertops-and-cut-offs pictures. The sex in a Ginger Lynn porno video and the violence in the latest Arnold Schwarzenegger film can't compare to this elite group of films that manage to make us feel — somewhat dirty...

Sleaze is a matter of attitude. The modern gore film trots out the new latex wonder to the indifferent masses, whereas the Herschell Gordon Lewis Sixties' snuff flicks shove chicken entrails under our noses where we learn to like it. The Hollywood hack may delude himself into believing his softcore romp with overpaid film stars says something about contemporary relationships; the funky regional hack, on the other hand, knows blood plus tits equal tix.

The purest distillation of cinema sleaze extant is the totally obscure, completely delightful *Sinner's Blood* (circa 1972). Words fail to do it justice. It's haunting your local video store in the "horror" section, but don't be misled — it simultaneously straddles "biker," "softcore" and "melodrama" genres, succeeding like a freeway ten car pile-up.

Sinner's Blood thrusts us into a smalltown milieu that's beyond *Peyton Place*, beyond *Twin Peaks*, beyond dysfunctional.

Two sweet young things breeze into town to stay with relatives after being recently orphaned; Patricia, a nice young girl, and her sister Penelope, a buxom wanton who resembles a cross-eyed version of Erica Gavin in Russ Meyer's *Vixen* (1968). They are to stay with a nightmarish couple, Clarence, a nerdy nebbish, and his miserable shrew of a wife Gladys, with their two adult children. Edwina, their repressed lesbian daughter, makes advances towards Patricia; their overgrown, mildly retarded son Aubrey, however, steals the show. Tall, gangly, wearing little more than a pair of white shorts and sneakers, Aubrey is an ostracized, voyeuristic "peep freak" who oversees the film's action. "I gonna tell on you" is his favorite phrase as he wanders in and out of the lurid chain of events. Working as an audience surrogate, Aubrey, more than *Henry, Portrait of a Serial Killer* (1986) hammers home the ugly truth that There Are People Like That Out There.

Both Penelope and Patricia pop in and out of the sack with anyone and everyone in a series of vignettes. The men wear Sonny Bono slacks, the soundtrack music is repetitious fuzzbox guitar feedback, ("wwwaaahhhh, waaaaaaaah, neeeer, neeeeer") and sub-plots involving biker gangs so tough they hit pacifist preachers over the head with chains enter and exit at random. The film reaches an epiphany of sorts when naughty slut Penelope catches clean-cut Gentry in congress with gay biker leader Shiv at a clam bake. Dosing Gentry's Fresca with acid, Penelope causes Gentry to die in a motorcycle crash. As punishment for thrusting her hooters at the camera at every opportunity and being partially responsible for his lover's death, the enraged Shiv performs a radical masectomy on Penelope with a buck knife. Heavy.

The video's box art, a child's chalk drawing of a preppie boy crashing through a motel plate glass window astride a Harley with his Farrah-Fawcett coiffed girlfriend should be enough to make this required viewing to Those In the Know. As it has been stated earlier, Sleaze is a matter of attitude and *Sinner's Blood* has attitude to spare. If the viewer approaches the film with the proper attitude, it will be impossible to settle for literally any other film instead. Sell or trade your 16-volume set of *Berlin Alexanderplantz* today.

TWISTED BUT TRUE

A no-budget film that developed a strong cult following when sold in a fright film package to television, *Horror High* aka *Twisted Brain* (1974) gains its power from it s fidelity to real life. The story is no great shakes, being a variation of *Dr. Jekyll & Mr. Hyde* in a high school setting, pre-dating the adolescent vengeance popularized by Brian DePalma's *Carrie* (1976). Little distinctive touches make it stand out in memory. Pat Cardi plays Vernon, an abused teenage nerd tormented by jocks and teachers. Vernon downs a potion, brushes his bangs in front of his face and walks with toes pointed in to settle the score after school lets out. The film's most memorable death occurs to an elderly lady English teacher. After shredding Vernon's report with a paper cutter, a chilling instrument we all remember from our Kindegarten days, the monstrous Vernon returns late at night to decapitate the old biddy with it in spite of her threats of *"I'll make sure you never get to college!"*

You have to come from a specific sort of background to appreciate scenes like this one.

Twisted Brain is the odd sort of film that works because it's so gosh-durned ugly. Blown up from 16 mm, the film is an eyesore that perfectly captures the atmosphere of a barren, sterile high school. There is no decoration or attempt at art anywhere. The cast is an unprofessional bunch o' uglies that all too readily conjures up memories of that dreaded four-year prison sentence. The minimalist synthesizer score has all the warmth of dentist drills. By chance or design, *Twisted Brain* is a genuine cry of teenage rage and alienation that I place ahead of *Rebel Without a Cause*.

MESSAGE IN A BOTTLE

It's just as well these films languish in obscurity; these many one-time directors will not reap enormous financial rewards, remake or parody their original works, or worse yet turn their backs on their original fans. And it's just as well that these films stay the property of a small clique of fans who see things in them that aren't really there. The person who sets out to make An Important Work of Art is most certainly doomed to failure. Let the film enthusiast find solace in these unintended happy accidents instead.

It was Jimmy Stewart who told Peter Bogdanovich that those in the film business give people "pieces of time" to return to over and over again. Stewart worked with six-foot invisible rabbits; we on this side contend with six-foot boogers with teeth that spit acid. But the sentiments are identical.

While we all appreciate the avowed classics, it's the little special touches in the unremarkable films that keep us all coming back for more. It's the small nuggets we uncover that drives us on in our search for buried treasure. To my blood kin, I offer a hearty "keep on digging!"

by Chas. Balun

Chapter One from the new novel to be published by The Chunkblow Press and FantaCo Enterprises, Inc.

The headlights cut jagged slices out of the darkened hillside as the car careened crazily down the winding, one lane road that led up to the cemetery. The incessant blasting of the horn sent shrill, staccato cries that echoed madly through the wooded canyon. A shaken, screeching night owl took hasty flight as the car sideswiped an ancient oak that marked the entrance to the grounds. Tires squealed as they lost their bite on the pavement— then, a shuddering metallic crunch rumbled across the land of the dead.

Smoke hissed from the crumpled hood of the late model grey Volvo as it lay groaning at the base of a monstrous elm. One of the headlights was broken out and the windshield was spiderwebbed with cracks. Blood, small slivers of pinkish grue and snatches of wet, dark hair oozed slowly down from the shattered point of impact. The horn wailed and did not stop. Suddenly the driver's side door flew open and a man tumbled to the damp, thick grass. He rose unsteadily to his knees and rubbed his scalp...and then the things were upon him. They howled as they dug their fingers into his flesh, sparking fresh, fevered cries from the struggling figure. One of the things bit into his upper arm, sending a warm, bubbling fountain of blood sloshing from the yawning, five-inch gash on the man's biceps. He yowled in pain as another one of them snapped at his face while it clawed at his neck and shoulders. Miraculously, the man regained his footing and shook one of the things off just as another chomped into the meaty part of his calf. Three of the creatures were still hanging from him but he maintained his balance and kept on moving.

Screams– jagged, gut-deep, relentless–split the night as the man saw more and more of them coming for him. They came from everywhere–behind him, from both the left and right and again, in front of him. Some wriggled right up and out of the wet, muddied ground, fighting and clawing their way to the surface in a frenzied, spastic struggle to join the hunt. Most left pieces of themselves near their escape holes–piles of grey-green desiccated viscera, shredded limbs, and unidentifiable dollops of putrescent flesh littered the landscape, especially heavy near the tombstone itself.

One creature was scrambling uncannily about on its hands–surreal crab-style–trailing a snakey, thickly-coiled pile of guts and glop that led back to a fancy memorial topped by a stone Jesus.

The hot, putrid stench of death splashed over the running man as one of them lunged, jaws snapping and grinding, right up and into his face. The black, broken teeth found his lips and he screamed. Another sank its fangs into his thigh and the man pissed his pants. He was choking on his own blood and the scream caught in his throat. His lips and most of his nose were now missing.

The creature that had just swallowed part of his face came at him again, teeth gnashing and dark, thin hands clawing for his throat. The man threw a hurried, yet solid, punch that caught the thing full in the mouth. It bit into him again and he pushed his fist down its throat. He heard the jaw crack and felt the cold, slimy mush in his fist as the thing gagged and flailed madly. He put his weight behind him this time and shoved hard. His forearm disappeared and he was up to his elbow in a frothing, curdled mess that began sluicing out of the thing's nose, mouth and ears. A deep, wet, sucking belch popped his ears as he forcibly withdrew his arm from the crushed fleshen cavern. Its head lolled crazily off to one side as the thing went down, hard. He smashed the rest of its face in with a well-placed mule kick and then began running again. He shook the others off and headed straight for a small grove of eucalyptus trees directly ahead. He saw no shadowy figures lurking within but he was still some seventy yards away and the creatures were coming from everywhere. He lowered his shoulder and continued to plow through them the best he could. Less than thirty yards to the woods now--lungs exploding, chest white hot with pain, legs going to rubber--but still he fought on.

As he passed a towering granite memorial, two of the things leapt onto his back. He felt their teeth burrow into his left cheek and neck as the warmth of his own blood washed rapidly down his shoulders and onto his chest. He bellowed in pain and then lost his footing. He skidded to an abrupt halt and pitched forward, gasping for breath while furiously beating at the ravenous things feeding on him. He hit the ground then rolled quickly over, only to see three more of them coming at him. Then, more still; jaws twitching madly, their eyes dead in their heads. They held him down and snapped at him again and again. And still more came. He was on his back now, kicking wildly when he saw the deep, vicious wound open up on his abdomen. He looked down, fearing the worst and getting it, just in time to see one of the things bite into a looping, slithering length of intestine and then yank it right out of his gut like so much bloodied rope. The other wounds stabbed into him with increasing ferocity as the crimson slush splashed to the ground beneath him.

He raised his head up high enough to witness two of the creatures go elbow deep into his stomach cavity and then begin fighting over a six-foot length of steaming gut when suddenly the night exploded. Bright, fiery orange thunderclaps erupted from the eucalyptus grove as he rolled his eyes towards the trees. Flaming tongues of fire leapt from the grove and then he heard the voices--human voices--coming from the tree line.

He glanced up again just as the hideous black, dripping maw lowered onto his face to finish the job. Then, in less than a heartbeat, the blackened head burst open in a chunky mist of bone and brains that splashed his face and filled his lipless mouth with a moist, crunchy gruel. The things momentarily stopped feasting long enough to look towards the grove as more and more fire from the trees found the flesh of the creatures.

One stared uncomprehendingly toward the gunfire, fresh entrails dripping down its chin, just before a high-powered blast tore a bowling ball-sized hole through its chest. The thing crumpled into a heap atop the downed man, its fingers and jaws still twitching furiously. Another flurry of explosions followed before he heard voices again, louder now, and much closer.

Six men, in both sweatsuits and fatigues, gathered around him and peered down at his ravaged body as he tried to raise his arm in signal. Nothing budged. He tried again to move an arm, a hand, even, but they were both gone. He couldn't move anything. He couldn't even blink his eyes.

"He's not one of them," said a blue-jacketed man holding a smoking AK-47 in his arms.

The man on the ground tried to acknowledge him but blood filled his mouth and choked off the reply.

"He shouldn't be anywhere near this place. How do you figure he managed to get through the roadblock?" said another man cradling a mammoth-sized pump action shotgun.

"Doesn't matter now, does it?" said the small one with the pistol.

"Fuck," replied Mr. Blue Jacket.

The fallen man groaned deeply as his eyes rolled back in their sockets. A second cough caught in his throat before it turned into a wheezing rattle that shook his body one last time.

The men looked up, impassively, and gazed blank-faced at one another.

Then suddenly......the figures disappeared, replaced by glowing, jangled static.

Raymond Tyler set his bottle of Black Velvet aside and punched the "eject" button on his VCR.

"That's not how I would have done it," he said to no one in particular. "Not at all."

He gingerly removed the ejected cassette and slid his well-worn copy of *Zombie Dawn* back into its box.

"You're OK Rollins," he said, fingering the bold-faced director's credit at the bottom of the box, "but you're losing it. Real guts don't look anything like that rubber shit you're using."

Tyler replaced the cassette in the shelf and reached for another. This one was in a black box right above his copy of *Cannibal Massacre*. He pulled it out and gently traced a pattern along the hand-drawn label. It read *Hammer Kill #2*.

"Now you'll see how it's done," he smirked as he slid the cassette into the machine. " You were good... in your day, Rollins, but it's time for the *new blood*", Tyler grumbled as he grabbed his bottle. He extended a thick, stubby finger and hit "play". He took another pull from the bottle, bending his head way back as the last of the nut-colored fluid gurgled down his throat.

"This is the way it really looks," he laughed.

The snowy, flipping picture steadied itself and revealed a hand-held close shot of a bespectacled young man cowering in fear. A dark, blurry object was seen crashing down upon his head. Tyler squealed as the claw hammer smacked into the guy's face.

"Now there's an effect that's *really* special," he chortled.

Several deep holes had been punched into the man's skull and he was screaming and crying at full-throttle. Blood bubbled up from the ragged craters and covered his head in a red sticky sauce. Tyler was mesmerized. Then the victim dropped out of the frame. The picture blinked a few times, went snowy again for a few seconds, then cleared.

A close shot of the bloodied head filled the screen, this time shown from an overhead angle.

" Now comes the good part," Tyler giggled as he drew himself even closer to the set. He licked his lips and extended a finger to the TV.

The red-ribboned face howled as the claws of the hammer sank into the eye socket, splintering the skull and popping the eyeball like an overripe grape. Then, levered against the nasal bone, the hammer slammed downward and a gash the size of a fist blossomed suddenly on the right side of the ruined face.

Tyler was clutching the whiskey bottle tightly with both hands as he watched the hammer come down again and again and again. The picture went dark. Then static and snow. He bent forward and switched it off.

"Now that's the ticket," he grinned. "I think there's a lesson here somewhere."

Tyler rubbed both hands together then slapped his knee with his right fist.

"I'll show these Hollywood jackoffs a thing or two," he beamed. " Show 'em all how it's really done... right."

Tyler stood up and reached for his jacket. He pulled it on and then picked up his camcorder from the chair. Moving over to the bureau, he opened the second drawer and withdrew a shiny object that he quickly hid in his coat.

"And this time," he hissed, "they're going to listen."

****

Jeff Rollins took a deep, lung-bursting pull on the proffered joint.

"Skunk buds. From Humboldt," said the attractive, red-haired woman sitting to his right. Rollins nodded and took another hit. He exhaled slowly through his nose, delightedly savoring the sweet, luxurious bite of the primo, $400-an-ounce stash. Rollins reached for his glass of Appleton Dark and ran his tongue over his parched lips.

"Fucking A."

The woman giggled. Rollins drained his glass, then quickly refilled it. He looked at his watch and sighed.

"Aren't we awfully early ? "

A neatly bearded young man in a fashionably-aged leather jacket turned around and addressed those in the rear of the van as the driver made a right turn on La Brea.

"They'd like you to sign a few posters and some publicity shots for the Academy before you speak to the members," said Paul Frandsen, the line producer of Rollins' last three films, including *Zombie Dawn* , their biggest hit to date.

"These people have been among our staunchest supporters in the past. Let's not forget that."

Rollins made a farting noise with his cheeks and reached into his pocket for the roach clip.

"Buncha wankers, college kids and couch potatoes... some in desperate need of mashing," replied Billy K.,the driver. Billy, a long-haired, lanky motormouth, was one of Rollins' production assistants and a part-time dope dealer to-the-stars. "Those whiney-assed yuppie wanna-be's haven't seen a real horror film since they blew lunch at *The Exorcist*. Buncha real lame cats."

"Maybe so," countered Frandsen, "but we've got a packed house for tonight's screening and plenty of European buyers have expressed interest in attending. They've been hungry for something like this for a long, long time."

Rollins, cocooned in a thick blue cloud of Class A gage, looked up and offered a cracked smile.

"We've printed up about 500 survey cards," continued Frandsen, "and if we get anywhere near the reaction we got in New York, well then, some serious ass is about to be kicked."

Both Billy K. and the woman nodded enthusiastically.

"If everything goes according to plan, then DDI and Lauren-Daniels are going to be at each other's throats for the North American rights...not to mention the cable and video pie." Frandsen smacked his lips and took another hit off the newly-ignited reefer.

"And the fans are going to eat it up big-time," Frandsen smiled, " the special effects are above and beyond anything they've ever seen in a splatter movie." He took in another lungful of the sweet smoke.

"Fuckin' zombies been mighty good to me."

Frandsen put his hands behind his head and exhaled slowly.

"Bread from the dead," he grinned.

Billy K. punched a button on the cassette player. Hendrix. The woozy wah-wah pedal intro to

Voodoo Chile: Slight Return wafted through the smoke-filled van. Rollins fell right into the groove.

"And, Jeff," beamed Frandsen, "this is the first time we've ever let them see your director's cut, right?"

Rollins nodded.

"Think they can handle it ?" added Frandsen.

Rollins sat up straight and winked.

"It's the Ultimate Chunkblower," the director replied. "Pure, one-hundred percent Butcher's Pride beef. Every conscientious, dues-paying gorehound will be coming in their shorts by the second reel. Hallelujah! Now I can die happy...and rich, too."

As the van turned the corner at Highland Avenue and made its way to the VIP parking lot of the Director's Guild theater, no one took notice of the muscular, long-haired kid leaning against the box-office window. When the van passed him, the kid stood erect, clicked his heels together and saluted smartly.

"The *new blood*," said Raymond Tyler as the girl in the booth handed him the ticket.

MAN MYTH AND MANIAC

An Interview with ***WILLIAM LUSTIG***

by Kris Gilpin

After working crew jobs on hard-core porn flicks at the ripe young age of 17, Bill Lustig directed two of his own XXX-rated epics before making Maniac *with Joe Spinell in 1980; it was a horror film so depraved it even pissed off many genre fans. Next came the revenge tale,* Vigilante, *followed by* Maniac Cop, *(which Lustig directed from a script by Larry (*Q, It's Alive*) Cohen.),* Hit List *and* Maniac Cop 2.

KG First off, how'd you come to meet and make a film with Larry Cohen?

WL Well, Larry and I have known each other for several years; we met through a mutual friend at a film lab in New York. It was in February of 1987 when we came up with the idea of *Maniac* over lunch in New York City.

KG What was it like to work with Cohen?

WL Well, once he'd written the screenplay I was basically on my own at that point. It was really a pleasure working with him; he came in during post-production and offered some very valuable suggestions on some of the editing choices and such in the film. It was mainly on the screenplay and in post-production that we worked together.

"I knew Argento pretty well...I was involved with the opening sequence of his *Tenebrae*."

KG Were you a fan of his work?

WL Oh, yeah, very much. I loved *It's Alive, Demon or God Told Me To, Special Effects*; I think Larry Cohen's an incredible filmmaker and a very interesting personality. An extremely bright guy, one of the smartest people I've ever met in this business.

KG Would you like to work with him again?

WL As a matter of fact, we're talking about doing another picture together; he was really happy about the way *Maniac* turned out. Larry's usually been an entrepreneur; this was the first time he'd done a project with a partner, let alone a partner who directed the picture. He justifiably felt a bit uncomfortable about that, so that's why he stayed away during the production; he figured it'd be like two chefs in the kitchen. But, when he finally did get to see the film, according to him it exceeded his expectations. We've screened it for buyers and it's been sold throughout the world, and it's now a profitable picture, and we want to do something else [together].

KG How about Bruce [*The Evil Dead 1 & 2*] Campbell?

WL He's great; he's terrific to work with. He does his work well, he's very well prepared when he comes to the set and he's a lot of fun; the crew loved him. He's a total pro, and I think *Maniac Cop* was a bit more demanding for him in terms of his acting ability because there's a lot more dialogue and character than in the *Evil Dead* films, which were more physical. Our film had physical stuff in it, but it was mainly a lot more interacting with other actors, and he handled himself great. He was so used to doing his own stunts. I'd have stunt doubles for him for just about everything, and he'd keep saying, 'Oh, I can do that!' He was surprised whenever anybody got a stunt double for him and, with some of the things, I think he was thankful for it [chuckles]. And he always had suggestions for his character. We were collaborating all along; he was the first person I hired on the film. He's a

"I think the horror films which tend to endear the audience to them the most are a bit more rough around the edges, like the *Evil Dead* films – the sort of Bad Boy movies."

very amusing guy, but we were working so hard there really wasn't too much time for laughter. All told, including pick-up shots, we had a 23-day shoot.

KG Do you have any anecdotes from the shoot?

WL We were doing some very hairy stunts during the film. Most of our 'fun' was being there when some really death-defying stuff was done. We had a guy hanging onto the side of a truck going 40 miles an hour who flew into the ocean. At the same time, the van turns over. It's a really spectacular stunt. We just had a lot of fun making the picture.

KG Have you always been a genre fan?

WL Oh, yeah. I was a *Famous Monsters of Filmland* freak and was always into monster and action films. I practically grew up watching movies on 42nd Street, so I got my fill of all the terror films that I really love, like the Dario Argento films.

KG Do you like making horror more than action, or vice-versa?

WL Well, when you're doing action, so much depends on stunts and effects and things like that, and no matter how much time you think [those things] will take, they take more. It's very tedious doing action films, but I enjoy them. I don't enoy the process of making an action film. I genuinely wish I didn't have to be there while it was being made because it's just so tedious, whereas with horror, you're really dealing with a lot of cinematic moments. It's hard to explain. For instance, *Maniac* is a balance between action and horror. We have this sequence in which there's a maniac cop killing people in a police station, and there's a lot of suspense and scares and stuff like that. I really enjoy working those camera moves and all that stuff out, and visualizing it. I'm thinking about the audience while I'm working, thinking about how to get the best scares and what'll work for maximum impact. It's a lot of fun and a lot less tedious [than directing action], because you're able to control it more. With action, because you're dealing with cars and traffic control and everything else, it just takes forever.

"We decided to pool our money, which came to a big $48,000, opened up a bank account and started a production – we called it *Maniac*."

"I'd always intended the film to be the equivalent of sitting at the dinner table, chewing your food and opening your mouth before you swallow it!"

KG Your first film was the hard-core porno, *The Violation of Claudia*. How'd you get that as your first feature?

WL I was working as a production assistant and an assistant editor in New York. I was a high-school drop-out, born in the Bronx and raised in New Jersey. Where I was raised was right across the George Washington Bridge, so I'd always go to New York. I related to New York. At the time *Deep Throat* was very popular, so the kind of film people were making in New York was some kind of hard-core picture. People who're now highly legitimate people [in the biz], whose names I won't mention, were making hard-core then because that was the genre. I guess, after *Friday the 13th*, there was the maniac and slasher genre. I had been working on several hard-core films as a production assistant in every position you could imagine. I knew nothing about cameras, yet here I was loading [film] magazines up. It was a great learning experience because there was a lot of hands-on experience on equipment. Quite frankly, I never really thought about what we were shooting. I was thinking technically all the time. I'd shot sections of XXX-rated films and, in 1976, the opportunity came my way to shoot an entire feature. I'd shot a lot of second unit stuff. No hard-core, but stuff with a lot of acting in it. I was 21 years old when I made *Violation of Claudia*. It was made for just around 40 thousand dollars and it went on to make about $2,000,000, gross. And I think we struck, all together, around 30 to 40 prints of the film! So it was a very, very profitable venture. I learned a lot, because I also took the film to foreign film markets and learned about foreign-film sales, which helped me in making my future films, since I was very comfortable dealing with the foreign marketplace.

KG Did you try to do something with *The Violation of Claudia* to differentiate it from the other current hard-core?

WL Actually my intention was — and I don't think it was the right one — to do it "classy." Because I had a *woman* who wrote the script and I tried to do something. Basically what I did was I ripped off [Luis Bunuel's 1967] *Belle de Jour*! It follows that story. I tried to do it with a lot of attention to production value, and the reviews of the picture all complimented that. I tend to think that hard-core films, just like horror films, need to be a little bit perverse to be fun, though [smiles].

KG In what way?

WL I think the horror films which tend to endear the audience to them the most are a bit more rough around the edges, like the *Evil Dead* films—the sort of Bad Boy movies. I think those films should be a bit more like Forbidden Fruit. I didn't do that with *Claudia* and, in retrospect, I think that was a mistake. A distributor once said to me, in my travels, "If you ever come across something which truly disgusts and bothers you, and you're afraid to shoot it because your mother might see it, shoot it!"

KG What led you into the horrors of *Maniac*?

WL Well, I'd always wanted to

make a horror film, even when I was doing *Violation of Claudia.* I was a fan of *Texas Chainsaw Massacre* and *Last House on the Left*. In fact, I'd met Sean Cunningham and Wes Craven in New York back then, and I'd met the actor Joe Spinell while I was making *Claudia.* He was coming out in *Rocky* and was a very prestigious character actor. He was a fan of genre films and we started hanging out together, seeing movies on 42nd Street, eating Chinese food and bullshitting. We'd have a great time and we wanted to make a movie together. We came up with an idea based on a father and son team who went around New Jersey killing women — a true story. The father would stand by and induce the son to rape and kill the women; it was really perverted. So we had this idea of doing a sort of *Honeymoon Killers*-type movie, and we wrote a screenplay called *Slayride*; I don't even know where the script is today. We went around to everybody but we couldn't raise the money [to make it]. Finally, then, I did *Hot Honey*, Joe had made some money from *Cruising* and a very close friend of mine at the time, Andrew Garroni, was doing the New York sequences for Dario Argento's *Inferno*. We decided to pool our money, which came to a big $48,000, opened up a bank account and started a production. We called it *Maniac*. What Joe and I did was come up with a compilation of personalities based on all these serial killers, then I came up with all these murder sequences I'd wanted to put into a picture. We took those to a writer who wrote a screenplay with us, which I think we never even looked at while we shot the movie [chuckles], because it was a traditional horror screenplay with police [and so forth]. We went out and basically improvised the movie as we went along. I knew the murder sequences, Joe knew the character, so it was basically divided between killing and Joe, killing and Joe. There was really not too much more [to it]. Total cash to post-production on that film was $135,000 and the film in this country has done five and a half million dollars, and overseas it's done equal that, if not more. The film just made a bundle and, all of a sudden, I became "legitimate." I started getting offers from studios to do pictures, and stuff like that.

KG *Maniac* pissed a lot of people off. How'd you respond to the cries of misogyny?

WL At first I kind of found it amusing. First off, suddenly getting all this attention for someone who'd never gotten any before was a lot of fun. Number two, I'd always intended the film to be the equivalent of sitting at a dinner table, chewing your food and opening your mouth before you swallow it! I'd always thought of it as a big joke to sort of upset people [chuckles]. But what happened was that, all of a sudden, people started to really give the film a lot more importance than I thought it deserved. I expected people to be outraged at all the violence, but I didn't expect the film to take on all these political things that happened with it. I started getting threat mail, all kinds of nasty things were sent to the [film] laboratory and to me, I came out here for the opening and there were people picketing the theatre. I really thought it was unbelievable. I stopped being amused by it. I never took the film seriously when I made it. I'd always had an irreverent attitute towards it. I thought, 'How can anyone take this seriously? It's so stupid.' The guy's going around scalping people. The violence in it was so outrageous it was ridiculous, and I always viewed it that way. It started to get kind of sad because I saw people who were taking everyday violence around them and trying to find very simplistic answers to what it's all about. I found it very sad that people would take very complicated problems and pin them on movies like *Maniac* and *Friday the 13th*, and books and records. I then became, in a sense, kind of "politically aware". I'd be on these talk shows with these women against [the film]. I had this one woman out here [protesting the film], Jean or Jeanie Something, and two years later she's arrested. She was involved with an actual murder! She was an accomplice to an actual murder. All I did was sit there with Tom Savini and splatter "blood" on people! It taught me a lot about hypocrisy — that there's a *lot* of it! I grew out of that experience.

KG So there wasn't any intentional hatred-of-women strain meant in the storyline?

WL What happened was that after we wrote the first draft, I said I wanted the best special-effects guy around. I'd seen *Dawn of the Dead* and I'd flipped over the effects. Tom Savini was in New Jersey shooting *Friday the 13th*. I gave him a call, he was dying to come to New York to live for a little while so we flew him up there, put him up in an apartment and he became our best buddy. And we sat around my apartment-office in New York and, over pizza and Chinese food, came up with the most outrageous things we could thing of to put in the movie. And we were laughing all the time we were doing it, as if no one would take this stuff seriously. It was a lot of fun, a lot of brainstorming. It was a gas. We were laughing as we were making the film, splattering blood all over the place. We thought it was hysterical. Tom was extremely efficient. Having had very little experience with make-up effects, I was expecting them to take a lot longer than they did, and it didn't. Tom was very well prepared and he did a first-rate job. He was energetic, enthusiastic and always adding more stuff to the show. The only thing which happened with Tom, which was hurtful, was that after the film started getting blasted, all of a sudden he started to change his tune about the movie. He started to, all of a sudden, call it trash, and here was a guy who, after we finished the movie, put his arms around me and told me how much he loved it. I never, to this day, understood why Tom did that.

KG Have you any involvement in the proposed *Maniac 2*?

WL I really didn't know what the hell to do for a *Maniac 2*. That's [my] number one [reason] — what didn't I do in the first film that I could do in the second? Obviously, somebody's come up with the answer, and they came to me, Joe and Andy Garroni and they bought the sequel rights to the film from us. Again, I could've done it for money, but I learned a long time ago not to do things for money. Step back from it; see if you can find out why to do it other than just for a paycheck. And I really couldn't find a reason to do a *Maniac 2* other than to make a paycheck out of it. I mean, maybe they'll come up with a script and it'll be wonderful, and they'll want me to direct it. I just don't know. Joe was the star of the movie. You can't have a *Maniac* without him. But I've had very little involvement with *Maniac 2*.

KG Have you always been a fan of gore films?

WL I've been a fan of horror and gore films, but, when you say "fan" ...I'm not really a fan of the Herschell Gordon Lewis films. I'm more a fan of the films of Dario Argento, Sam Raimi, George Romero and Cronenberg. A lot of people sort of enjoy revelling in mediocre films but I don't. I enjoy seeing a quality film, like *Texas Chainsaw Massacre*.

KG If you made *Maniac* again, today, would you do it any differently?

WL [Answers immediately.] I'd put more humor into it. Although we weren't mean-spirited when we made it, in retrospect, looking at it today I think the film is too mean-spirited.

KG And that's what pissed people off?

WL Maybe it did. I looked at it [recently] and I didn't see any humor in it, and I think it needed it, because what we were thinking was not up on the screen.

KG Have you ever planned to make a movie with Dario Argento?

WL We were gonna do one together, but it just never came together. I had a project he liked. I was going to shoot it in Rome and New York. But, for reasons I don't even remember, it just never came together. I haven't spoken with him in at least three years. Sam Raimi's a friend who I speak to once a month. He has a very brief role in *Maniac*. He was a ball to work with. He's a great guy. I knew Argento pretty well. We'd spent a lot of time together in Rome and New York. I was also involved with the opening sequence of his *Tenebrae*, which is called *Unsane* here. I did New York service work for the opening scene. It was very brief, about three minutes of screen time. I haven't been there for a while but the next time I'm in Rome, I'm going to give him a call. I'm dying to see [Argento's latest film] *Opera*! The guy is a technical master. I enjoy his movies because I get a lot of ideas when I watch them.

KG Where would you like to steer your career from here?

WL Well, my first step — when I got my XXX-rated films — was to learn my craft. My next step was to get involved with making independent pictures and handling the financing, and all the rest of it. Now I'm doing pictures with other people's money, and for my next step I'd like to do movies with [big] stars in them and I'd like to have more time to shoot my movies. The common denominator on most of the pictures I've done is that there's just never enough money. And, many times, if you have stars in your film, it gives you the budget and ability to spend more time doing things which, sometimes, you're not able to give the proper amount of time to. With these two

"I found it very sad that people would take very complicated problems and pin them on movies like *Maniac* and *Friday the 13th*, and books and records."

action projects, I have budgets in the five to six million dollar range in mind. Whether or not I'm able to go up to that level I'll soon see. But that's my goal right now. I've proven myself and my films have been successful. *Hit List* was bought by Warner Bros. for overseas distribution, and RCA Columbia has it for home video in this country. So now I'd like to move up a level, to try to grow a little bit and get into bigger films. And the major common denominator in my films is that I try to make them visceral pictures, where they get you. I try to create a sustained suspense throughout.

A FRENZY OF BLOOD!

THE BLOOD SPATTERED BRIDE

EASTMANCOLOR

R RESTRICTED Under 17 requires accompanying Parent or Adult Guardian

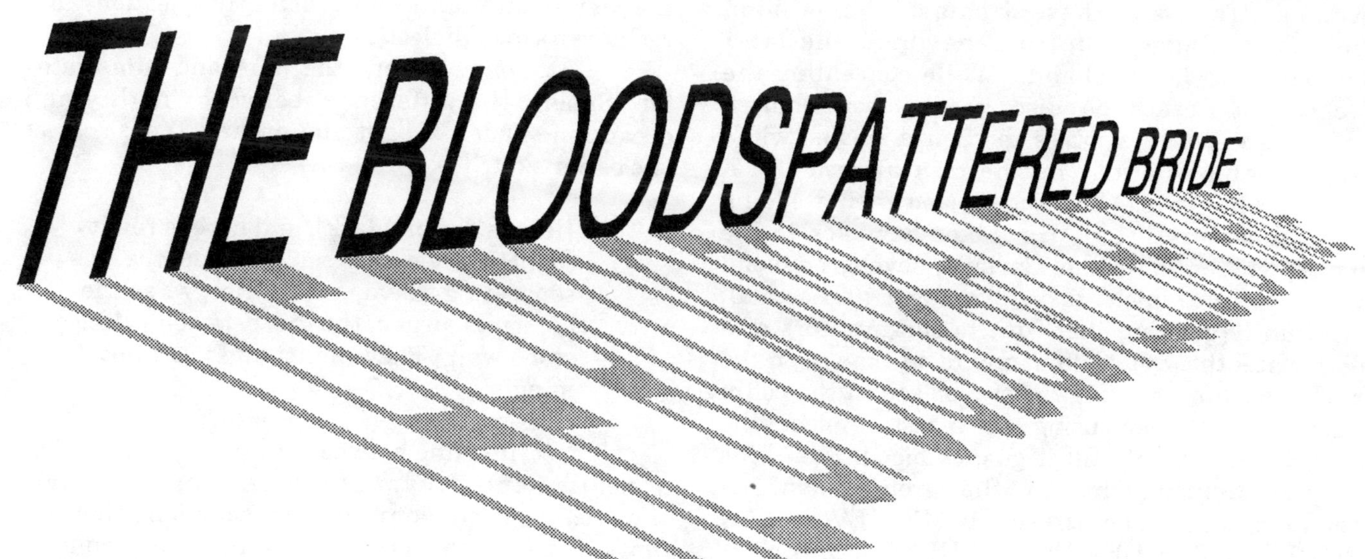

THE BLOODSPATTERED BRIDE

THE LESBIAN VAMPIRE AS REVOLUTIONARY

"The good are content to dream what the wicked actually practice."

Plato

by Steven R. Johnson

The Bloodspattered Bride was one of the most misunderstood of the seventies' spate of lesbian vampire films, which also included the likes of Joseph Larraz's *Vampyres* and Stephanie Rothman's *The Velvet Vampire*. Though often compared to Vadim's *Blood and Roses* and Hammer's *The Vampire Lovers* because of its basis in J. Sheridan le Fanu's Carmilla, the film more rightly compares to Harry Kumel's 1971 film, *Daughters of Darkness*, both movies involving the brides of sadistic husbands who are driven to murderous relationships with charismatic women vampires. *Bride*, while obviously inspired by Kumel's film, goes beyond that film's sexual politics and adds an ironic subtext alluding (as did many other Spanish films of the time) to the wider political climate of its native Spain under the Franco dictatorship. Much maligned and underappreciated in most genre texts (though gaining in reputation), it's time to take a second look at this important work by director Vicente Aranda.

Produced in 1972 by Aranda's own Morgana Films (named for his 1966 feature, *Fata Morgana*, and implying right off the bat that what we think we're seeing may be an illusion), *Bride* presents a constantly conflicting dialogue between two characters' fantasies, never giving us a clear perspective on anything. The method is perplexing yet never without its logic, and provides an argument to those who misread the film as a macho treatise on the threat of lesbianism, for what may come off as the filmmakers' own misogynist attitudes often turns out to be the vengeful or paranoid fantasy of a character of highly questionable motivations. The nudity, which is clearly voyeuristic, and the editing, which sometimes seems to have been done with a trowel, were a source of some criticism as well, though they, too, have their function — mainly in throwing off Franco's censors from the film's highly volatile criticisms of his regime, one which did not take kindly to such upbraidings.

The story begins with a pair of newlyweds arriving at their hotel, where the bride, Susan, notices a mysterious woman in a red car and black cloak watching her. Up in their room she experiences a masochistic fantasy involving a man who resembles her husband, and insists that they leave. They move to the husband's huge estate, where Susan endures his abusive behavior while apparently fantasizing visitations by the woman. In one of these dreams, the woman passes a dagger on to her, which she later transfers to her husband. While concealing the weapon on a beach, he discovers someone buried in the sand who resembles the figure in his wife's dreams and who may be the reincarnation of a woman who killed his ancestor on their wedding night a century before. He takes her back to the house, where the woman, Carmila, develops a bond with Susan which turns vampiric and sexual, eventually goading her on to the murders of a doctor and the groundsman and to attempts on the husband's life. Finding the two asleep in the coffin Carmila has been using as a resting place, the husband shoots it till it gushes blood, then kills the pubescent daughter of the groundsman. A headline appears on screen, HOME NEWS: MAN CUTS OUT THE HEARTS OF THREE WOMEN.

Given these circumstances, it's easy to misread the film, especially as Aranda eschews most of the technical artistry which might suggest a more refined political sensibility. Much feminist criticism would also seem to argue *Bride*'s portrait of its lesbian character, as the depiction of her here is true to the predatory archetype which usually casts her as a threat to the manhood of our focus of audience identification. The error in applying such readings to this film lies, however, in mistaking any character's point of view for the director's, and in a failure to fully appreciate the barbarism and cruelty of the husband himself, whose fantasies frequently impose themselves on the action of the film. Such episodes as his tearing open Susan's bridal gown, lifting her by the hair, assaulting her in the aviary, intruding on her innocent fun with Carol, a servant girl, in the cellar, and subsequently snapping an ancestor's bone before his wife's very eyes, all indicate someone few rational viewers would want to identify with and support. And if male audience members are encouraged to side with him, female viewers as well could derive satisfaction from her retribution, serving to balance the conflict, if nothing else. The number of shots from behind banister railings, headboards, footboards, and fences, suggest both sexes as caged animals acting instinctually, unreasonably, and finally destructively, the most stirring demonstration of this being a shot appearing toward the end of the film in which the husband touches a bloody dagger to the bloodied teeth of a fox trap, uniting the murderous phallus with the vagina dentata. The film further balances the masculine and the feminine in its accumulation of deceptively subtle recapitulations of scenes, each one with a twist (usually a switch of the genders initially assigned) that puts the viewer off guard and constantly questions and restates its own dialectic.

At one point, the husband illustrates for Susan the difference between reality and dream, in shades of light and dark in the corner of one of her sketches:

> Here is dream [dark], and here is reality [light]. When a person is asleep, the line separating them is imprecise; when the person is awake, the line between is like a stone wall. They cannot and must not mingle.

Yet the line between our own apprehension of reality and dream is blurred by Aranda's thwarting of conventional expectations, for the film's leaps from one to the other are seamless. When the mysterious man in black springs from the closet to attack Susan, there aren't any fancy wipes or dissolves, it just happens; when the husband digs up Carmila on the beach, the scene is played totally straight, the obviously artificial hand protruding from the sand a footnote to another film essay on fantasy and reality, Maya Deren's *Meshes of the Afternoon*; finally, when the husband sleeps through a knifing by Susan and later finds Carmila and his wife asleep in their coffin after a killing spree, we are no longer certain where reality left off and the fantasies even began. Both "attacks" on Susan and all of Carmila's early appearances take place in bright light, first in the sunshine and later with the bedroom lights full on, Susan's eyes wide open. This is either to imply that what's taking place is, according to the husband's illustration, reality (since it occurs in the light), or that, for these women, the principles of light and darkness are a reversal of his own (as is their sexuality, growing nocturnal nature, and, for the allegedly "undead" Carmila, very state of being).

Whether Carmila is real or fantastic, living or dead, human or vampire, is never made explicit. The doctor who administers to Susan after her attacks insists that Carmila is flesh and blood, but he's off base on other matters, and may be so on this one, as well. Her explanation of how she wound up naked and buried in the sand doesn't wash, either (she was scuba diving and "lost track of time," she says — next thing she knew, the husband was digging her up), but is accepted by everyone. About all we know is that, metaphorically, the husband's sexual violence (as symbolized by the phallic dagger) is responsible for the production of this, in turn, sexual avenger.

When the husband returns home from the seashore with Carmila, the scene is shot from the same perspective as his arrival at the hotel (and soon after at the house) in the beginning of the film, his honking for the servants tying the scenes together; it's at this point that the many recapitulations of scenes, imagery, and dialogue kick in, reinforcing the feeling of restarting and restatement. Even though the husband appears to represent order and logic, certain things, such as the uncertainty as to Carmila's physical existence, and the obvious wish-fulfillment fantasy of the ending (Carmila and Susan somehow conveniently remain asleep — naked, of course — while the husband sets about their destruction, just as the girl Carol willingly submits to her own execution) indicate that we haven't necessarily entered a verifiable reality. The continuing surreality of events implies, instead, that we have rather gone from Susan's fantasy of violation and retribution, into her husband's fantasy of threat to and reassertion of his dominance.

It's also worth noting the similarity between a shot in Aranda's film and a scene in the original *Cat People*, in which the sexually repressed Irena (Simone Simon) claws the back of a couch in frustration; this is recalled in *Bride* when Susan claws the surface of a desktop with a set of inverted rings as she tries to get to the dagger her husband has hidden within. That film's fear-of-sex motif rhymes with *Meshes* and *Bride* also in the delusion Illona suffers of turning into a murderous panther if aroused, with the suggestion that this animal might actually be the agent of her jealous subconscious. (The relation between the two earlier films wasn't lost on Curtis Harrington, either, whose first commercial feature, *Night Tide*, paid homage to both.)

Beyond this psychosexual subtext, however, Aranda's references to the husband's family and ancestry suggest a larger, cultural perspective as well, the repression of the feminine in the husband suggesting the oppression of all women by the patriarchal society he represents. The unsatisfying feeling of the ending — the sudden freeze-frame and blur on the image of the dagger against Carmila's breast (the only camera effects in a movie told entirely in shocking, crude jump cuts) — is intended to leave us hanging, thus to startle us into a realization of the failure of machismo in this macho society.

Even further beyond this cultural dimension is the deeper, political reading the film demands, however. Coming in the last years of the Franco regime, *Bride* ultimately acts as a commentary on the absurdities of a macho and, not coincidentally, repressive government trying to stifle the larger spirit of, more than just a subculture or gender, an entire people. That Aranda should have chosen a violent, exploitative genre format such as this to disguise his inflammatory viewpoints is no wonder, given the censorship under which Spanish filmmakers worked at the time, as John Hopewell describes in his authoritative book on Spanish cinema under Franco, *Out of the Past* (London: BFI Books, 1986). In it, he refers to the problem and to certain measures ("censor-evading techniques best described as a resort to diffusion"; p.69) taken by Aranda's contemporaries, directors who used the formal and theoretical implements of their trade too complex or elusive for Franco's boorish censors to pick up on to render their political allegories.

The portrait Aranda draws, then, of Franquista rule, is hardly a flattering one.

The Spanish Civil War was a clash between Loyalists defending the newly-elected Republican government, and Nationalist rebels led by Franco, who stood for the established landowners, military, aristocracy, and the Catholic Church. Afterward, the General presided over an array of quasi-fascist cabinets for 35 years, and many who disagreed with his policies were either imprisoned, exiled, or put to death. Franco himself is frequently characterized as an oafish, patriarchal, ineffectual though well-meaning dictator, fond of hunting (a popular metaphor for filmmakers, according to Hopewell, for its "political connotations as the favorite sport-cum-slaughter of Franco and his ministers"; p.27) and other macho occupations.

It's not too far a leap, then, to associate the husband in *Bride* with this man, or to associate his estate with the state, suggesting Susan as representative of the Spanish people as a whole. Marriage, given the attitude Aranda displays toward how the sexes relate, may be analogous to civil war, and the figure of Carmila given to represent the spirit of revolution itself, especially as implied by Carol's last words (preparing for her execution, she tells the husband, "They'll come back. They cannot die").

Also amplifying the political allegory is Aranda's constant veiling of the victims during the aforementioned violations or "unspeakable" acts: when the stranger emerges from the hotel closet to rape Susan, he wraps her wedding veil around her face, the image also suggesting the subjugation of women through marriage. Similarly, Susan's face is veiled by her own hair in the aviary, as it is in the chapel with Carmila; Carol also drapes her hair over her face at her own execution. This suggests a blinding of the people — even by their own hand, at times — to these violent actions, a maintenance of secrecy or ignorance of which the aforementioned censorship may be an example. It's also analogous to the removal of the face in Mircala's portrait in its obscuring of identity, whether that identity be the oppressor's, as in the husband's stockingfaced assault, the victim's, or the revolutionary's. (Significantly, Susan is immediately sedated after her visitations from Carmila, a further suggestion of the blinding or numbing of upstarts to quell fomenting rebellious sentiment.) Considered in this light, then, the film becomes an allegory of the will of the people to live free from oppression, repression, and dictatorship, and the lesbianism becomes more or less a positive force in rising up against such rule.

The film stands as an uncompromising, if ambiguously related, document of the regime at its worst and of the violence of the reactionary feeling it inspired in its artists, and as a vivid portrait of the spirit of the people, once politicized, under any totalitarian rule. Specific political associations aside (where Aranda's ambiguous attitude toward this one suggests he would rather leave them), the message the film sends out to all oppressors is clear: you can deface or defame the people who stand up against your inhumanity, you can deny them their identity, legitimacy, try to blind the people to your "unspeakable acts," you can even cut their hearts out trying to rid yourself of the source of their resistance, but as long as you force them to live under tyranny and dictatorship there will always be a "return of the oppressed". They may be silenced or put down for as long as you live, but, unlike individual men like Francisco Franco, "They'll come back. They cannot die."

GORE SCOREBOARD

THE RATING SYSTEM

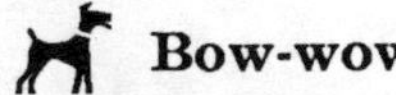

Bow-wow

Nearly worthless

Average

Above average

Classic, Must see

The Gore Score

The GORE SCORE concerns itself with **nothing** but the quantity of blood, brains, guts, slime, snot, puke or other assorted precious bodily fluids spilled, slopped or splattered during the course of the film. A simple, straightforward indication of just how moist and meaty the movie really is.

Like this...

1 — **TERMS OF ENDEARMENT, GANDHI, WILLOW, THREE MEN AND A BABY**

10 — **DR. BUTCHER M.D., MAKE THEM DIE SLOWLY, NEKROMANTIK, CANNIBAL HOLOCAUST**

REVIEWERS:

Chas. Balun (CB) Shane Dallman (SD) Walter Gay (WG) Greg Goodsell (GG) Paul Sammon (PS)

VIOLENT SHIT (1989)
d: Andreas Schnass

This German gore bomb may cause you to revaluate your views on the demolition of the Berlin wall. And, if you were one of the unfortunates who actually *purchased* a copy of this atrocity, well then you've probably bricked it up and salted the site, right?

This amateur backyard splatter-toon garnered an undeserved underground reputation in the wake of *Nekromantik* as the "next big thing" from the German gore brigade. Oh, it's gory alright, perhaps even *the* bloodiest film ever made, but don't take that as any sort of recommendation from *these* shores.

In fact, this "film" is really a shoddy video, presumably shot by people attempting to match the cinematic artistry seen in such butt-numbing spectacles as *Lunchmeat*, *Video Violence* or *Cannibal Campout*. They fucked up. Big. *Violent Shit*, aptly named and execrably executed, is even an *insult* to these films. You may even find yourself savoring the fact that *Shit* is in German, without subtitles, thus sparing you dialog no doubt just as punishing as the on-screen action.

Oh yeh, the *Shit* really starts flying when a lumbering maniac attacks and hacks a number of dimwits with his plywood cleaver (spray painted silver for maximum verisimilitude). Sure, there are endless, loving close-ups of garden hose gouts of the red stuff every few minutes, but so fucking what?

The filmmaking techniques employed by the *Shit* crew never progress past page three of the camera owner's manual and the script must've been jotted down on a cocktail napkin after 30 or 40 Heinekens.

Don't be fooled by the hype you may have heard about this Teutonic turd. *Violent Shit* sucks hamster dicks and that's a fact, Jack.

(CB)

SOCIETY (1989)
d: Brian Yuzna

5

BRIDE OF RE-ANIMATOR (1990)
d: Brian Yuzna

The unabashed adulation heaped upon Brian Yuzna's *Society* by the British genre press seems even more puzzling in the wake of the sound thrashing given the more accomplished *Bride of Re-Animator* in recent U. K. journals. Perhaps the fact that *Society* deals with social paranoia, class consciousness and the tyranny of a small but powerful minority group appeals to the Brit's frustration over mass unemployment, youth group malaise, a crumbling social order and the questionable antics of the rich, snooty layabouts that compromise the "Royal Family." Shit, we fought a revolutionary war over the same gripes. It's not that we can't *comprehend* the situation, it's just that it's not a good *enough* reason to call *Society* a five-star classic and refer to it as "Film of the Year."

True, *Society* aims high. It's refreshingly imaginative storyline and ferocious originality eclipse the somewhat predictable *Bride* in terms of ambitious thematic concerns, but ultimately *Society* never really lives up to it's portentous ideals.

Billy Whitney (stiffly played by low-wattage soap star Billy Warlock) is *Society's* token innocent; a kid who appears to have everything, yet still suffers from unrelieved anxiety, paranoia and a deep-seated fear that his family and their friends have risen in conspiracy against him. Turns out his fears are founded; they *are* out to get him. A weird slime cult plans to make Billy an entree during the surreal, bizarre sexual ritual they call "shunting."

Society saves nearly all it's FX sequences for the final 15 minutes as hyper hedonists engage in an orgy of shape shifting, body melding and sexual sliming that sounds much more exciting than it actually is. FX artist Screaming Mad George has concocted a formidable array of creature creations that, unfortunately, will never be mistaken for anything other than methacyl-soaked latex. Several sequences are rendered clumsy and ineffective despite their outrageousness simply because the Screaming one chooses to show *too* much rubber and not enough restraint.

Society is a high-concept film, full of fascinating and compelling ideas that never seem to be fully realized or exploited. In short, a film whose whole is far less than the sum of it's parts.

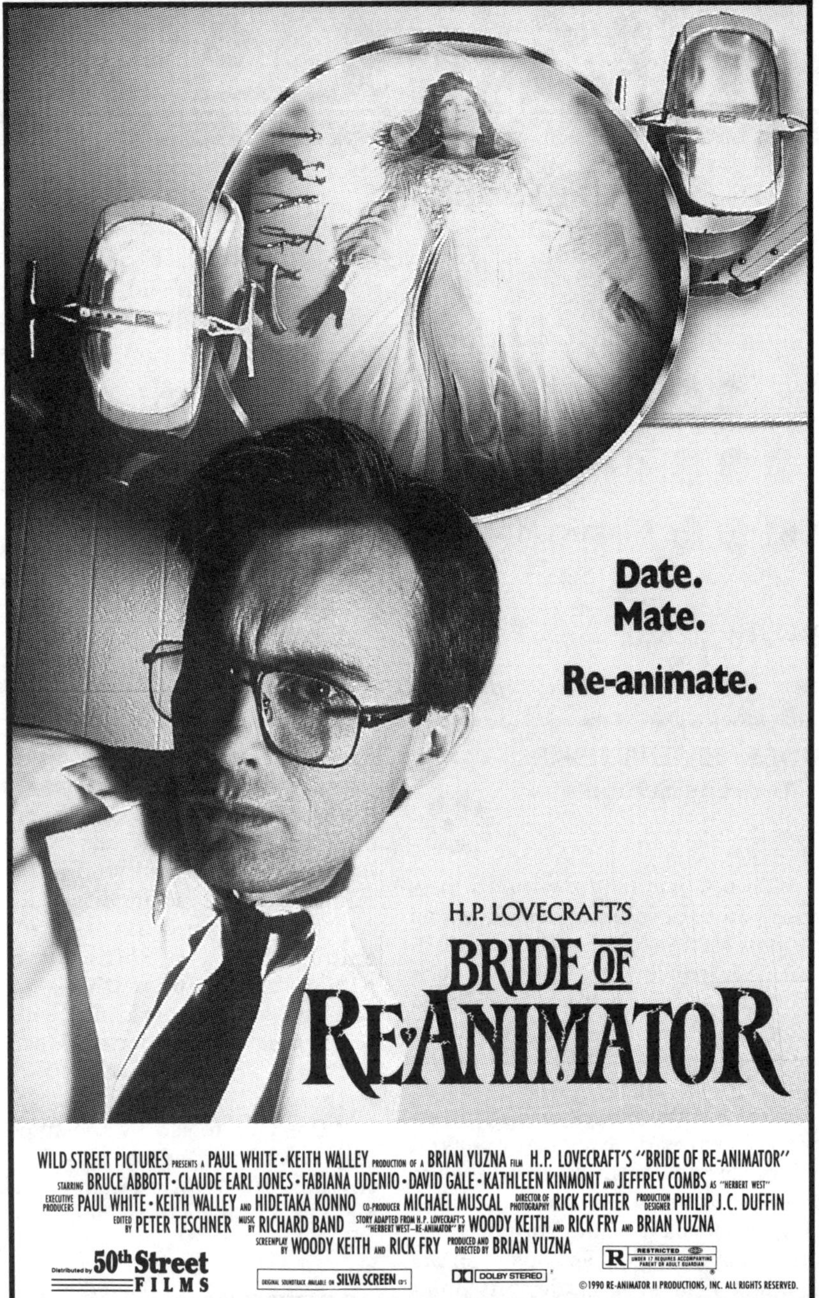

Bride, however, succeds in a more conventional sense. Besides being a heartfelt, sincere homage to Mary Shelley and the Frankenstein mythos, Bride is also a satisfying and logical follow-up to it's predecessor that sacrifices little of the eclectic formula that went into making *Re-Animator* such a scream. Only this time there is a bigger budget, better zombies, gorgeous sets, freaky creatures and another rousing climax that highlights a show-stopping creation sequence that reveals the *Bride* in all her gutsy glory.

Jeffrey Combs commands the screen in a robust, self-assured performance that celebrates the peculiar megalomania that seems to infuse all who specialize in creating life in the laboratory. Bruce Abbott's Dan Cain is now no longer the whimpering, apologetic acolyte he essayed in the first film, but rather a consenting conspirator who gets far more than he bargained for. Hats off to David Gale's user-friendly performance as the famous Talking Head of the Miskatonic Massacre, despite the fact that the good doctor's noggin is propelled about by a very questionable method of locomotion.

Though numerous FX studios were employed in *Bride*, none shine brighter than the Boys at KNB EFX for their marvelously detailed, lovingly rendered titular figure, sensitively played with heart-rending pathos by Kathleen Kinmont.

Brian Yuzna, who cut his film teeth producing Stuart Gordon's *Re-Animator*, *Dolls* and *From Beyond*,

Howard Berger adds the sauce to the Bride's gory demise.

shows considerable progress as a filmmaker with *Bride of Re-Animator* and deserves kudos from the fans for preserving both the quality *and* the integrity of the series.

Though *Bride* was shot a year after *Society* wrapped, it now appears that *Bride* will walk down the theatrical aisles first, allowing distributors time to strategically target a release date for *Society* and capitalize on a film no doubt being touted as one brought to you "by the creator of *Bride of Re-Animator*." That's show biz, folks.

(Editor's Note: The above reviews have *not* been influenced one way or another by the fact that I got only *one* measly close-up as a slime-slurping party dog in *Society* nor by the recent gift from KNB studios of the prop body of the *Bride* used in the laboratory assemblage sequence. Honest.)

(CB)

THE HELTER SKELTER MURDERS (1970)

4

I've seen a good share of the films directly inspired by the Manson bloodbath, plus a few *I Drink Your Blood*, *Thou Shalt not Kill--Except*, and *Igor and the Lunatics* which are tenuously connected to the original case via Mansonoid characters. However none of them were as mercenary, pointless, sleazy, mean or downright cruddy as this thing, shot almost as soon as the corpses were cold.

The "documentary" style touted on the video box is actually a euphemism for Neanderthal acting, nonexistent continuity, primitive editing, simian sound recording, and, except for one color dance sequence, the worst black and white cinematography imaginable. "Mechanical Man," written and sung by Manson himself, is included on a soundtrack that would've been a disaster even without it. The murders are accurately recreated with a slobbering zeal that even sickened Yours Truly. Lacking the stupid amusement-value of Michael Findlay's *Slaughter* (aka Snuff), devoid of *Helter Skelter's* brains, talent and restraint, this bleeder comes across as exactly what it is--a crass commercial insult to the memories of Votjek Frykowski, Abigail Folger, Jay Sebring, Steven Parent, Leno and Rosemary LaBianca and Sharon Tate. Viewers who thought they were renting a well-thought-out piece like *Manson* or *Helter Skelter* should likewise be insulted.

(WG)

Bruce Abbott and Kathleen Kinmont.

GHOUL SCHOOL (1990)
d: Timothy O'Rawe

7

Ghoul School is an amiable junky monsterfest with the golden touch of noted auteur David (*Creepozoids*) DeCoteau smiling from the wings. Two *Fangoria*-reading dorks stay late at their high school in preparation for a big school dance when, for some inexplicable reason the swim team is turned into flesh-eating zombies. The rest of the film concerns them running up and down hallways trying to convince stragglers that they're in imminent danger of becoming ghoul chow.

Ghoul School is beneath amateurish, but it has a plucky sensibility and good spirit about it that's hard to dismiss. In an era of harsh, coarse exploitation films that go for the jugular a *Ghoul School* emerges as a refreshing junk food treat.

(GG)

HAUNTED (1976)
d: Michael de Gaetano

The soundtrack album to this little number clogged record store shelves for years. This writer was very intrigued as I never saw this film mentioned in any reference book. This film is now marketed in a plain black-and-red box with little more than the film's name and an incorrect synopsis on the back cover. The reason for the soundtrack album becomes quite clear when one sees the film; every minute or so, a character breaks into song or a jazzy instrumental blares over the action.

That's the chief reason for this film's existence as it is execrable ca-ca doo-doo, taxing even the patience of the most ardent Aldo Ray completist (yup, he's in it). *Haunted* is an indescribable mess involving a murdered Indian princess, reincarnation and revenge set in an Arizona ghost town. The film has no other real purpose but to showcase music; in a superfluous scene, characters go into a pizza restaurant and we get a few minutes of rinky-dink organ music (remember those Pizza 'N' Pipes places of the seventies?). To it's credit, however, the film has the most disturbing scene in recent memory: a nude love scene between Virginia Mayo and Aldo Ray. AAAAAARRRRGHH! Flabby, hairy backs slapping together with mummified, powdered flesh--brrrrrrr. *Nekromantik* has nothing on this 'un, friends.

(GG)

SOMETIMES AUNT MARTHA DOES DREADFUL THINGS (1970)
d: Thomas Casey

It's too bad that this Florida cheapie is so obscure as to most battle-scarred viewer it emerges as one of the most *sick*, *bizarre* and *sleazy* films in existence. *Aunt Martha* tells the story of Paul/"Aunt Martha," a homosexual jewel thief forced to hide in drag with his hippie boyfriend Stanley. Stanley is too much into girls and hard drugs to pay Aunt Martha any mind, so the jealous Auntie takes it upon herself to thin out Miami's bikini squad with a kitchen knife. The domestic life of the two is one long battle as Aunt Martha tells Stanley to cut his hair and get a real job while Stanley rips off Auntie's wig at inappropriate moments. It only gets stranger from there on in, with a junkie roommate, slaughtered bimbos, drugs, death and hysteria culminating in an emergency C-section on a dead middle-aged matron. Whip out the air-sickness bag!

It's a story suitable for Fassbinder but writer-director Thomas Casey never loses sight of the expoitive elements in his demented story. Filmed on bright, obvious soundstages with chintzy lighting, hammers from the fever dream aura surrounding the action. Recalling the squall and squawk of Herschell Gordon Lewis, Aunt Martha is so off kilter it's the closest a film can come to in approximating real life.
(GG)

VAMPYRE (1990)
d: Bruce Hallenbeck

Loosely based on the Carl Dreyer 1932 film *Vampyr*, and announced back in *Ghastly Ones #1*, Bruce G. Hallenbeck's tribute to the Vampire Cinema has finally arrived. After two years of pre-production, production, post-production, Millaganesque money and disputes with doofball distributors, *Vampyre* proves to be well worth the wait.

Vampyre opens like a supernatural version of the gangland/vengeance flick *The Summertime Killer*. Traumatized by vampires as a youngster, David Gray becomes an adult dedicated to fighting the bloodthirsty forces of evil. Gray (Randy Scott Rozler) is called to the remote village of Cortempierre, in which innocent humans have become a minority; witches and vampires hold sway over the countryside thanks to demonic doings of an evil doctor (John Brent) and his partner in crime, seldom-seen but all-pervasive vampiress Margurite Chopin (Kathy Seyler). Well before the final showdown, the audience, and Gray himself, wonder if he has bitten off more than he can chew.

Filmed mainly in Eastfield Village, a restored Rensselaer County hamlet near Nassau, *Vampyre* is set in a nebulous time and place, the French sound of "Cortempierre" not withstanding. This, and the film's dreamlike--in some cases nightmarish--atmosphere give the director free rein to be as weird as he wants with little opening for criticism. The "no children--no dogs" dialogue is intentionally strange, rather like the fragmented exchanges we hear in dreams of our own. Flouting Hollywood convention, vampires stalk their victims in broad sunlight (which happens quite frequently in vampire folklore). A peasant woman is tied upright to a piece of farm machinery and murdered. Blood flows from the mouth of a horned cattle-skull during a demonic ritual. Black-and-white footage and a sepia-toned sequence are used to good advantage. The local Igor-type is de-legged in loving close-up; later, believe it or not, a character with a musket-ball crater in his face rips off Igor's peg-leg and kills him with it. Anything is possible in the macabre non-linear world of Bruce G. Hallenbeck.

Surprisingly for the low budget, Al Adamson or H.G. Lewis-style gaffes are nonexistent. The director has called *Vampyre* a case of "David Lynch Meets Hammer Films" but for the money, the film at it's best recalls Piers Haggard instead. As in *Blood on Satan's Claw*, shots of solitary figures walking into foggy valleys and stark, bare trees outlined against the sky give one the impression that the countryside itself is steeped in evil, that there is a demon or vampire lurking behind every bush.

Acting, for the most part, takes a back seat to the eerie tone. Most of the players are adequate but dwarfed by the weird overall ambience. (The only bad actress is a big-boobed Bimbolina-- pardon the redundance--who is killed in the interests of good horror cinema before the main credits.) Rozler stands out as Gray; his considerable thespian talent and Carradine-like appearance make him a natural for this sort of production. John Brent as the evil doctor displays a flair for the screen villainy unseen in recent horror flicks. In fact, if laws against scene-stealing are ever enacted, Brent will find himself up on Grand Larceny charges, First Degree.

The first time out, Hallenbeck may not have made the *Carnival of*

Souls or *Horror of Dracula* of 1990 but it's not for lack of trying. Bloody in certain scenes, fleshy in others, loaded with inside-humor and made by a fan rather than just another profiteer, Vampyre is an hour-and-a-half of good solid entertainment for the broad-minded fans of the ghastly and the weird.
(WG)

THE MASQUE OF RED DEATH (1989)
d: Larry Brand

If one was to gather ten people at random, at least one upon instruction could probably act. Alas, the thirty people gathered for the lavish remake of *The Masque of Red Death* beat the odds by presenting an ensemble of performers who do anything *but*. Decadent Italian princes stare at the ground, mumble their lines, stare into space wondering what to do next.

In mounting this production, Roger Corman was either extremely tight-fisted with sheckels or just didn't care. 1989's *Masque* is as poverty-stricken as it is devoid of imagination. The titular Masque, in fact is staged with elementary school choreography (one can almost see the actors count baby steps) and with paper dimestore masks.

Nobody expects a Super 8 ketchup-and-cow-intestines project to elevate the art form and enhance the spirit. That this theatrical presentation is so barren of visuals, literacy and theatrics the resulting effect is one of overpowering despair. A desecration of the Roger Corman Poe series, the '89 *Masque* emerges as one of the very worst films of the past five years.
(GG)

SLIPPING INTO DARKNESS (1988)
d: Eleanor Gaver

When a trio of rich schoolgirls inadvertently lead a young retarded man to an ugly death on train tracks, the brother of the 'tard enlists the aid of two biker buddies to bring the three bimbos to justice. They abduct the girls and drive them to the countryside. At first threatening, defenses soften and the boys and girls pair off for nookie. One of the dudes, Otis, isn't playing with a full load and strangles a debutante in the heat of passion. In the next 24 hours, things go from frightening to devastating to shocking with alliances ever shifting between the girls and guys in a painfully protracted battle of the sexes. It's not giving away too much when we learn that one of the girls turns out to be more psychotic and evil than the other five put together, and we discover what *really* happened at the railroad crossroad.

Owing a heavy stylistic debt to Terrence Malick's *Badlands* (1974), director Gaver films her story of amoral youth against the sumptuous backdrop of the American Midwest. Unlike the working class kids in *River's Edge*, murder and madness has no class structure here. Stunning photography and acting make *Slipping Into Darkness* a white-knuckle trip into smalltown depravity with two knock-out gore sequences. Highly recommended. (GG)

HOUSE OF EXORCISM (1975)
D: Mario Bava/Alfred Leone

According to Spanish critics who saw Mario Bava's *Lisa and the Devil* (1972), the weird, sleazy tale of Elke Sommer in a house of degenerates and a possessed mannequin was hypnotic and well made, up there with the director's best. In the mid-70s, Alfred Leone got ahold of *Lisa*, excised twenty minutes, then spliced in new footage of Sommer, possessed, swearing, puking and doing the Linda Blair horizontal twist with the worst of them. One of her antics, which even gave me the queasies, entails the oral expulsion of green toads. In the doctored *House*, remnants of Bava's original are flashbacks of the cause of Elke's possession, revealed to perplexed priest Robert Alda. The *Lisa* footage, featuring Gabriele Tinti and a lollipop-slurping pre-Kojak Telly Savalas, has enough mayhem, perversion and necrophilia to give Leone's new, gratuitous scenario a run for its money. Confusing to first-time viewers; not as incoherent as *The Rats are Coming, The Werewolves are Here*, but that's not for lack of trying. (WG)

EPITATH (1987)
d: Joseph Merhi

The Fulton family are an upwardly mobile clan living in sunny Southern California who are "challenged" by a nagging personal problem. Mrs. Fulton (Natasha Pavlova, a zaftig Elizabeth Taylor-type) is a murderous, psychotic *bitch*. When she offs dear old dad, the Fultons try to carry on the best way they know how, but momma is out to prove you always hurt the ones you love by keeping them prisoners and killing them off one by one.

She power-drills granny, she keeps her daughter prisoner in her bedroom (we see her wee-wee in her jeans a la *Last House on the Left*) and sets her daughter's boyfriend on fire. There's even a scene where Mrs. Fulton ties up an innocent neighbor and has a rat burrow through the victim's stomach by strapping on a bucket and forcing the mousie to eat through flesh using a carefully placed torch! Now that's entertainment!

Joseph Merhi is an Andy Milligan of the 90's. His straight-to-video hits (*The Newlydeads, Mayhem*) are atrociously acted and constructed but contain enough exploitive verve to cater to any gorehound's demands. Despairing, no-budget tales of human lambs to the slaughter, the video-films of Merhi are sure to purge the viewer of all remaining positive feelings toward mankind. The family in *Epitaph*, in particular, are so dim-witted and devoid of personality we don't feel pity for them even through the worst of it.

Faster, Merhi! Kill! Kill!

(GG)

FRIGHT HOUSE (1990)
d: Len Anthony

Fright House is a stone unwatchable. At 110 minutes, viewing it straight through is analogous to huffing paint thinner as an ill-advised hangover cure.

Composed of two different stories, "Fright House" and "Abadon," *Fright House* is edited in such a way as to induce acid flashbacks. Two people will be talking, the action will cut to a naked lady devil worshipper, people will be walking in a hallway, the camera will focus on a bloody sacrificial knife, etc., etc. *Fright House's* editing schemata surpasses mere coming attractions trailer disintegration; the editor reaches into a plastic Hefty garbage bag containing millions of pieces of film and splices them together at random!

What of the two "name" stars, Al "Grandpa Munster" Lewis and Duane (*Night of the Living Dead, Ganja and Hess*) Jones? Lewis appears briefly as the leader of a clandestine naked lady devil worshipping cult that was obviously more fun to participate in than to watch. Poor Duane Jones, in the second tale about an ageless succubus college professor looks visibly ashamed and embarrassed. His recent untimely death comes as no surprise; appearing in *Fright House* would make the heartiest soul die from humiliation.

(GG)

BARN OF THE NAKED DEAD (aka TERROR CIRCUS, NIGHTMARE CIRCUS) (1973)

d: Alan Rudolph

This 1972 effort by the future director of *Trouble in Mind*, et al., features Andrew Prine as a mother-fixated maniac who runs his own carnival in the Nevada desert. His star attractions are females held captive in the titular barn; whenever the action flags he marches them around the homestead to the tune of his cracking whip or sics his pet cougar on them. The action takes place near a former nuclear test site, which gives the filmmakers an excuse to throw in a badly made-up mutant toward the end. Despite its inexplicable reputation as a splatter flick this is short on gore and for the most part pretty lame, but the scenery-chewing Prine manages to keep things moving. It's always a pleasure to watch this performer at work, even in a geek-show like this. Alan Rudolph now makes pretentious-art films with retarded titles like *Choose Me*; he'd probably like to buy up all prints of *Barn of the Naked Dead* and burn them.

(WG)

ATTACK OF THE BEAST CREATURES (aka HELL ISLAND) (1983)

d: Michael Stanley

A dog it may be, but fans of the "so bad it's funny" group should go out of their way to check this little number out. In 1920, survivors of a North Atlantic shipwreck wash up on a seemingly deserted island, only to discover such inconveniences as pools of acid masquerading as water, the obligatory infighting and bickering among the group, and...hold on...an army of tiny plastic dolls! Resembling cut-rate miniature versions of the Zuni fetish doll in *Trilogy of Terror*, these blank-eyed, sharp-toothed, stiff-limbed little devils come chugging through the grass and swinging from vines to land on the hapless crew, who scream, jump, thrash, and hold the dolls tightly to make sure they don't drop them! Another unforgettable moment has a fellow trip and fall onto a pointed stake. He kicks and screams for a while before expiring while a fellow shipwreckee remarks, "He never knew what hit him." The hell he didn't! The fairly high amount of gore is the only clue that this is an American film shot in the 80's, and it's highly unlikely that you'll find anything else like it again. If you think that's a pity, seek this out. If you think it's a relief, you know better.

(SMD)

THE BODY BENEATH

d: Andy Milligan

This Milligan horror is one of his best. Foppish Reverend Ford (Gavin Reed) is actually an anemic vampire whose clan of bloodsuckers takes over Carfax Abbey and neighboring Highgate Cemetery. Ford wants to move to the U.S. ("London is a police state after dark," he proclaims, as if America isn't.) Before the migration, he plans to replenish the weak family bloodline at the expense of pretty young Jackie Skarvellis. Milligan saved a few bucks on costumes by setting this film in modern times, though he does indulge his passion for archaic wardrobe during the closing blood ritual. His photography is commendable here, splashed with hues of black and red. Especially memorable is the crimson-filtered vampire chowdown at film's end culminating in the immolation of Milligan standby Berwick Kaler. Other mayhem includes vampirism, fun with leeches, knitting needles in a servant's eyes, and crucifixion. With an eerie soundtrack and authentic London graveyard setting, Milligan attains a high level of weirdness here that's all too absent in some of his other work. He and his cohorts were thrown out of Highgate Cemetery for operating sans work permits. While one person distracted the caretaker at the gate, the others hopped the back wall and went on filming. THE BODY BENEATH is one Milligan film that was definitely worth the trouble.

(WG)

THE SEVERED ARM (1973)

d: Thomas S. Alderman

Much of my affection for this film has to do with the fact that I grew up with it on TV — but it still has its moments. Six explorers, trapped in a cave-in, reach the point of starvation. Ultimately, they decide to slice off the arm of one of their own for food. But the very moment the operation is completed on the unwilling donor, the rescue team arrives. The facts of the case are covered up, but one-armed Ted swears "I won't forget." Years later, sure enough, the other five begin to loose their right arms, one by one. The script has some silly dialogue and lapses of logic, but the direction is good and the suspense is quite solid. The violence and gore is surprisingly strong (but only in the uncut Video Gems version — the print found in the cut-out bins of various stores is hacked up even worse than its own characters), and the last ten minutes scared the hell out of me when I first saw it, and still get to me today. Comedian Marvin Kaplan appears as disc jockey "Mad Man Herman," and yes, that's Deborah "Gidget" Walley as the daughter of the original "Lefty."

(SMD)

THE HEAD (aka DER NACKTE UND DER SATAN) (1959)
d: Victor Trivas

Sickly, overweight Professor Abel (Michel Simon) has discovered Serum Z, a strange fluid which successfully sustains the severed heads of dogs. Wanting to further pursue his researches but fearful of the dangers poised by his ailing heart, Abel arranges to be the recipient of a heart transplant, one overseen by the mysterious Dr. Ood (Horst Frank). But Ood is actually a jealous maniac, and instead of giving Abel a new heart he decapitates him, keeping the unfortunate Professor's head alive through an application of the man's own Serum Z. Ood then embarks on a murderous reign of terror – one which involves grafting the beautiful head of a crippled nurse (Karin Kernke) onto the spectacular body of a statuesque stripper (Christiane Maybach).

Writing the above plot synopsis was almost embarrassing, and indeed, in terms of narrative or acting, there's not much to recommend in *The Head*; this is basically a slow, badly dubbed, West German horror/sex exploitation film. On the other hand, I distinctly recall the frighteningly grotesque ambience this film *oozed* off the screen when I first saw it, on a double bill with *Horror Hotel*, in 1963. Gloomy, bizarre and morbid, this really is one uniquely creepy little chiller, an ultra-expressionistic exercise in creating unnerving atmospheres. For that achievement alone, *The Head* deserves some sort of (semi) serious respect.

I won't go into *The Head*'s plot, which is both silly and sleazy, especially during the stripper sequences or when Dr. Ood (love that name!) is graphically fondling a woman in bed. No, *The Head* strictly succeeds through a polished, and highly technical, manipulation of sound and image. There's the ominous, low-key score by Willy Mattes and Jacques Lasryi; a sound recording/sound effects track which is spare and somewhat muffled (leading to the sense that much of the film is taking place underwater); the striking black & white photography of Georg Krause, stylized to the point of depression (sickly-looking moons float in smoky, sooty skies while skeletal branches paw at country roads like bony fingers). In fact, *The Head* is constantly oppressive, whether the action is taking place on a shadowy front porch, a road hemmed in by thin, menacing trees, or in the grainy artificial light of Professor Abel's laboratory.

Which leads me to warn you - this is not a film for the chronically depressed.

(PS)

Paul Sammon's latest book, Blood and Rockets, will be published in Summer, 1992.

VAMPIRE CIRCUS (1971)
d: Robert Young...no, not Marcus Welby!

Though the output of Hammer films certainly doesn't qualify as obscure, many people, in listing their finest accomplishments, tend to end the list by around 1970, citing the product of their last few years as pale shadows of a former glory. While it's probably true that the original Horror of Dracula (1958) has never been topped, the 70's films had their share of great moments — and this film is one of the best Hammer ever put out. A plague-infested village is offered some much needed entertainment in the form of a gypsy circus — but the true motive of the performers is to resurrect Count Mitterhaus, staked decades ago by the villagers, by means of claiming the children of the very villagers who did the deed. Not resembling the Dracula films in the least, this is an original concept featuring several of Hammer's familiar faces, as well as dwarf actor Skip Martin, Lalla Ward ("Romana" on the British TV favorite Doctor Who), and Dave "Darth Vader" Prowse as the strongman. Those only familiar with the TV print won't believe what they've been missing.

(SMD)

CELIA, CHILD OF TERROR (1988)
d: Ann Turner

The packagers of this Australian melodrama have done consumers a disservice by marketing it as a horror film. While there are horrific elements in the story, the emphasis is plainly on wistful nostalgia.

Celia concerns a little girl who grows up in a small Australian town in the 1950's. Her next door neighbors are a leftist leaning bunch who are ousted by the less tolerant townfolk. Deprived of her playmates, the mean town constable takes her pet rabbit away where it dies in quarantine after an outbreak of plague. Slowly, but surely Celia slips over the edge and it's not long before the mean ol' constable winds up on the receiving end of a rifle wielded by the film's precocious heroine.

How this sunny view of childhood abruptly lurches into *bad seed* territory comes as a bit of a shock. We are left to wonder if the little girl has gone mad, seeing woodland monsters hiding in the shadows (superb monster make-up glanced only briefly) or has merely embraced ruthless evil. *Celia's* denouement--or lack of one sets it apart from others. *Celia, Child of Terror* really isn't a horror film but is an interesting yarn nonetheless.

(GG)

WOODCHIPPER MASSACRE (1989)
d: Jon McBride

Although technically it ranks among *Black Devil Doll From Hell* in the "America's Favorite Home Splatter Movies Stakes," this shot-on-video opus has an ingratiating charm you can't shake off. Three obnoxious children (suffering from *Goonies* syndrome, i.e., screaming in the direction of the microphone) must contend with their harridan Aunt Tess over the weekend at their ritzy suburban Connecticut home while dad is away on a business trip. When Aunt Tess accidentally falls on Junior's Rambo-survival knife, the kids elect to throw the corpse in the wood chipper machine and tell daddy his sister " just had to go home." Aunt Tess' ex-con son is rumbling in the neighborhood, and after threatening and beating the children, winds up in a similar Black-and-Decker demise.

Jon McBride peppers his script

with witty comments on spoiled adolescents; moments after Aunt Tess is killed, a little girl's dismay turn to jubilation when the new cute boy in her class calls her up on the telephone. The music, composed on a portable synthesizer is excellent. The acting is a bit rough but spirited. It's amazing how quickly the sheltered tots turn to homicide without second thoughts; Woodchipper Massacre is a John Hughes movie by way of Roald Dahl, and I like that.

(GG)

THE WEIRDO
d: Andy Milligan

A teenage whipping-boy goes berserk, butchers his oppressors and comes to a bad end in this West Coast horror. Unlike Andy's early shockers like THE GHASTLY ONES, which featured murder and mayhem before the titles, this takes awhile to get going. To keep the first half afloat Milligan throws in his usual contempt for authority-figures, paints a black picture of family life and showcases abuse of the handicapped. Then one obnoxious character cuts a cake with a meat cleaver and it's non-stop violence from there on. Cleaver-carnage, dismemberment, immolation, electrocution, a severed head in a trash bag, and one victim's impalement by a cross in a church sanctuary are more audacious in concept than in actual execution. Despite his money-saving modern setting and a budget unhampered by anyone named Mishkin, Milligan's mayhem too often sinks to the rubber-hand level. The death by fire of one character is especially amusing; aflame, face blackened (probably by KiWi polish) and in agony, she doesn't scream. Watch her corpse's eyes blink, also. THE WEIRDO, suffering from slow pacing and chintzy gore, is further hurt by one of those twist endings often ascribed to CARRIE (a finale, in fact, that Brian DePalma ripped off from DELIVERANCE.) Could this mean WEIRDO II in the future? When it comes to that bargain-basement weirdo named Milligan, nothing would surprise me any more.

BRAIN DEAD (1989)
d: Adam Simon

For the hardcore fan, there's no finer thrill than stumbling across a genuine sleeper, a distinctive little movie you've read or heard nothing about that zings in out of nowhere and suddenly validates all the wasted, disappointing hours you've spent watching dreck. And to find such a gem on *video* is like stumbling onto a single, beautiful rose...one growing out of a manure pile.

Brain Dead 's that kind of movie.

Neurosurgeon Dr. Martin (Bill Pullman) is persuaded by a corporate friend (Bill Paxton) to retrieve an important formula from the brain of psychopathic mathematician Dr. Halsey (Bud Cort). There's only one problem; Martin's method entails the use of an untested surgical procedure, one which could possibly lobotimize Helsey if Martin miscalculates. The surgery proceeds anyway, and Halsey is seemingly cured. But why does Dr. *Martin* suddenly start to hallucinate?

"Am I a man dreaming that I am a butterfly, or a butterfly dreaming that I am a man?" That famous riddle comes from the 3rd Century B.C. Chinese writer Chuang Tse, and is the philosophical bedrock upon which *Brain Dead* rests (it also explains the film's second-to-last shot). Yes, I said "philosophical." For despite its science fictional and horror/mystery/thriller/anti-corporate trappings, *Brain Dead* is actually nothing less than an examination of reality itself.

Having written that, don't be put off. *Brain Dead* isn't just an absorbing intellectual exercise; you can further enjoy it on a number of other levels.

Science fiction addicts will take to *Brain Dead* 's surgical concepts, and all those Bud Cort fans who've been wondering whatever happened to their eccentric hero after *Harold and Maude* and *Brewster McCloud* will here discover one of Cort's meatiest, far-ranging roles. Rock fans will uncover two songs ("Brain Dance" and "Mystic Revelation") by Bill Paxton's band Martini Ranch (probably best known for his energetic portrayals of a cowardly space Marine in *Aliens* and good-ole-boy vampire in *Near Dark*, Paxton has a second career as an LA-based rock musician).

Mystery buffs should enjoy trying to figure out just what the hell is going on in *Brain Dead*, because after Pullman operates on Cort, the movie makes a mystifying left turn: Dr. Martin not only starts to see horrible visions, but there seems to be a conspiracy aimed at putting him in a mental hospital. Horror fans will like the brain operations themselves, where sizzling hot probes dig deep into the meaty recesses of exposed craniums. And effects fans will enjoy the surreal sight of a skinned and blinking human face stretched across a wire frame, one sitting on a scientist's desk.

Interestingly, the *Brain Dead* story is based on a screenplay by Charles Beaumont, an American scenarist and horror story virtuoso who died in 1967. Beaumont/Simon really lead you down the garden path here; by the end of the film, you realize that *everything* you've seen in *Brain Dead* is subject to doubt.

I realize I'm giving you very few plot details concerning this film, but that's intentional. Half of *Brain Dead* 's fun lies in trying to follow the twists and turns of its increasingly fragmented story. Is Dr. Martin sane? Insane? Paranoid? A victim? By *Brain Dead*'s climax, you still don't know. Our world is what we perceive it to be *at the moment*, even if that's an incorrect perception, or one we've had forced upon us by someone else. Which is, of course, the film's frightening point.

NOTE: *Brain Dead* scripter Charles Beaumont is no stranger to the worlds of fantasy/horror. An influential and well known genre contributor during the 1960's, Beaumont wrote many of the original *Twilight Zone* episodes, including "The Howling Man" (Satan locked up in an old monastery), "The Jungle" (Charles Dehner as a disbeliever menaced by voodoo in contemporary Manhattan), and the 1962 episode "Person or Persons Unknown" (a segment which greatly resembles *Brain Dead*; Richard Long plays a hungover man who wakes up one morning to discover a world where nobody knows him). Beaumont also supplied the screenplays for Corman's *The Haunted Palace* and *The Masque of the Red Death*, which explains Corman's knowledge of the unfinished

Brain Dead screenplay, one which director Adam Simon completed twenty-two years after Beaumont's death.

Finally, Charles Beaumont died from the ravages of a true-life disease just as grotesque as anything he put down on paper. In 1964 Beaumont contracted a form of progeria, a rare and terrible ailment whose strangest symptom is premature aging. Three years later, Beaumont passed on. He was only 38 years old.

But he looked like he was a hundred.

(PS)

CREATURE FROM THE BLACK LEATHER LAGOON (1990)

Trash rockers the Cramps received a setback when MTV refused to air their video for *Bikini Girls With Machine Guns* due to a patently phony plastic toy machine gun wielded by the scantily dressed Poison Ivy that included a glimpse of a bikini bottom sliding down her thighs. For their next promotional clip, the black clad ones damned the torpedoes and set out to offend everyone and everything with this three minute visual and aural assault with more joyous nihilism than you can shake a crutch at. Extremely hip in their selection of schlock horror film references, *Black Leather Lagoon* directly swipes from Herschell Gordon Lewis' *Just For The Hell Of It* (1968), *Humanoids from the Deep* (1980) coupled with softcore tease and flashing strobe lights. It all culminates with a 99¢ Creature from the Black Lagoon in black leather jacket and spiked heels carrying away a damsel in distress into the sunset, the camera lingering just long enough to catch the monster tripping and dropping the girl. If the Cramps pursue this current path, they'll never get played on MTV, win a grant from the National Endowment of the Arts, or go to Heaven – making our lives all the richer for it.

(GG)

NIGHT OF THE BLOODY TRANSPLANT
d: David W. Hanson

One might expect just a little something more from a film that carries a hyperbolic warning claiming it's "Not for the squeamish! This intense film contains actual footage of open-heart surgery!" Who-oa, I'm shakin'!

My manhood challenged, I plop down my $2.98--for *purchase*, not rental (I'm serious here). I soon discover that even the title is a raging bogosity, way too cool a moniker for a film dumped onto the Blockbuster Video clearance table. Actually, it *is* intense, for about 90 seconds anyway, then the spliced-in surgery sequence ends and Dave King and the Royal Knights kick into a valium-fueled performance of "You Wonder Where Your Heart Can Go." Whew!

This movie plays like a bad acid trip. It does deserve slight mention here for it's unassailable, cheeky nerve in the face of such insurmountable odds as monosyllabic, semi-comatose actors, King Cornball dialog, painful modern dance routines set to dreadfully dated jazz scores, and pecker-wilting strip routines featuring people who should remain fully clothed at *all* times. These elements alone should provide ample warning to all other sentient beings, squeamish or not.

(CB)

HORROR HOUSE ON HIGHWAY FIVE (1985)
d: Richard Casey

Unconvincing wanna-be maniacs, including one addled by brain parasites and another wearing a Richard Nixon mask, wreak predictable PG-13 type havoc upon some dim-bulb college types in this throwaway killer directed by the allegedly "notorious rock videomaker" Richard Casey.

The rockin' musical interludes *do* afford brief relief from the snooze-inducing antics provided by a cast of Little Dick's personal friends, family and investors, but even a Metallica soundtrack couldn't bring much life to this stiff.

Feeble little twist thrown in at the end, too, as art imitates life. *Big* Dick lives!

(CB)

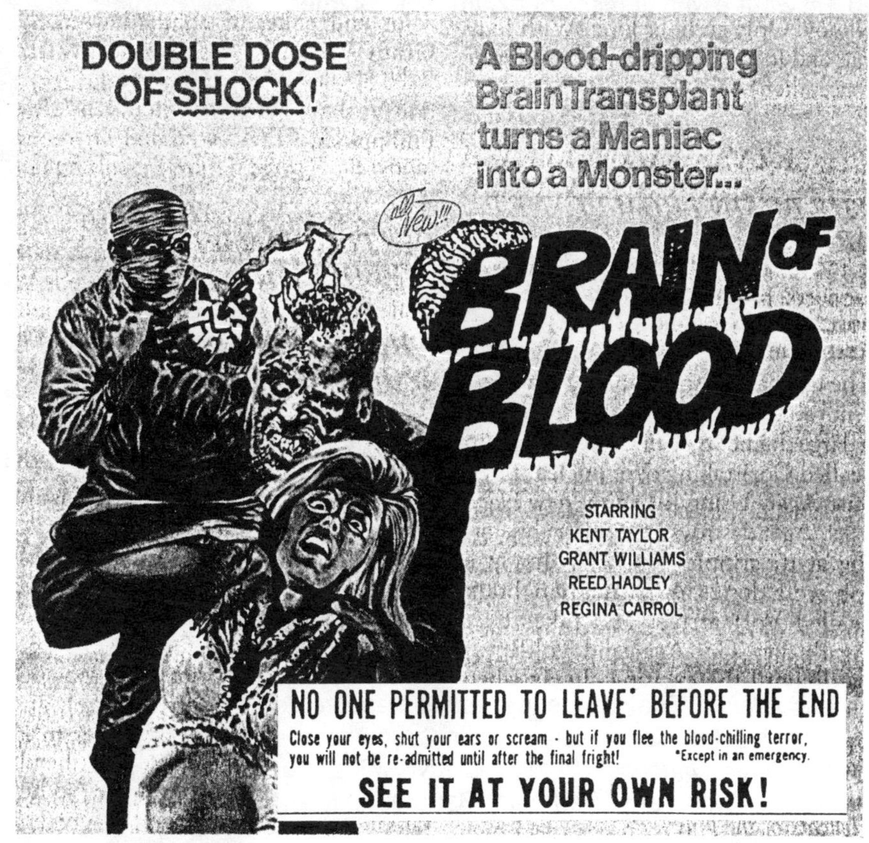

DEEP RED POSTSCRIPT

COMPILED BY CHAS. BALUN

In our first six issues, we were happy to feature the talents of many enthusiastic fans, semi-professionals and practicing pros who we felt were not getting the attention they deserved. Soon, what were once mere names on a return address label became close and trusted blood brothers. Much of my inherent, fatalistic cynicism was held in check knowing that a new assault force of horror shock troops was forming from the ranks of our friends. That is the way it should be.

BUDDY GIOVINAZZO, director of *Combat Shock*, wrote *Dead and Married* (aka *She's Back*) and is collaborating with ROY (*Street Trash, Document of the Dead*) FRUMKES on the deliciously titled *123 Depravity Street*. Frumkes is working on a new film called *Mr. Softee* with James Lorinz, the acid-tongued doorman in *Street Trash* and the star of Frank Henenlotter's *Frankenhooker*. Both Roy and Buddy G. continue to teach filmmaking at separate New York universities.

PERICLES LEWNES, director, star and FX artist of *Redneck Zombies*, has worked on several other Troma productions including *Troma's War*, *Toxic Avenger II and III* and *Sgt. Kabukiman NYPD*. Peri has several original scripts in various stages of development at this time.

SCOTT SPIEGEL, whose *Night Crew* (aka *Intruder*) was profiled in *Deep Red 4*, co-scripted *The Rookie* for Clint Eastwood (!) Scott is again teaming up with Sam Raimi on a screwball mondocomedy called *The Nutty Nut*.

KNB EFX, which supplied the grisly FX (conspicuously missing from the "R" print) for *Intruder*, has gone on to work on nearly every major genre film shot in the last couple of years including *Night Angel*, *Horrorshow*, *Leatherface*, *Nightmare on Elm Street V*, *Bride of Re-Animator*, *Tales From the Darkside: The Movie* and *Misery*. They also supplied the slaughtered and mechanical buffaloes seen in Kevin Costner's much-acclaimed *Dances With Wolves*. KNB will share makeup duties with Tony (*Darkman*) Gardner on the upcoming *Evil Dead 3*.

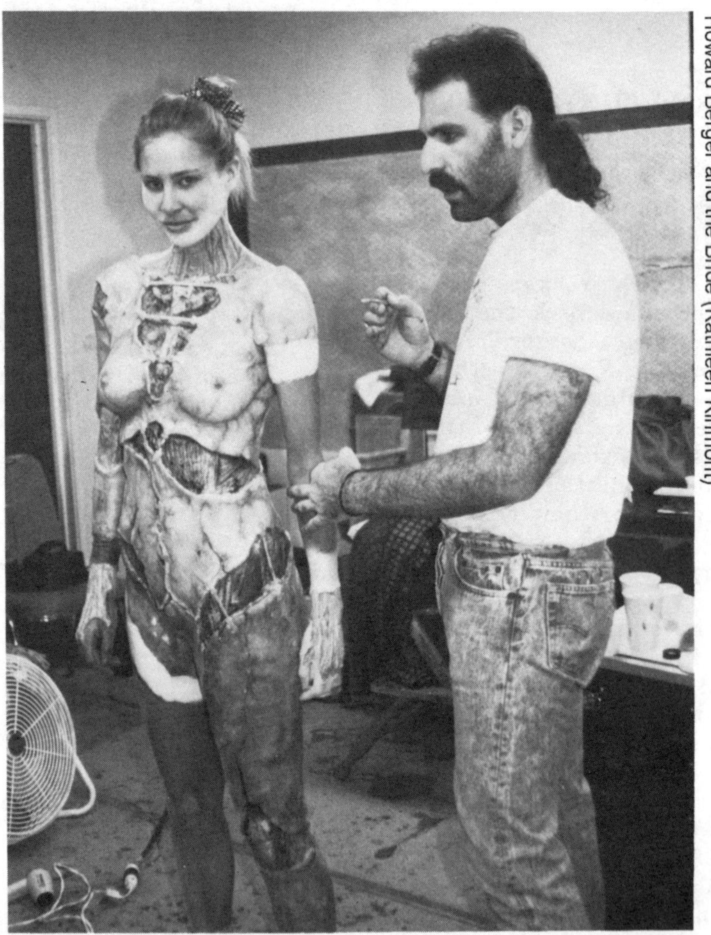

Howard Berger and the Bride (Kathleen Kinmont)

Kurtzman and Balun do lunch with the Bride of Re-Animator.

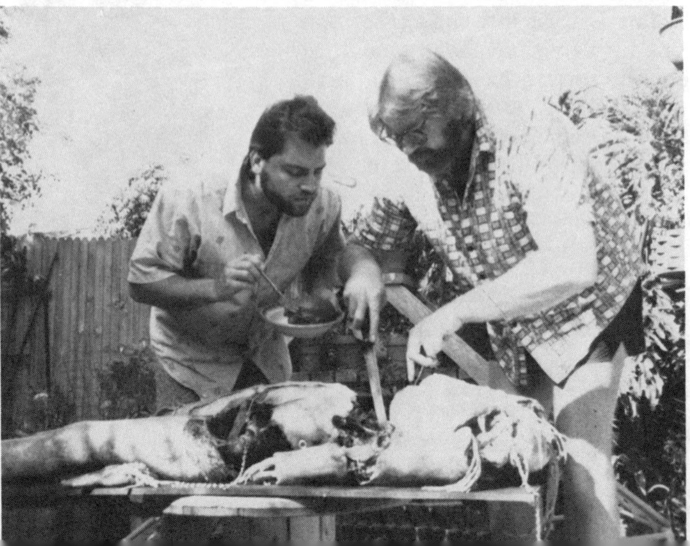

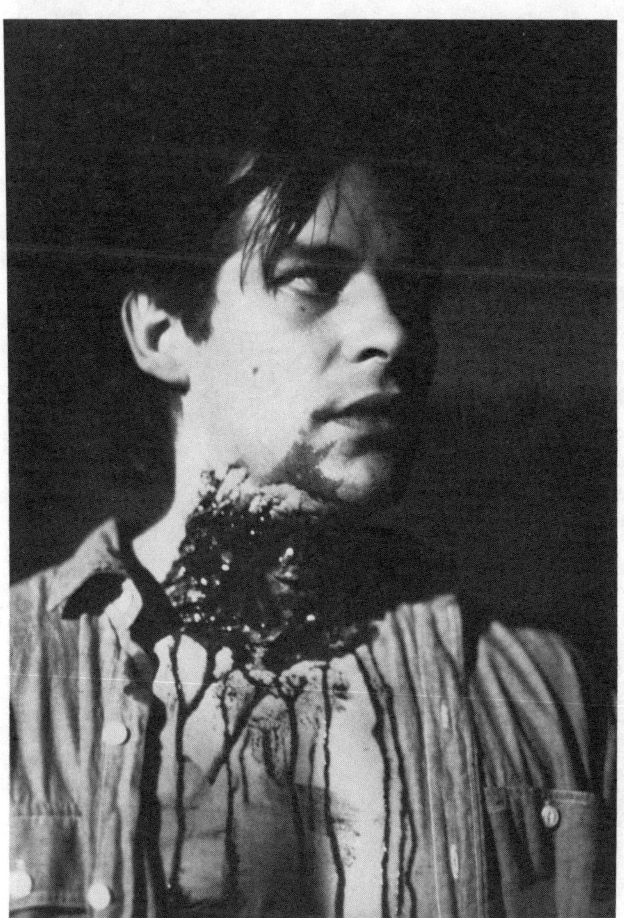

James Remar gets ripped in *Tales from the Darkside*.

Kurtzman applies final touches to the baby gargoyle in *Darkside*.

Mike Deak in KNB make-up from *Monsters* episode.

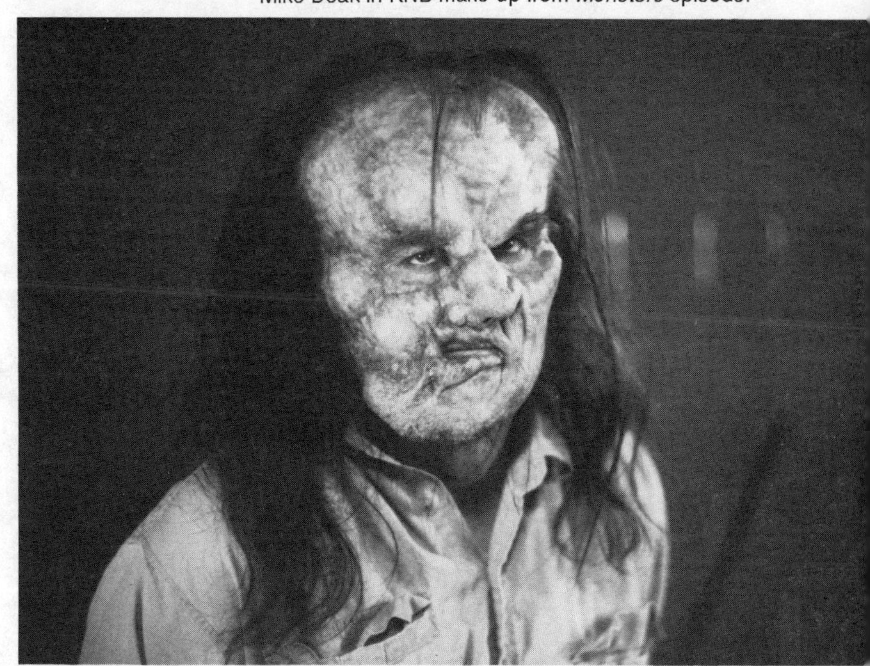

KNB Shop during *Gross Anatomy*.

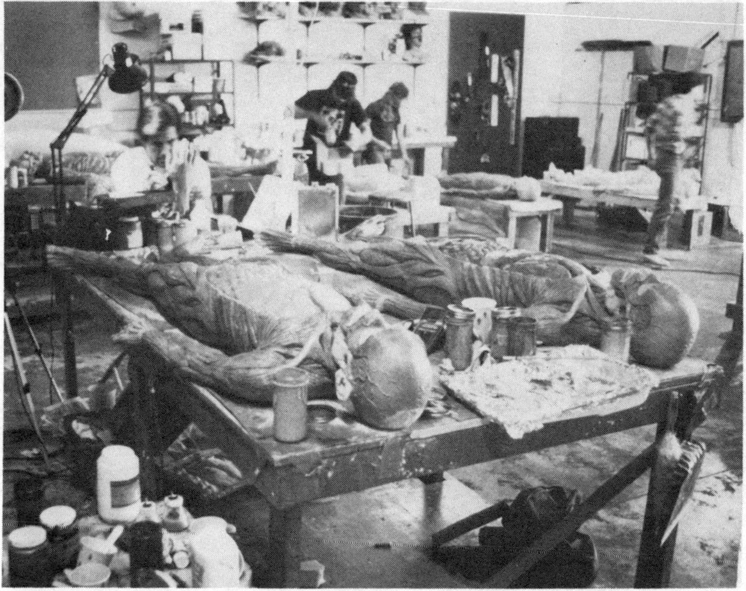

Tim Gore and barking buddy.

Bruce Spaulding Fuller paints "King Willie's" severed head from *Predator 2.*

BRUCE SPAULDING FULLER, former *Gore Shriek* cartoonist and commercial artist, went from *Deep Red 3* straight to Hollywood and *Dick Tracy* and hasn't looked back since. In a scant two years out West, Bruce has provided FX on such films as *Misery, Edward Scissorhands, Predator 2, Bride of Re-Animator, Leatherface, Nightmare on Elm Street V*, and *Tales From the Darkside: The Movie*. He's just finished *Terminator 2* and *Mom and Dad Save the World* with both *The Addams Family* and *Lovecraft* (for HBO) next on his slate.

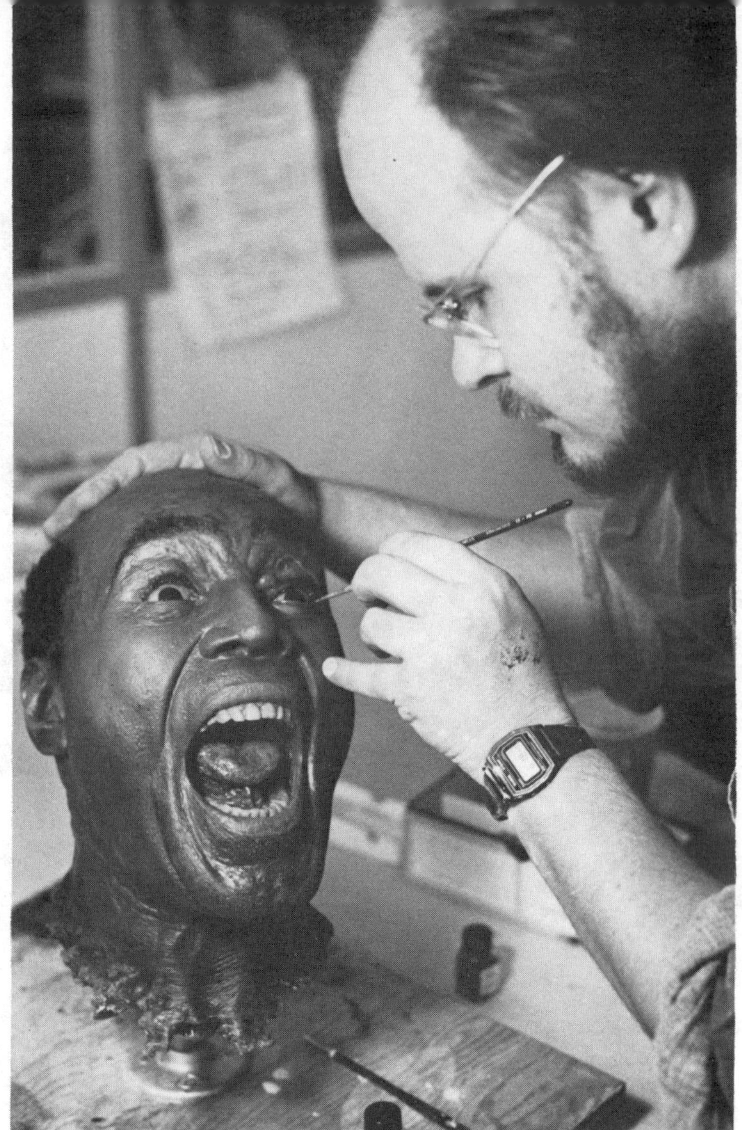

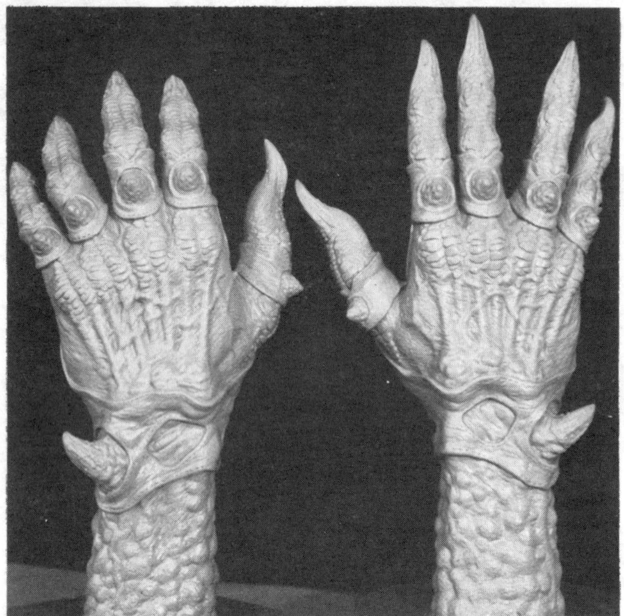

Sculptured hands for *Predator 2*.

Autopsy body from *Shadowzone* by Fuller, Mark Shostrom and Greg Smith.

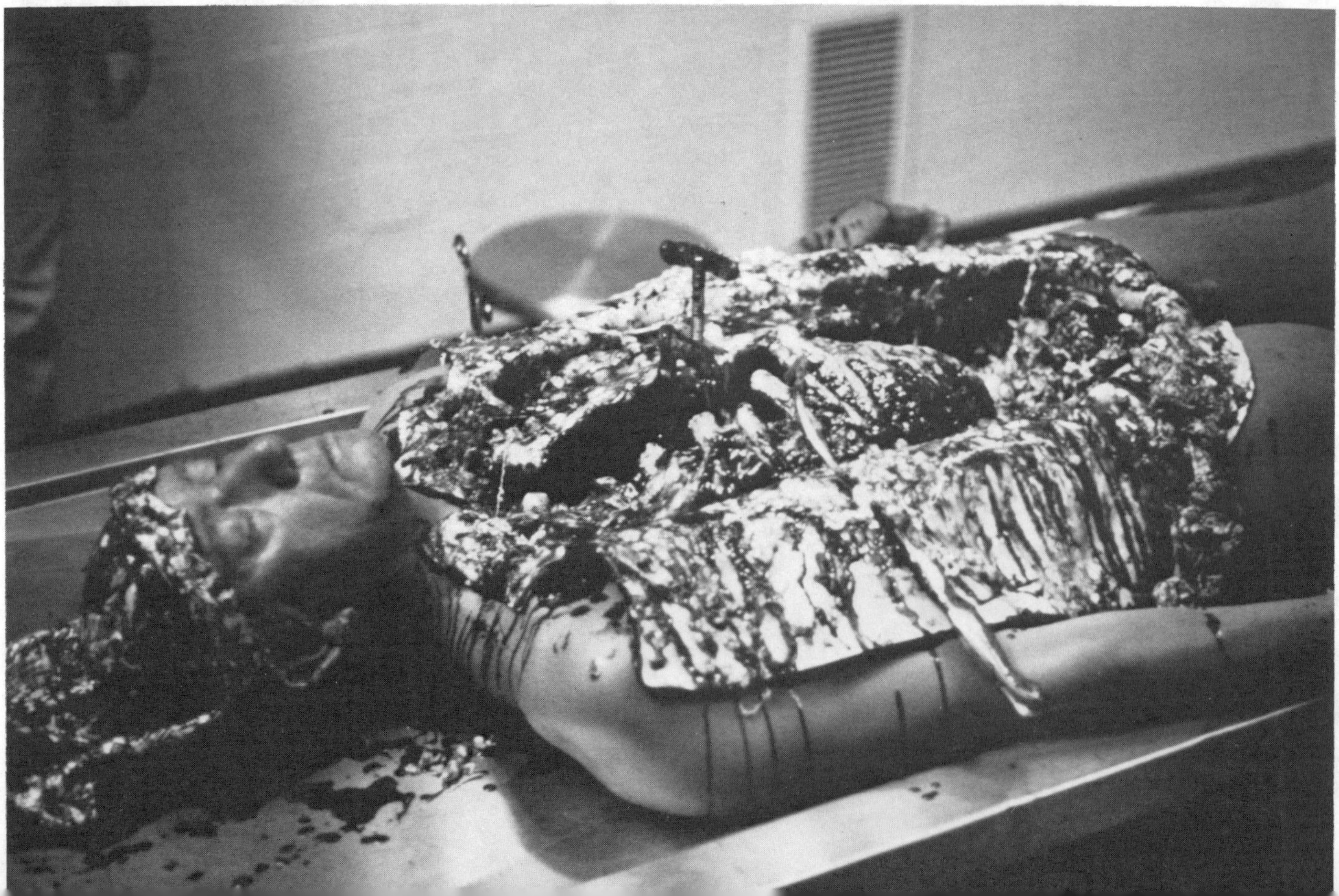

Fuller and Wayne Toth sculpting the full-sized gargoyle from *Darkside* at KNB Studios.

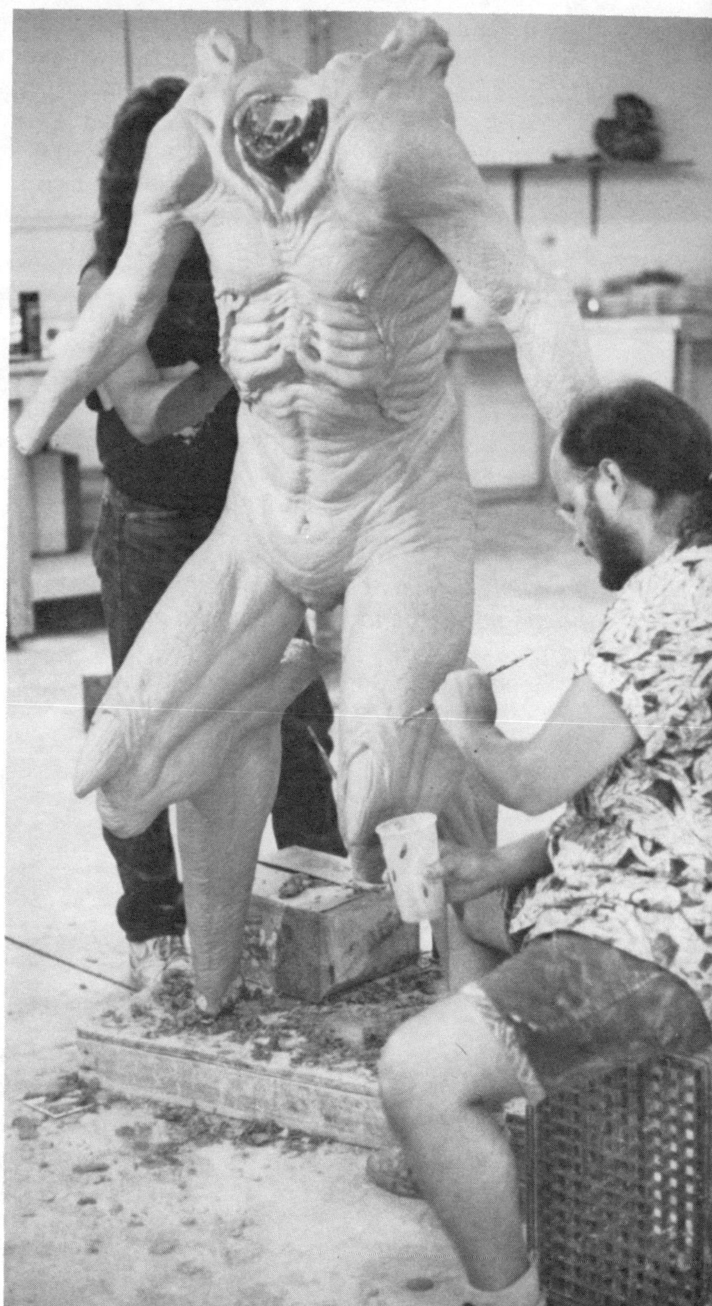

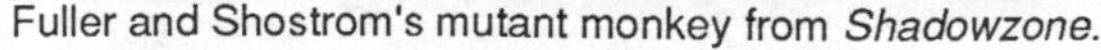

Fuller and Shostrom's mutant monkey from *Shadowzone*.

STEVE WANG, featured winner in the Hollywood-based "1st Annual Monster Makers Halloween Contest" has worked on *Predator*, *Monster Squad* and *Hell Comes to Frogtown*. He has also co-directed (along with Screaming Mad George) *The Guyver* a fantasy-monster-thriller produced by Brian (Bride of *Re-Animator*, *Society*) Yuzna.

MARK WILLIAMS, cover man of issue #5, has recently supplied FX for *Syngenor* and the Martin Short/Charles Grodin comedy *Clifford*. He has sold an original script for the sequel to *Psycho Cop* and will direct his own script as well as furnish FX for the upcoming voodoo/thriller *Baron Samedi*.

Mark Williams with Syngenor mask.

TIM (GORE) LARSEN, a young FX talent first featured in *Deep Red*'s "New Blood," has worked on *Slaughterhouse*, *Dr. Caligari* and *My Mom's a Werewolf.* Tim was the first place winner at "Fangoria's 1988 Weekend of Horrors" Makeup Contest and has successfully marketed his own unique makeup creation "Goreknobs." Tim also rigged the makeup and FX for Skinny Puppy's 1990 American Tour.

NATHAN SCHIFF, renegade filmmaker of such backyard chunk-blowers as *Long Island Cannibal Massacre*, *Weasels Ripped My Flesh* and *They Don't Cut the Grass Anymore* has just put the finishing touches on his two hour and twenty minute magnum opus *Vermilion Eyes.*

Here, then, are the True Believers.

"We are constituted that we believe the most incredible things; and once they are engraved upon the memory, woe to him who would endeavor to erase them."

Goethe ("The Sorrows of Young Werther" 1774)

Go for it. *We* are the New Blood.

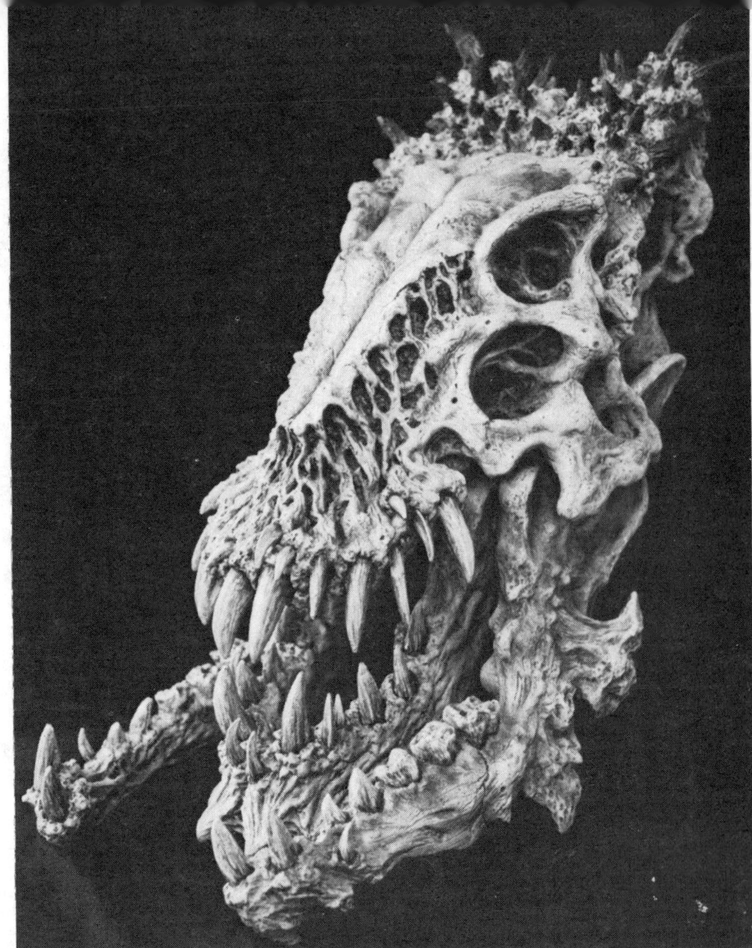

Giant alien skull for *Predator 2.* Built and painted by Bruce Spaulding Fuller.

Tim Gore's dead heads.

CHUNK BLOWER THE MOVIE

Plasma Films, Inc., a Canadian production team responsible for several Skinny Puppy rock videos, has announced plans to begin principal photography on *Chunkblower*, a hardcore full-throttle splatterfest written by REDitor Chas. Balun from a story by Alan Zweig and and Gary Blair Smith. Scheduled to be shot in and around Vancouver, British Columbia in Spring 1991, *Chunkblower* chronicles the lives (and deaths, 'natch) of a severely dysfunctional nuclear family that has learned the art of the Highway Harvest in order to supplement the income from their foundering towing service. Numerous gory deaths precede a devastating familial apocalypse that climaxes with a spectacularly splashy, gratuitous flesh feast that should have card-carrying splatterhounds howling like hyenas. Barf bags will be provided during selected theatrical engagements and included with the videocassettes.

At a budget just under $1 million, *Chunkblower* will be directed by Ohio filmmaker Jim VanBebber, whose previous features, *The Last Days of John Martin*, *Deadbeat at Dawn* and *Charlie's Family* showcase a ferociously talented young auteur whose work may help re-define the genre in the Nineties. The 26 year-old director also earned himself a new nickname while shooting a trailer for the film last year as panicked victims of a fire gag gone slightly awry christened him "Jim VanLandis." At the fiery climax to the 3-minute promo reel, two punks handcuffed to the steering wheel of a firebombed car really feel the heat when the flame bar used in the stunt unexpectedly kicks into overdrive. The sequence is cut just before crewmembers rip open the car doors and extinguish the two manacled hot heads. Nerves were shot, hair was lost and both toastees quit the production on the spot.

The cast was undetermined at press time, though Canadian thespians Peter Devorsky (James Woods' partner in *Videodrome*) and Les Carlson (*Deranged, Videodrome*) are being sought for the leads. Deborah Harry has been approached to appear in a cameo role during a revoltingly oozy scene illustrating the dangers of unsafe sex.

FXers including KNB, Optic Nerve, Bruce Spaulding Fuller, Tim Larsen and Robert Comer are being considered for the gore chores.

Skinny Puppy bandmates Cevin Key and D. Rudolph Goettel will contribute an original soundtrack and noted cinematographer Cyrus Block will act as Director of Photography.

For further information on the film and details for obtaining a videocassette of the promo reel, contact the producer, Gary Blair Smith, at Plasma Films, Inc. 310-1510 Nelson St. , Vancouver B.C. , Canada V6G-IMI .

DEEP RED
TASTE SOME
BODY BITS
DEAD BLIND
HEADCASE
BLOODY SHOTS
"the GURCH © 91